Young Jim

The
Jim Parks
Story

Young

Jim

The
Jim Parks
Story

Derek Watts

Foreword by Ted Dexter

TEMPUS

To Gerry, for all her love and support, and to my father,
who taught me to love the game.

First published 2005

Tempus Publishing Limited
The Mill, Brimscombe Port,
Stroud, Gloucestershire, GL5 2QG
www.tempus-publishing.com

© Derek Watts, 2005

British Library Cataloguing in Publication Data.
A catalogue record for this book is available from the British Library.

ISBN 0 7524 3550 7

Typesetting and origination by Tempus Publishing Limited
Printed in Great Britain

Contents

J.M. Parks at Tunbridge Wells

Parks takes ten in two successive balls from Wright,
A cut to the rhododendrons and a hook for six.
And memory begins suddenly to play its tricks:
I see his father batting, as, if here, he might.

Now Tunbridge Wells, 1951; the hair far lighter,
The body boyish, flesh strung across thin bone,
And arms sinewy as the wrists are thrown
At the spinning ball, the stance much straighter.

Now it is June full of heaped petals
The day steamy, tropical; rain glistens
On the pavilion, shining on corrugated metal.
The closeness has an air that listens.

Then it was Eastbourne, 1935; a date
Phrased like a vintage, sea-fret on the windscreen.
And Parks, rubicund and squat, busily sedate,
Pushing Verity square, moving his score to nineteen.

Images of then, so neatly parcelled and tied
By ribbons of war – but now through a chance
Resemblance reopened; a son's stance
At the wicket opens the closed years wide.

And it is no good resisting the interior
Assessment, the fusion of memory and hope
That comes flooding to impose on inferior
Attainment – yesterday, today, twisted like rope.

Parks drives Wright under dripping trees,
The images compare and a father waves away
Applause, pale sea like a rug over the knees,
Covering him, the son burying his day

With charmed strokes. And abstractedly watching,
Drowning, I struggle to shake off the past
Whose arms clasp like a mother, catching
Up with me, summer at half-mast.

The silent inquisitors subside. The crowd,
Curiously unreal in this Regency spa, clap,
A confectionery line under bushes heavily bowed
In the damp. Then Parks pierces Wright's leg trap.

And we come through, back to the present.
Sussex 300 for 2. Moss roses on the hill.
A dry taste in the mouth, but the moment
Sufficient, being what we are, ourselves still.

Alan Ross

Foreword by Ted Dexter

I suppose you have to be an optimist to be a half-decent games player. Thinking about all the things that can go wrong is halfway to failure before you start. Happily there was much for me to be optimistic about on those fine mornings, travelling on the *Brighton Belle* from Victoria, looking forward to winning the toss and having a bat on that excellent Hove pitch.

It was only a short step from that thought to hoping to be involved in a partnership with the sublimely gifted, sandy-haired Jim Parks. You could pick out his style from a mile away, open stanced with his hands high on the handle. No furrowed brow for this prince of sweet ball strikers. Come hell or high water, there was always the same quiet smile and a mere nod of the head to appreciate the crowd as they applauded yet another curvaceous swing of the bat.

Batting with such a stylish, unaffected, unselfish character simply made the whole business seem much easier for anyone the other end. What it was not wise to do was to take him on at table tennis, shove-halfpenny, darts or tiddlywinks, to name but a few of his other talents. You were lucky to get away with your shirt.

Jim was just one of the 'pros' when I started, with Robin Marlar captain and Don Smith senior pro. Then he was my senior pro and went on to captain the county. None of these moves ever changed the way he played. Nor did the sudden change from the amateur and pro days to the more liberal regime when all who played were deemed to be cricketers, paid or not. In fact Jim was a role model whom others would have done well to emulate.

There was a period from the early sixties till late in the eighties, and even into the nineties, when many of the new breed taking to the paid ranks of county cricket seemed to put their earnings first and the game second. It was hard to put a finger on the form and substance of that suspicion, but whatever it was, it was never even faintly true of this particular representative of the great Sussex cricketing family carrying the name of Parks.

I was a great supporter of Jim's decision to don the wicketkeeping gloves half way through his career. Of course he was a loss as a superb fielder and catcher in any position, but it was a way of getting him into the England side. He should have been in long before, in my opinion.

One thing that might have been held against him by selectors was a slight reputation for playing the faster bowlers less well than the slows. But for every bit of that silly tittle-tattle, I could cite an innings of superb quality and not a flinch of any kind, such as playing Jackson and Rhodes on a green top at Derby when he stroked them all over the ground. The rest of us were struggling even to make contact.

Jim has continued to bring great benefit to Sussex as a keen supporter and administrator ever since he hung up his boots, always with the same welcoming smile. I remain wary, however, lest he should want to take me on at snooker, billiards or cards, for I am sure the result would be just the same as it always was.

Introduction

I watched my earliest first-class cricket at the Central Ground in Hastings around 1952. It would have been County Week or the Festival, and I was at once captivated by the ebb and the flow, the grace and the power, the names and the history. Here indeed was a game with a glorious past, a thrilling present and an infinite future. Summer, it seemed to an eight-year-old, would go on forever.

I followed Sussex, of course, and Tom Marchant, our neighbour, ran Hollington United, a thriving outfit in the East Sussex League with a promising goalkeeper named Alan Oakman, who got me all the autographs. I read them today as I write – George Cox, Hubert Doggart, Ted James, John Langridge, Charlie Oakes, Gordon Potter, David Sheppard, Ken Suttle, Ian Thomson, Rupert Webb, Jim Wood – and Jim Parks. He was the one who excited me and my friends the most: the player who, like Botham or Flintoff, would empty the bars, who in 1952 had schoolboys rushing down Queen's Road to see if he was batting, who hit with joyous abandon, who pounced on a cover-drive like a cat on a rat and who, when he was out, still smiled at the cricketing fates. Then my dad told me that he knew his uncle Harry. Wonder of wonders, we were practically related! 'Yes,' said Dad, 'he played left-back for Hastings when I was in goal.'

This book tells the story of one of the county's favourite sons. It is a Sussex life born of the warp and weft of the Weald, part of that dynastic tradition enriching the cricketing past of the county which is the cradle of the game. The story sets 'young Jim', as he was always known, in the context of his family's past; it also sets his family in its socio-geographical and historical milieu, for roots are integral to our story. Finally, it relates Jim's sporting chronicle against the background of Sussex's fortunes as he grows and matures as a player and a man.

I am deeply grateful to all those former players who gave so generously of their time in research for this book: David Allen, Keith Andrew, Trevor Bailey, Bob Barber, Don Bates, Geoffrey Boycott, Frank Clarke, Brian Close, Ted Dexter, Hubert Doggart, Peter Graves, Mike Griffith, Raymond Illingworth, Ted James, Alan Knott, David Mantell, John Murray, Charlie Oakes, Alan Oakman, Gordon Potter, Don Shepherd, David Sheppard, Mike Smith,

Mickey Stewart, Raman Subba Row, Ken Suttle, Ian Thomson, Derek Underwood, Peter Wales, Alan Watkins and Rupert Webb.

'When you play so many games they all merge into one,' John Murray told me. I have therefore identified what I term the 'memory shift syndrome', in which a player may be talking about an innings which he played in a different game against a completely different bowler in a different town and five years earlier – but why let the facts get in the way of a good story?

I also received anecdotes, memories and memorabilia from many school-mates, friends, supporters and RAF colleagues: Fred Cleary, Paul Dallaway, Bryan Dolbear, Gordon Fowlie, Malcom Greffen, John Hall, Al Hams, George Haspell, H.J. Hedges, Nigel Hepper, Alan Hill, Flyle Hussain, Jimmy James, Ron Lack, John Loarridge, Tony Millard, Gwen Newcombe, Dennis Nicholls, Alan Pratt, Geoff Sear, Gordon Smith, John Stanbrook, Bruno Stratta, Jack Sydenham, John Tester, Ray Thompsett, Nick Turner, Doug Turville, Lorraine Voss née Whitehead and Percy Williams. I am indebted to all of them.

I should like to thank also Rob Boddie, librarian and archivist at the County Ground, Hove, for all his help and advice; Christopher Martin-Jenkins; John Woodcock; Malcolm Woolley, for his assistance with the archive photography; Blatchington Mill School, Hove, and St Wilfrid's School, Haywards Heath, for allowing me access to their school records; and the British Newspaper Library and Sussex Archives at Lewes.

For permission to reproduce photographs thanks are due as follows: the *Argus* for plate 37; Blatchington Mill School for plates 6, 7, 8 and 14; the Newcombe family for plate 5; Jim Parks for plates 4, 16, 18, 24, 38 and 39; Mark Peel for plate 36; Geoff Sear for plate 9; and Sussex County Cricket Club for back cover image and plates 1, 2, 3, 4, 15, 20 and 28 and John Wallace for plates 13, 23 and 26. While every endeavour has been made to trace and obtain copyright for the other photographs, apologies are offered if any copyright has inadvertently been infringed.

My special thanks go to Bobby Parks – and of course, 'young Jim', who was invariably approachable and unfailingly courteous through over six months' research, interviews and questions, questions, questions… Thanks to him and to Jenny for the coffee!

Most of all, the entire project would have failed without the constant support and encouragement of my partner, Gerry, chief critic, proof-reader and copy editor. Finally, to Che, Roger and Rod, and all the other friends of Bill W. and Dr Bob – thanks for your belief in the project, and in me.

Derek Watts
Lewes
December 2004

Prologue
Down the Brighton Line

In August 1997, the Old England XI took the field against Haywards Heath Cricket Club on the Recreation Ground in Sydney Road. Captain for the day and playing his last ever game of cricket was Jim Parks, whose presence created a personal link between that game and events on the ground a century before. Haywards Heath was 'so called, according to tradition, from the fact of a highwayman named Hayward being captured in the vicinity, and hung in chains on the heath'.[1] Historians tell us, however, that Hayworth, the earliest form of Haywards Heath, was known in the thirteenth century. The afforested Weald possessed enclosures called *haiae* or hays, in which game was conserved for hunting. Thus the name Hayworth seems to mean 'an enclosure for keeping animals for sport' – a connection to the game of cricket which is of course purely coincidental. In 1879 Haywards Heath could 'scarcely be described as a town, nor can it condescend to the appellation of a village'.[2] Half a century before, it did not exist as a distinct settlement. The origins of the present town lie in the entrepreneurial vigour of the early Victorian age.

At a quarter to seven on the morning of Tuesday 21 September 1841, the first-ever train to link London and Brighton puffed out of Victoria and arrived soon after nine o'clock. The train passed through a lonely station at a point on the Sussex Weald chosen so that neither Lindfield nor Cuckfield need suffer the noise and indignity of having this new fangled transport system shatter their rural idyll. The line had been built through a swathe of heath between the two villages. Its construction had been threatened when the railway navvies found themselves a couple of miles from the nearest source of beer: they were on the verge of striking until a boy was employed to fetch and carry essential supplies. By the early 1840s Haywards Heath and other centres like Burgess Hill and Hassocks – which had begun as 'urban villages' on commons enclosed by an Act of Parliament – became suburban dormitories. By 1860 many residents of Haywards Heath commuted to Brighton for commerce, leisure and employment and, with the advent of more frequent services, London increasingly became within daily reach.

Five years after the arrival of the railway, the number of daily coaches on
the turnpike from the capital to the coast had dwindled to one, and the railway pressed on to Bognor, Hastings and Worthing. A combination of poor
agricultural land and a reliable railway system led to increasing urbanisation
in rural Sussex. These factors, together with the construction of substantial
homes for the growing Victorian middle class and 'a desire for rural quiet'[3]
stimulated the development of new towns.

By 1862 Haywards Heath Common had been enclosed, making land
available for building, and by 1870 Haywards Heath was described as 'the
abode of civilisation, many villas and pleasure residences having sprung up
almost by magic'.[4] St Wilfrid's church was built in the 1860s, and under the
1894 Local Government Act the scattered hamlet became a town and a civil
parish, and an urban district council was formed. There followed a gas company, hotels and banks; a new lunatic asylum provided a third of the 3,717
inhabitants in 1901. A minority of these were inmates, but this institution,
located strategically just far enough outside the town to assuage the sensi-
bilities of the populace, also provided employment. The growing sense of
community fostered new schools, churches and a local press and the dynam-
ics of urban commerce attracted people from the rural hinterland of Sussex
– and of neighbouring counties too.

Chapter 1
Runs in the Family

Horace Parks was born in Maidstone in 1842 and in his twenties moved to Haywards Heath. In 1867 he married a local girl, Jane Skinner, and is described as an 'attendant' at the St Francis Asylum in the census of 1881. In that year the *Mid-Sussex Times* was founded, stimulating both civic consciousness and new employment opportunities. In 1891 Horace's son, Mark, was working there as a fifteen-year-old apprentice printer, and a decade later he had become a printer/compositor with a young son of his own.

What clinched the town's regional importance was the weekly cattle market, established in 1868, which was allied closely with the railway; a cattle train left for Brighton after the Tuesday sales. *Clarke's Directory* mentioned in 1879 that it was 'a rising township after the American States style'.[1] The coming of the railway, the farming hinterland, the establishment of banks, hotels, churches, schools, newspapers, trading posts and a market – even the stagecoaches – are the elements which underpinned the town's evolution. It is an exquisite evocation of these factors in the town's growth that Horace's great-grandson, Jim, should enjoy the Westerns at the Perrymount cinema in the late 1930s. They were Jim's favourite genre, and they reflect the flavour of the early years of his birthplace.

More people meant more business. A growing population also fostered more social interaction, which found expression in the British penchant for forming clubs. There was a demand for more recreational amenities, and the council provided footballers with facilities in the new park in the centre of the town. Summer games were catered for too. Victoria Park was also the base for the Haywards Heath Lawn Tennis Club, and stoolball, that strange game virtually unique to Sussex and Kent, saw two clubs – the Bluebells and the Asters – playing there.

Cricket, the main summer game, had flourished in the county for over 150 years and in 1882 the Haywards Heath club 'removed its headquarters from Sydney Road to a spacious field at Great Haywards'.[2] In 1894 the new urban district council became the focus of much civic energy in the provision of better recreational amenities.

Mr Jesse Finch, a prominent local businessman, had long nurtured a scheme to tidy up a polluted watercourse which was spoiling a large part of the recreation ground. His plan was adopted by the council and completed at a cost of almost £450, Haywards Heath Cricket Club contributing a significant amount. The *Mid-Sussex Times* for Tuesday 29 June 1897 records, in florid prose, the 'Opening of the Haywards Heath Cricket Ground'. The whole tenor of the report is redolent of the *Pickwick Papers*, and the opening sentence of the piece has distinct overtones of Jane Austen:

> It seems a peculiar characteristic of many Englishmen that having fixed their minds upon achieving a certain object, and having set the ball rolling, so to say, they immediately become despondent and despair of their mind's object realising a successful issue.[3]

The paper describes the grumblings about council delays, but, on Wednesday 23 June 1897, the first match was played on the ground, which was opened by the chairman of the district council, Mr Bannister, who was also the president of the cricket club. A Mr Nye asked if working men might play on the ground. The president replied that the ground was for everyone in the district and if working men applied to the council their application would receive every attention. It is interesting to note how the issue of class in late Victorian society underlies something as apparently un-controversial as the provision of a leisure amenity.

The ground may have opened with due fanfare, but there was no pavilion: players and scorers used a marquee. The match itself was a one-sided affair. Fourteen of the Haywards Heath Club played against thirty-two assembled from the district. In glorious weather the latter batted first and scored only 67, the scorecard recording that one F.W. Tate was 'caught Thring bowled Golding 7'. This was Fred Tate, a Sussex cricketing legend, who five years later was playing for England against Australia at Old Trafford. Fred, often known as 'Chub', was the father of the great Maurice, voted by Sussex supporters in 2004 as the finest cricketer ever to play for the county. Maurice spent his early life in the town and in 1911, aged sixteen, was playing for the club. By 7.30 p.m., when play was stopped, the Haywards Heath XIV had knocked up 166 for 12, which included 'M. Parks b Higgs 9'. The printer/compositor, son of Horace from Kent, and grandfather of Jim, played in the inaugural game.

Three years after that first match, Mark Parks senior appeared in another when he married Ellen Mary Ede, from Cuckfield, and over the next decade they produced seven children. The three eldest sons, Mark junior, Jim and Harry all played their early cricket on the ground. Charles and Percy were twins, born in February 1908, but sadly Percy died only a month later. A similarly tragic fate befell a sixth child, born late in 1908, who died in 1913. The last of the line was Ivy Mary, born in 1910. Ivy inherited her father's sporting genes, for during the 1930s she captained the Bluebells Stoolball Club to the county championship four times in five years. It was two of her brothers, however, who achieved the most.

James Horace, born in May 1903, did not play cricket at school. In his teenage years, soccer was the leading sport in the Parks household, with his mother Ellen a formidable coach, cheerleader and critic. 'She expected, even demanded, us to do well', Jim senior recalled, 'and it could be embarrassing for us as she egged on the rest of the crowd to cheer us in the town matches.'[4] In the wind and rain, Mrs Parks must have cut a striking figure as she marched up and down the touchline brandishing an admonishing brolly at those churlish fans who failed to cheer on her boys. In the early twenties Jim was an inside-forward, brother Mark played on the left wing and Harry at left-back (he later played for Hastings in the Southern League, with the author's father in goal).

Jim was in his late teens when he started to think seriously about a career in cricket. After the First World War he became a first-team regular for Haywards Heath, noted for his top-class fielding. A good performance against Sussex Club and Ground attracted the interest of the county. Jim scored 50 – the next highest score was 9 – and took 6 for 44. 'With his round face and ruddy complexion, old Jim looked every inch a countryman cricketer.'[5] He made his debut for Sussex in 1924 and in only his third game, against Leicestershire at Horsham, he took 7 for 17 with his slow medium off-cutters and in-swingers. Jim skittled the Foxes for only 51 in their second innings, leaving Harold Gilligan and Ted Bowley to knock off the 5 runs needed to win.

Jim found batting a much harder discipline, but under Albert Relf and George Cox senior he developed into a sound opener. Careful and compact, he was a skilful cutter, playing late and close to the stumps. Relf had been Sussex's leading all-rounder in the first two decades of the century and in the thirties became an outstanding coach. George Cox was one of the new generation of professionals fostered by the county in the transitional years following the Edwardian era of Ranji and Fry. Duleep, Ranji's nephew, was a source of pride and a natural link to that golden age, but a quartet of brothers, Parks and Langridge, were on the thresholds of great careers. Henry William G. (Harry) Parks, born in July 1906, began his county career in 1926 and over the next twenty years he and his brother became indispensable stalwarts of Sussex cricket.

In 1929 Jim scored 110 and his mentor Ted Bowley 280 in an opening stand of 368, then a record for the county, against Gloucestershire at Hove. Bowley, a gifted batsman and unselfish partner, had a profound influence on the younger players. 'He set us a marvellous example and it was an education to bat with him. In my view he was the finest professional batsman to play for Sussex.'[6] By 1934 Jim Parks had become one of the leading all-rounders in the country and a year later he achieved his first double of 1,627 runs and 101 wickets. This gained him selection for E.R. Holmes' MCC side to tour Australasia in the winter of 1935/36, along with his county colleague Jim Langridge. The Sussex pair showed good all-round form but it was a long tour. The MCC opened in Perth at Hallowe'en, spent Christmas in Christchurch and left for home in mid-March.

Jim senior's six-month absence in the Antipodes came at a difficult time for the family. In 1930 he had married Irene Heaver, a Brighton girl three years his junior, and the couple set up home at 129 Western Road in Haywards Heath. On 21 October 1931 at the family home, a son, James Michael, was born. Family life, however, was to last only five years as Irene contracted tuberculosis in 1935. She convalesced at Darvell Hall, near Robertsbridge, where coincidentally the author's father was a patient at the same time. Irene was gravely ill and there was an energetic four-year-old to look after. She declined during 1936 and returned home, where she died on 8 October with her husband by her bedside. Young Jim 'can't remember much about my mother as a person at all – I can vaguely picture her standing in the lounge once and that's about all.'

In 1937, Jim senior set a record which will almost certainly never be beaten. His feats of that summer are attributed by his son to the grief of that bereavement: 'Mother had died in the previous year and Dad just threw himself into his cricket to try to forget the loss.'

Jim senior scored 3,003 runs in that season and took 101 wickets. He scored 11 centuries in 63 innings, setting up a county fifth-wicket record of 297 with his brother Harry against Hampshire at Portsmouth. He also made his only Test appearance, opening the innings for England with a young Len Hutton against New Zealand at Lord's.

Jim senior's unique record and the 19,720 runs he scored for the county – not to mention his 795 wickets – assure him his place in the Sussex cricketing pantheon. Yet his younger brother Harry scored more runs – 21,763 – and more centuries – 42 – than Jim. In August 1930 he made 123 against Lancashire at Eastbourne, while brother Jim scored 115 in the same innings – an event unique at the time. Taller than his brother, and blessed with the balanced poise of an athlete, Harry was an outstanding outfielder and an aggressive middle-order batsman, who drove impressively off the front foot. Perhaps Harry's greatest pre-war performance was at Leyton in 1933 when he made an unbeaten 114 in the first innings and scored 105 not out in the second. At that point only four other players had ever scored two unbeaten centuries in a match.

Although Jim senior and Harry were the professionals, the other brothers – Mark, the eldest, and Charlie, the youngest – also played for Haywards Heath at football and cricket.[7] Their father, Mark senior, was 'a fine footballer as well as a cricketer'. Aunt Ivy captained the Bluebells, who as well as being county champions gained the Jubilee Challenge Cup for the best stoolball team in mid-Sussex. In 1938 she married Dick Richards, a slow left-arm bowler from Bognor, who played eighteen matches for Sussex between 1927 and 1935. The real sports fanatic was Ellen, the matriarch and touchline termagant, who died in Blackpool in 1978 at the age of ninety-nine. Jim remembers that she was mentally as sharp as a button well into her late eighties. 'She would often be watching cricket on television. Sometimes they'd be playing old footage of me and she would say "Why did you do that?", even at that age.' Throughout the thirties, therefore, young Jim grew up in a family whose life was ruled by the rhythms of professional sport. 'For Jim Parks was born into the cricketing purple, the great family tradition which startles and sparkles through the history of Sussex cricket.'[8]

Jim remembers a bat in his hand at five years old, having a daily net in the garden before his father went off to play for the county. Number 129 Western Road is an unremarkable, solidly built semi-detached house; between the wars the large garden housed both the cricket net and a substantial vegetable patch, for Jim senior was very keen on his garden. Young Jim was urged to hit the ball hard, and in one summer in the thirties he shattered twenty-seven windows in neighbours' houses. Jim senior paid up with good grace and a smile: 'He always taught me with good humour and was very encouraging.' Jim senior also taught him leg-spinners: 'I thought bowling fast was too energetic.' The early development of his football skills was not neglected either. 'My father used to make me kick left-footed, so although I was a right-footed player naturally, I became an inside-left, until I got a bit older and moved to left-half.' Valuable as this early coaching was, and as much as it created a sporting bond between them, Jim and his son were parted for much of the year. Young Jim was barely five when his mother died, and since 'my father got on very well with his mother-in-law she moved to Western Road and brought me up. My grandfather was a tailor by trade and had his own business down in Brighton. He used to look after the garden and greenhouse for my father as he was away so much in the summer.'

Although the town's population in the year young Jim was born was only 7,344, it had doubled in thirty years. Still, Jim's recollection was that 'Haywards Heath was only a small market town: the biggest shop was a Co-op in Wivelsfield Road.' Cars were rare and Johnny Johnson delivered the milk on an old handcart. 'He had only one arm. He'd lost the other in the First World War but he was a very good footballer.' Recreational activities for boys of Jim's age were largely ones they made themselves. 'During the winter we'd go up to St Wilfrid's Boys' Club twice a week and play table tennis and five-a-side football in the hall.' The town had two cinemas the Broadway and the Perrymount, which Jim preferred. 'My favourites were the Westerns – especially the Lone Ranger and Tonto. I remember being on my own a lot. I don't remember there being too many friends around,' although Dennis Nicholls, who was at the same primary school, recalls 'going to Western Road and playing cricket up against the garage door with his father, Jim, trying to teach us… to bowl a spinner. We used to bat down the little alleyway that led up to the garage.'

Dennis was a schoolmate at St Wilfrid's, the church primary school where Jim was enrolled in the infants' department in September 1937. Also at St Wilfrid's were Doug Turville, a good footballer who later became a school-mate of Jim's in Hove and a team-mate for Haywards Heath, and the Young sisters, Pam and Irene. Jim's education had begun a year earlier at Belvedere, a private school in Bolnore Road, which boasted amongst its alumni the legendary Maurice Tate. Jim recalls that Belvedere gave him a flying start academically and 'I had been at St Wilfrid's two or three years before they caught up'.

In the summer 'my grandmother took me to cricket and we always sat at the top of the ground with Joe Vine[9] and his wife.' Jim's earliest memory of a game at Hove was in 1937 and the redoubtable Laetitia Stapleton, a Sussex member for over half a century, remembers 'seeing his grandparents wheeling him round the ground in his pram, for they would never miss a match in which their sons, Jim and Harry, were playing.'[10] The day's cricket in late July, against Lancashire, would have stuck in the memory of the least committed spectator, let alone a boy whose father and uncle were involved in the fray. Eddie Paynter hit 3 sixes and 39 fours on that first day before Jim senior bowled him for 322. 'I loved watching him even when he hit my Dad for 6 – because he hit the ball hard.'[11] Cyril Washbrook scored 108, Lancashire amassed 640 for 8 declared, and Jim's dad toiled in the sun for 5 for 144. Yet that apple-cheeked countenance bore a resigned smile – 'Cricket's a game, son, and a game to be enjoyed.'[12]

Young Jim had an enquiring mind and was always asking the groundsman about the wicket. He also spent a lot of time with Jim and Harry in the home dressing room. He became almost as familiar a figure at Hove in the late 1930s as he was thirty years later – and not only in the pavilion. He had both the Langridges bowling to him in the nets, but they made no attempt to coach the youngster. Jim was an instinctive stroke-maker and remained so – although George Cox did say to him on one occasion, 'One day, I guess, you'll be a fast bowler.'[13] Rubbing shoulders – so to speak – with the Sussex professionals, household names like Cox, Langridge, Cornford and Tate, did not make Jim blasé about the game. He had his heroes – the greatest of them Denis Compton, then making his way in Test cricket as a dashing young shot-maker of carefree genius. Jim still remembers the thrill when Harry got him his hero's autograph, the dream of finding his boyhood hero in the side when he made his Test debut in 1954 and the chagrin of catching out the great man in his last game against Sussex three years later.

Young Jim's other cricketing images of the thirties included a visit to Hastings in August 1938 for the derby game against Kent. Jim senior made 78 on the first day, but he was overshadowed by the hitting of Hugh Bartlett, who cracked 114 in 105 minutes, including 4 sixes and 14 fours. Then Jim Langridge skittled Kent for 115; Tich Cornford was hit in the mouth and Uncle Harry donned the gloves and held two catches in Kent's second innings as Jim Langridge took 6 for 91 to clinch a win by an innings and 15 runs. Hugh Bartlett features again in Jim's memories of 1938 as he played one of the finest innings ever seen at Hove, against the might of the touring Australians. Fielding a side not markedly changed, apart from the omission of Bradman, from the one that had played in Hutton's record-breaking Oval Test, the tourists were, at one stage, in danger of defeat. Batting first, they made a solid 336, and in reply Sussex were 109 for 3 when Bartlett was joined by Jim Langridge. Then the fun began. Bartlett reached his 50 in half an hour and his century came up in 57 minutes as he added 195 with Langridge. He took 21 off Frank Ward's leg-spin in one over and struck 18 fours and 6 sixes, one of which ended up on the grass by the tavern beside the main gates.

After the war Bartlett reappears in Jim's story as his first county captain, having seen service at Arnhem and been awarded the DFC. When Jim saw him strike the Australians to all parts, the war was a gathering storm, a menacing aspect of that late summer when the clouds lowering over the international scene darkened. This looming peril affected local communities all over the country: Haywards Heath did not escape. The log book of St Wilfrid's records in late September: 'In consequence of the international crisis and the threat of war, daily fire drill is being practised this week, the children being trained to obey unexpected orders swiftly and silently.'[14]

It was a wet autumn and a hard winter. Jim enjoyed an early Christmas holiday as heavy snow forced the early closure of school. The snow persisted into January and attendance was low during most of the Lent term, as the children were suffering with coughs, colds and influenza, although 'I didn't suffer very much – I've never had flu in my life.' Considering the heating with which the school was blessed it is scarcely surprising that the pupils succumbed to these ailments – indeed it is a wonder that many of them attended at all. Jim remembers the cheerlessness of the Victorian school: 'It was a big old building and the ceilings seemed about fifty feet high. The rooms were always bitterly cold.' Dennis Nicholls recalls the only heating being 'large coke stoves in the classrooms…. The only people kept warm were the teacher and the front row of desks. If you sat at the back you froze.'

Creature comforts were almost totally lacking. Children walked to school, and if it was teeming with rain and blowing hard many would have stayed at home, especially as there were no school dinners and everyone walked home and back in the lunch hour. Other elements of Jim's early educational environment were positively Dickensian. The school always seemed dark 'and it was… a great and rare occasion in midwinter when they actually lit the gas light in the class and we could see'[15]; 'all the inkwells were stored in a cupboard in a corridor and in a large classroom… there were a lot of old pens sticking into the ceiling, thrown up javelin-style over the years.'[16] The author can alas confirm that conditions had altered very little fifteen years later when he went to primary school in Hastings, and the following memory has an uncomfortable resonance: 'There was a toilet… which was so dark and smelly you made sure you waited till you got home.' However, by contrast, 'the boys' toilet was brick-built and open-topped. To be able to pee over the wall was most boys' ambition but only a few show-offs could do it. You only stood the other side of the wall once and you never warned any newcomer.'

The kids at St Wilfrid's indulged in the playground games of the day, which had changed not one bit by the mid-fifties. 'I remember playing marbles, tops and conkers, collecting cigarette cards and cardboard milk bottle tops,' Jim remembers; and during the frequent cold snaps the boys would make slides in the snow down the slope from the top playground. Jim had 'a very big stamp collection and I got quite good at geography through the stamps'. The teachers tended to assume the guise of mythical, half-human creatures: 'There was a Miss Tedham, a very buxom lady, who wore a blue overall and was called Miss Teddybottle. We had music in this class, which amounted to some triangles and cymbals and not much else.'[17]

School holidays in the thirties were much shorter. The children had only four weeks to enjoy the brilliant summer of 1939. Breaking up on 4 August (ironically the silver jubilee of the outbreak of the First World War), the school was due to reopen exactly a month later. Young Jim of course played cricket and watched his father. At Eastbourne, there was an unlikely victory for Sussex as Worcestershire scored 372 on the first day, Sussex replying with 475 for 9 declared, including 115 from Jim senior. Left to score 200 to win in 105 minutes, John Langridge, usually the epitome of watchful defence, made 65 at a run a minute and Hugh Bartlett hit 59 of the last 76 in half an hour.

That last summer of peace was Jim senior's benefit year and his actual benefit game was the final, potentially attractive, fixture against a Yorkshire side containing Hutton, Leyland, Yardley, Verity and Bowes. It began in a somewhat unreal atmosphere: 'The collection for Jim Parks came to £75, whilst the Queen of Holland and the King of the Belgians were offering to mediate and Poland was accepting their offer.'[18] Nearly 500 runs were scored on the first day as Cox drove and cut for 200 minutes, hitting 28 fours and a six in a brilliant 198. It was an innings guaranteed to last for the duration of the war in the mind of all who saw it. Play on the last day took place in an ambience which bordered on the surreal; news had come through at six o'clock that Friday morning that Hitler had invaded Poland. War was inevitable. As the late summer sun blazed down on a rain-affected wicket, Sussex were bowled out for 33, Hedley Verity taking 7 for 9 in 48 balls.

By midday on the Sunday, Britain was of course at war. Young Jim heard Neville Chamberlain's fateful broadcast at his grandmother's and as he and his father walked home on that bright September morning, already the sirens were wailing. Soon Jim senior became a reserve police constable and young Jim prepared to return to a school at war. But not just yet. The Director of Education had ordered that schools be closed until Thursday 13 September 'on account of the outbreak of war and the absorption of evacuees into Sussex.'[19] Concrete air-raid shelters were built at the top of the playground and could still be seen early in 2003. Underneath the school was a basement cloakroom where the children used to sit if it was wet at playtime. This basement was turned into an air-raid shelter in 1939, as the log-book explains: 'An air-raid shelter is shortly to be constructed in the senior basement playroom. Practice in quickly collecting gas masks and outdoor clothes and reaching the playroom by appointed routes has been taken by each class.'[20]

That autumn, although he can't remember having birthday parties, young Jim received a memorable present. For his eighth birthday, Jim senior gave him a miniature bat, which he autographed for him. In the early days of the war, young Jim and the other lads used to have a scratch game in the evenings after his father had played for the Heath and Jim senior used to bowl at them. As Dennis Nicholls writes:

There were no games or sporting facilities at the school; we may have walked over to the park and had a few running races, but certainly nothing like cricket or football. St Wilfrid's can't claim fame for producing a professional cricketer like Jim.[21]

The credit for that must go to his father – and to Harry – and to the increasingly competitive cricketing environment which his wartime education provided. The country boy from the railway town was on the verge of becoming a star.

Chapter 2
Hove in Sight

War and its trappings came early to Haywards Heath. Canadians were stationed at Borde Hill and there was an Army camp at Maresfield. Every Sunday morning the troops paraded at the cenotaph on Muster Green: the Black Watch were Jim's favourite – 'I used to love their pipes and kilts'. Meat, salt and sugar became increasingly scarce:

> I never had sugar and I don't take sugar now. We always had lots of vegetables, chickens and eggs and I remember my dad killing the rabbits. We bred very big Flemish Giants, although I always had my pet.

The phoney war had become all too real by the summer. School had to be shared with the evacuees, which meant Jim had lessons in various halls in the town. By early June, France had fallen, Dunkirk had been evacuated and, to add insult to injury, a week later St Wilfrid's log book records two cases of German measles!

Day after day during that blistering summer, the Battle of Britain was fought out over the skies of southern England. Inevitably, Jim's education was regularly disrupted. In the last week of June, school attendance was 'extra low on Wednesday… owing to an Air Raid warning lasting four and a half hours (11 p.m. to 3.30 a.m.) during the previous night.'[1] Jim remembers the Battle of Britain:

> Once I counted a hundred bombers with fighter escort on their way to London, and we saw the odd bomber off-loading on the way back and fighters chasing stray Germans. If one came down, I used to collect shrapnel – bits of German planes, bullets, things like that.

By September there were night raids all week and the children were allowed to arrive at school up to 10 a.m.

In May 1942 Jim senior took his son to see him play for a Civil Defence XI against the RAF at Lord's. When young Jim was introduced to the Bedser twins, he was struck by their enormous hands – but they were not the only legends of the game Jim encountered. 'I met Denis Compton, my hero; by that time I was old enough to appreciate it. When I had met Hugh Bartlett before the war, he'd impressed me but Compton was more accessible and I knew what he was talking about.'

This must have been heady stuff for a cricket-mad schoolboy, but Jim had not neglected his studies. Although Dennis Nicholls didn't think 'we had a particularly good start to our education', in late 1942 Jim won a scholarship to Hove County School. His admission card for September 1943 is illuminating. It shows that pupil number 864 was never lower than ninth out of thirty-five in his form, scoring A for intelligence, B for industry and A for character in his second and third years.

His educational horizons were being expanded beyond what was still virtually a village primary school:

> Getting the scholarship entailed a lot of travel, much of it in the blackout. There were dim lights on the train and you always had to have the blinds down – twenty to eight in the morning in winter was a bit bleak and if there was snow on the ground, which was quite often in those days, no buses ran. They wouldn't come up Western Road, which was very steep – so we had to walk to the station. It was an hour and ten-minute journey to school via a change of trains at Brighton.

Jim's schoolmate Jonathan Austin recalls: 'The novelty of travelling for over two hours a day soon wore off, and going to school so far from home did little to improve your social life.' Jim did well at his new school, but when he did fall foul of authority his sporting background came in useful. 'I didn't get detentions very much but if you did have a half hour detention, you sprinted across Hove Park to Preston Park to get the fast London train from Brighton.'

The school had extensive playing fields comprising several cricket and football pitches. A nostalgic contemporary remembers that most summer lunch hours were spent in impromptu games of cricket 'with our coats as wickets. My one memory was bowling Jim first ball although I think the tennis ball hit a ridge before breaking sharply to hit the coats! Jim just smiled and handed over the bat to the next player.'[2] Peter Wales, who played for the school XI three years ahead of Jim and joined the Sussex staff on exactly the same day, recalls:

> Jim was a minor celebrity as a result of his father – most people who knew cricket knew he was coming to the school. Cricket equipment was very difficult to come by and I persuaded Jim to join our group, not only because of his

reputation but because he could supply reasonable quality balls from his father. Even then we could see that he was going to be a very good cricketer.

Those lunch hour knockabouts presaged crucial events some fifteen years later. 'He liked to keep wicket and he kept properly standing up to the stumps.'[3]

John Stanbrook was in Jim's year, but not in his class – in more ways than one. 'This meant that I competed against him for my house in most sports each Wednesday afternoon and he was outstanding.' In one of his first games for Gloucester House Jim made 82 not out and took 8 for 2, which won him a place in the school under-14 team. The selection pleased Jim senior, who gave him a new bat, ball, pads and batting gloves, with the advice: 'A nasty knock can not only cause an injury but make a player lose confidence. That's why you must always wear gloves.' The bat was not the only present his father gave him:

My dad bought me a beautiful new Raleigh. In the summer we'd cycle to cricket matches with our pads and bat on the handlebars. We'd go up to Horsted Keynes, Ardingly, Burgess Hill – quite some way.

Jim senior did not confine his advice to his son. He was ready to impart his knowledge and experience to Jim's schoolmates, as the school magazine for March 1945 records:

We were fortunate in having visits for net practice from Mr J.H. Parks, the Sussex and England cricketer, and we are most grateful to him for finding the time to come in spite of the exigencies of war-time duties.[4]

Don Bates, a year behind Jim at school and later a Sussex colleague, remembers: 'His dad came to watch the matches quite a lot and we were all in awe of him.' Geoff Sear stressed, however, that Jim, whilst always totally confident about his cricket, never bragged of having a famous father; indeed, he said that Jim was slightly shy but would occasionally venture the odd dry quip. The magazine records a moderately successful season, one in which 'Parks and Gates bowled with steadiness and consistency and Parks, Colwell and Goodwin batted consistently.'[5] John Hall played for Lewes County School for Boys:

In those days, kit was very short, and few people owned their own. But Jim Parks had a bat, which was of great interest to us. On the back of it, he had inscribed the words, 'hundreds I have made with this bat'. It was an impressively long list for an under-14. We never looked like getting him out.

They never looked like getting him out in 1945 either, when 'Parks was undoubtedly our best batsman, although he was not in quite the same devastating form as last year and as he also took the most wickets, he contributed considerably to the side's success.'[6] That August the *Mid-Sussex Times* carried perhaps the first-ever picture of young Jim in cricket gear. A match on Lindfield Common featured the local club against a Mark Parks XII in aid of the Pavilion Extension Fund (see Plate 6). A fortnight later Jim made his first competitive appearance at Hove, playing for East Sussex Juniors against West Sussex Juniors, scoring 15 not out in a total of 70.

The 'hundreds he had made with this bat' were probably scored for a team formed on the train to school. It was difficult in wartime for young players to get a game and Jim and some like-minded friends formed a club called the Rangers. Inevitably Jim was appointed secretary, treasurer and captain. Members were asked to pay 1s a week and soon the club attracted many schoolboy players. It was an under-14 side, but 'we felt like a proper cricket club and it was very satisfying to run things without adult help.'[7] The local council decided the municipal pitch could be used one Sunday in every four by a club other than Haywards Heath – and Jim successfully applied on behalf of the Rangers. They played mid-week games starting after 7 p.m. to allow for prep – and there was a lot of that: 'We got a lot of homework. We'd play table tennis, handball and five-a-side football at the boys' club three nights a week – but it was homework mostly.' Geoff Sear[8] recalls playing table tennis on the Morrison shelter at Western Road – and losing to Jim!

In that sense, Jim's upbringing was not unusual, 'although I suppose it was different. I didn't think much about it – I just got on with school and my sport. I learnt pretty quickly that a batsman's duty was to score runs and as quickly as possible.' Jim frequently ignored his father's advice on sound technique: 'Remember, if you hit the ball along the ground, you can never be caught out.' Near the pitch there was a big house with a lovely pear tree. As captain and leading batsman Jim saw it as his duty to hit the sixes so that his team-mates would have to rush to retrieve the ball and incidentally pilfer some pears!

It was not only cricket that the young Jim Parks excelled in. The games curriculum of a provincial grammar school in the forties and fifties followed an established rhythm: football in the Christmas and spring terms, with cross-country in the snow and mud of January and February to build character and cricket and athletics in the summer term. Somewhere in the mix was a swimming gala, with the added ingredient at Hove of inter-house boxing. Jim was soon in the school under-14 football team and played full-back for Brighton Schools. Quick and well-balanced, 'he had that sense of advanced anticipation which most sportsmen of any calibre have.'[10] An old schoolmate remembers his enthusiasm for the game:

> During the winter holidays Jim used to gather a team from his mid-Sussex school friends to meet an eleven which I raised from our Hove school pals to play the occasional game at Hove Rec. Jim's father would referee these games with such enthusiasm and encouragement for the less able players.[11]

Jim was an athlete too. A contemporary notes 'a cross-country race in the junior school in which Jim came third and he competed in house athletics, mostly at 440 and 880 yards.'[12] Naturally enough Jim came into his own in throwing the cricket ball – an event on sports day. John Stanbrook remembers Jim as being 'the complete master of all sports', but not quite – 'I kept clear of the house boxing teams.'

His early years at Hove County School were set against the background of the war. 'My father came back one lunchtime and told us that a doodlebug had crash-landed at Ansty – it must have been 1943 – and then the V2 came in which you could actually hear on a quiet night, followed by terrific explosions in London.' Enthusiastic youngsters would flock to the County Ground for the wartime games. 'Maurice Tate used to play for the Home Guard and they had services teams, with a sprinkling of County players.'[13] Jim recalls with affection Sussex's greatest cricketer: 'I used to get off the bus at Sussex Square and sometimes Maurice Tate would be there. He was stationed at a big house in Oathall Road and we would have a little chat.'

At Hove County Jim had some talented schoolmates. Don Bates, the son of the games master, Basher Bates, was an outstanding footballer, boxer and cricketer. Tall, with a whippy action, he became a team-mate at Hove for many years. Other contemporaries were Dinsdale Landen, the celebrated actor, and the splendidly named Moggy Oldfield:

> I was in my final year. We already had a Music Society and a lot of us were keen on traditional jazz – I used to listen to a jazz programme on Radio Luxembourg – and Moggy liked modern jazz. We went to the headmaster and he said, 'Fine, go ahead – but make it educational.' It was one of those after-school clubs and we did it all ourselves.

Jim still has an extensive jazz library today. Though he played chess he 'wasn't a tremendous reader – I can't remember books in the home, although I did read some comics. We used to have a paper every day and I used to have a scrap book with maps in it of how the war was going – like the stamps, it was probably geographical.'

Jim took a characteristically pragmatic attitude to his education – 'I took French and German instead of Classical Greek – my theory at the time was that they would be more use to me'. An added incentive was that the modern languages teacher, Mr Griffiths, was in charge of cricket. 'We used to call him Jumbo because he was a very big man with a big nose: he was quite a good cricketer – bowled quick.' Mr Carpenter – inevitably called 'Chips' – helped him. 'Carpenter was a batsman and bowled little leg-spinners – he taught maths. I was good at maths and got on well with Tabby [Mr Tabrett, deputy head and maths teacher] – many didn't.' Don Bates was one: 'Mr Tabrett used to frighten the life out of us in class.' Bates' clearest memory of school cricket was of limited opportunity to bat. 'Peter Wales was an excellent opener, Jim went in number four and that was it. I hardly got a bat all season at number five. Anyway, I was in the side for my bowling. Jim bowled leg-spin quite a lot and he pitched it very well.'

Jim pitched it so well that by the summer of 1946, when he was only fourteen, he made the school First XI. His father must have been proud but it was doubtful that he saw much of his son's progress. By mutual agreement Jim senior was not re-engaged by Sussex and he moved north again to Accrington. He had been posted there in late 1944 and he spent eight years in the Lancashire and Northern Leagues. In his debut season young Jim headed the batting averages and was undefeated in over half the innings he played. As the school magazine noted: 'J. Parks, although young for the XI, made some sparkling runs, with the promise of many more to come.'[14] Lest readers surmise that Jim made his runs and took his wickets against weak sides, the school also played Brighton College, Collyer's, Ardingly and Hurstpierpoint – educational establishments with some cricketing pedigree. Jim made his first-team debut for Haywards Heath that summer and, unbeknown to him, played against Mickey Stewart, a future England colleague: 'I first saw Jim at West Surrey CC in about 1946 – it was my second game for them. He was fourteen and on a sporting wicket he got about 30.'

Jim kept up his football though: that winter he was scoring goals for house and school and his growing maturity as a cricketer gained him an invitation for a trial in the nets at Hove. 'Billy' Griffith, then both captain and secretary of the county club, spoke to Jim senior and recommended to the county committee that they invite him. With his customary aplomb, Jim 'looked forward to showing the county coach and the committee of Sussex Young Amateurs what I could do.' It had certainly been a season of progress. 'This season … we have seen some interesting and enjoyable cricket… J. Parks has shown considerable improvement with the ball in addition to his sound performances with the bat.'[15] He was still not quite sixteen, yet the *Sussex Cricket Association Handbook* for 1948 noted:

> As an instance of keenness and efficiency... may we draw attention to 'young Jim's' figures for 1947. Playing for his school [Hove County], the Young Amateurs, Haywards Heath, the Cricket Association, and certain other matches, he batted in all sixty-six times for 1,636 runs [average 32.72] and 211 wickets [average 6.43]. More than half the matches were in senior club cricket.[16]

Early in August 1947, 134 young cricketers assembled at Hove. Twenty-six were chosen for a trial match and a final sixteen were selected. Four days later, Jim received a letter inviting him to join the Sussex Young Amateurs on their tour of Leicestershire, Derbyshire, Nottinghamshire and Yorkshire. Robin Marlar, a member of that squad and later Jim's county captain for five seasons, remembers the reputation which Jim brought with him to that tour:

> When the main bunch of the Sussex Young Amateurs gathered in 1947 there was much nervous looking round the squad. Who would play in the best XI? ... All agreed that one youngster, the youngest in fact, was certain of a place.'[17]

John Stanbrook, a Hove school-mate, recollects that Jim 'was only of average build, but he had all the batting skills, natural timing and he bowled leg-spin – unusual for a schoolboy player then.'[18] As Marlar put it:

> He could bat better than anyone, he bowled leg-spinners at a brisk rate... If this were not enough he was a flying machine through the covers, swooping like a hawk on anything travelling at speed off the bat. As for catches they stuck, as if he was always in place, ready to receive... All in all, Jimmy Parks was destined for stardom.'[19]

Don Bates agrees: 'He was clearly in a different class. After all, it was in the genes and he was a natural.'

Opening for Leicester Young Amateurs at Wyggeston Grammar School was Maurice Hallam, who fourteen years later would score 203 not out and 143 not out at Worthing. He made 18 as Leicester reached 108 for 8 in reply to the visitors' 204 for 6 declared, to which Jim contributed 14. After the game against Derby, the squad, in quaint post-war prose, 'enjoyed a glorious drive up the Derwent Valley through Matlock and Chatsworth. A grand run through Wharfedale via Harewood brought us to Harrogate' for the first match against Yorkshire at St George's Road. A youthful Brian Close scored only a couple in his side's 194 as Jim took 3 for 32.

Thursday's game at Huddersfield was an illustrious affair. At the Fartown ground there was a civic welcome and lunch, at which the mayor welcomed the legendary George Hirst, who in 1906 had scored 2,385 runs and had taken 208 wickets for Yorkshire. Jim senior was also there and so Hirst and Jim, two great all-rounders, met for first time. Jim senior was then playing for Accrington, but as the *Huddersfield Daily Examiner* for 14 August had it, he came from further afield: 'included in the side is J.M. Parks, son of the old Sussex player, who came over from Africa, where he is a professional, to see his son play'[20] (and drove back in the evening no doubt). Brian Close was not playing that day as Sussex dismissed Yorkshire for 150, Jim taking 4 for 46. When Sussex replied, Jim came in at 66 for 4:

> Parks, facing Fielding, a fast slinger, slashed alarmingly at his first over and three snicks careered through or over the slips to the boundary; but after these escapes he settled down to play the stroke properly and he and Mallinson put on 67 valuable runs.[21]

Jack Arlidge, the doyen of sporting journalists in Sussex, covered the tour: 'His father came into the press-box while he was batting, watched very intently as young Jim made 30 or 40 runs, and said to me, "Jack, he'll do. He'll make a county player, you mark my words."'[22] Sussex won at Huddersfield, were shown over Headingley by the Yorkshire president, beat Nottingham by 9 wickets and watched some of the county match at Edgbaston. It had been an instructive week – and to cap it all, Jim senior gave his son £10 to cover the cost of the tour.

Jim did not have time to put his feet up, though. In the Haywards Heath Cricket Week, five games in five days for the Sussex Cricket Association were capped by an exciting win for the Young Amateurs over Buckinghamshire. Jim made only 15 in Sussex's 193, a total which featured Robin Marlar's cavalier approach to batting. He made 25 from his first eight balls and was out on the ninth. In reply, Tanner and Newman put on 148 for the first wicket, 'but then Newman sliced an off-drive which gave Parks a difficult caught and bowled' and Jim finished with 4 for 46.[23]

He had just a week to scrub up before his father remarried at St Wilfrid's. His bride, Sybil Parker, lived close by in Western Road, and young Jim moved to his other grandmother's house in Wivelsfield Road when Jim senior went off to New Zealand to coach. In 1948/49 his father coached at the Lancaster Club in Christchurch, and the following winter took another coaching post at Napier.

A sign of young Jim's development as a cricketer came a week after his father's wedding as he captained the Young Amateurs against Middlesex Grammar Schools at Hove. The following day was his sternest test so far against a strong Kent side. Jim took 3 for 38 as Kent made 187 in reply to the hosts' 167. Sussex, including eighteen-year-old David Sheppard, were in trouble at 89 for 5 when 'a splendid partnership by Randall and Parks added 150 in 65 minutes, a feature being the running between the wickets.'[24] Sussex declared at 239 for 5 and then bowled Kent out for 165, to win by 54 runs, Jim taking 3 for 39.

Jim returned to a newly named school in September and between then and November scored nine goals for the County Grammar School for Boys. At Christmas, 'I first played for the football club. My father was manager of Haywards Heath. On Boxing Day he came back at lunchtime and said they were one short so I went and played centre-forward.' He was still catching the train to school, of course. One of his travelling companions was Irene Young, who had been at St Wilfrid's with him. 'Rene was at the girls' school and I was at the boys' school. We became friends mainly by travelling on the train together: we had to wear school uniform – blazers and caps, and a satchel.' Don Bates corroborates this charming picture of teenage innocence: 'I remember Jim rushing from school down Nevill Road every day to Hove County School for Girls and waiting faithfully outside for Rene to get the train back to Haywards Heath.'

Girlfriend or no girlfriend, Jim's cricket in that year of Australian dominance went from strength to strength. He made 267 runs at 24.27 with a highest score of 100 not out. That century was made against the staff in what was always the last match before the summer holidays. John Tester recalls that knock: 'When "Chips" Carpenter came on to bowl his very slow leg spin, Jim dispatched each ball of his first over for six to all parts of the school field.' Another old boy, Bruno Stratta, remembers Jim hitting a six and striking the school clock off the bowling of 'Buster' Burnett, who was short and bowled off the wrong foot. The author can confirm that to this day the Blatchington Mill School clock sports a horizontal crack across its handsome face.

Jim was selected to represent Sussex Young Amateurs for his second season, which opened with a game against Yorkshire Owls at Haywards Heath in June. He was bowled for 11 by the future Test spinner Bob Appleyard. If it was not already a formality, a half-century and a couple of wickets in the trial game at Hove in late July confirmed his place.

The next week was the turning point of his young life. Against Gloucestershire YA at Hove, the pressure of a one-day game, the need for quick runs and the intense concentration whetted Jim's appetite for the first-class game. Sussex opened with a brisk 112 of which Jim scored 30, then dismissed the visitors for 63, Jim taking 3 for 11. In the afternoon, Jim led the hunt for quick runs, with 'a brilliant 90 in under 45 minutes, containing 5 sixes and 5 fours'.[25] Sussex left Gloucester 180 to win but once again they had no answer to Jim s leg-spin, crumbling for 66 as he ended with 6 for 22. 'I became aware of definite Sussex interest. 'Billy' Griffith began to have discussions with my father. It was also about then I was thinking of going to Loughborough.' That summer saw Sussex entertain Leicester and Yorkshire YA in return for their hospitality of the year before. Jim opened the bowling against Leicester at Worthing and took 6 for 42, his first four wickets for 2 runs, all clean bowled. He then put on 43 in 22 minutes with Chappell, 'before Jim's propensity for hooking the ball just under good-length again found him out'.[26] Brian Close got runs in a rain-affected game at Hastings and on the Friday at Hove made a brilliant 127. It was quite a side that the visitors fielded – 'they were all there – Close, Illingworth – Closey was quick and bowled seamers down the hill. Even then Fred had a beautiful action and I remember him steaming up the hill.'

A pleasant trip to Buckinghamshire, where Jim captained the side, and a first sighting of Colin Cowdrey completed a memorable season. At Gerrards Cross Jim made an attractive 88 before being stumped and 'safely judged an awkward catch' as Sussex won by 52 runs.[27] 'A delightful drive back via Staines, Kingston and Leatherhead completed a most enjoyable day'[28] – ah, the delights of the open road before the M25! At Canterbury, Sussex were all out for 177 on the first day, and had Kent 17 for 3 before Cowdrey, then fifteen and at Tonbridge School, made 159 and even had the temerity to bowl Jim for 18! 'It was the first time we met and he played beautifully.'

Jim had qualified for exemption from London University Matriculation and had achieved two distinctions – in mathematics and geography. He was now a sixth-former and undecided what to do. Billy Griffith spoke to Jim senior, who felt it would be better for Jim to join the Lord's ground staff, 'but I didn't want to go. What really swayed me was when I fell out with the headmaster and was banned from school sports teams.' This spat with the head highlights Jim's sense of loyalty and commitment. Selected to play for Haywards Heath in a Sussex senior cup tie, he had

cleared it with Basher Bates – Don Bates's Dad – who said, 'Yes, of course you can play.' When the school teams were announced at assembly on the Friday my name was in the side so I went straight round to Basher and said, 'What about it ?' He said, 'Sorry, the headmaster says you've got to play.' I said, 'Sorry, you've given me permission – I can't drop out of Haywards Heath now' – so I went and played for the Heath. I was then banned from all sport at school.

My housemaster, Mr Andrew, was so furious about it that I was allowed to play house matches – but I never played for the school again. If Basher had said 'no' straightaway when I queried it, fine, but having been given permission, I felt that a commitment was a commitment.

Jim then decided on a cricket career. 'Dad had no problem accepting my reluctance to go to Lord's. It just didn't appeal to me and I couldn't see the point of it.' For Jim had no choice: it was inescapable, almost predestined. He was a Sussex man and Sussex was his first love:

> I'd played a few club and ground games, Hendren was coach, so I was going to get as good a grounding here as anywhere else. I was also a very independent person. I'd been travelling around quite a bit: having had no mother I was left to my own devices. Dad was just delighted that I wanted to play cricket'.

In the autumn of 1948 Jim senior again spoke to Griffith and it was decided that Jim would join the ground staff at Hove in the spring. On Monday 4 April 1949, young Jim became a professional cricketer. He took the train to Brighton, met up with Ken Suttle, whom he had played against in club cricket, and reported to Patsy Hendren, who became his coach, boss and friend. Hendren's geniality shone through from the first: 'Welcome, lads. Never be afraid to ask me anything. That's the only way you'll learn.'[29] Jim's wages were £3 a week and, if he was selected for the First XI, the match fee would be £6: for the Second XI it was £4. As the season approached Jack Arlidge wrote:

> With the arrival of the Sussex County professionals at the County Ground, Hove, the other day, we drew an exciting step nearer the start of 'the beautiful game with the beautiful name.'… And who are the likely stars of tomorrow? Young Jim Parks, eighteen-year-old son of the famous Jim Parks, 'literally possesses unbounded possibilities', to quote Sir Home Gordon.[30] Patsy Hendren has told me that he may well be a second Denis Compton if he has the capacity for taking pains, for no sportsman ever reaches such heights without striving, practising, learning, and then striving, practising and learning all over again. Young Jim is a grand fielder in any position, which is really saying something, and I well remember his all-round ability on the tour of the Young Amateurs of Sussex to the North and Midlands two seasons back. At Huddersfield his father joined us in the press box, watched the lad doing his stuff with bat and ball, and uttered the significant phrase, 'He'll do'.[31]

It was now up to young Jim to prove it.

Chapter 3
Called to the Colours

Patsy Hendren was a cockney with Irish blood who loved a bit of slapstick to amuse the crowd: small wonder then that his fledgling pros found practice fun. Though he was largely self-taught, Hendren's profound knowledge and wide experience of the game perceived chinks in the armour of even the most gifted of his brood. He thought that young Jim 'had too many shots and not enough defence'.[1] This echo of his father's advice fell on stony ground. 'One of the weaknesses of modern cricket,' thought Jim, ' is that few players seem to realise that they're handed a bat for offensive purposes',[2] and he determined to hit the ball hard whenever he could.

Hendren worked the lads rigorously for two hours every morning and afternoon; in addition they performed all the normal ground staff duties – helping roll the wicket, looking after the deckchairs – and of course playing in club and ground games. While he might not have been the most strictly technical of coaches, Hendren had a human touch and a wealth of cricket stories which kept the youngsters in stitches when it rained. These breaks often included games of table tennis in the refreshment hut, which Jim always won. Ted Dexter said of Jim, 'His eye-hand co-ordination was quite extraordinary – if you played him at table tennis he'd win – and probably left-handed too.' Apart from Peter Wales and Kenny Suttle, other contemporaries were Alan Oakman, a team-mate for twenty years, Gordon 'Gilly' Potter and Peter Laker, later the cricket correspondent of the *Sun*.

Seven weeks after joining the staff, Jim made his Second XI debut against Gloucester at Hove wearing his father's cap as he hadn't got one. He fared better than he had feared. Ken Graveney, Tom's brother, dismissed both openers with his pace and accuracy, whereupon Jim made an aggressive start, but was out just before lunch. Jim took 4 for 62 in Gloucester's reply and the experience made him practise all the harder. One lunchtime, tired, hot and hungry, he was about to tackle a salad when one of the ground staff patted him on the back and said, 'Congratulations, Jim – you're in the county side against Cambridge University at Horsham. It's on the notice board.' Jim was thrilled and his mentor was encouraging: 'It's a big chance for you, lad.

Good luck, play your normal game, and don't forget the things I've told you to do.'

More than a decade had passed since Jim had seen Hugh Bartlett hit the Australians for a breathtaking hundred and on Jim's arrival at Horsham the veteran of Arnhem treated the seventeen-year-old debutant like a seasoned professional. Jim, who never had any doubts about his ability, had slept well and he listened intently while the Langridge brothers told him about the Cambridge players and things to watch for. Jim was played as a bowler but was given only four overs. Nonetheless the *Evening Argus* recorded Jim's first senior scalp:

> Jim Parks, bowling slow off-breaks, in his third over in first-class cricket, broke up the stubborn partnership between Popplewell and Hall. The ball came in sharply to bowl Popplewell off his pads.[3]

The Cambridge side was virtually county strength, including Doug Insole, the captain, Hubert Doggart, John Dewes and John Warr, all future Test players. Horsham could sometimes seam around but that June it was its usual benign self. 'Even so, I'd never seen anyone of Warr's pace and I soon realised the gulf between minor counties and first-class cricket.'[4] Eighteen months later Warr would play for England in Australia and early on bowled Jim a ball he didn't see; later Jim was elated to hit him through the covers for 4 before being bowled for 12.

After this taste of the senior side it was back to club and ground – and the Second XI. The youngsters played at fairly inaccessible venues, as Gordon Potter recalls: 'Jim and I used to be fairly close as teenagers. I lived in Frant and you had to go by train to matches in places like Midhurst or Petworth. I often couldn't get back to Tunbridge Wells after the game so I used to stay with Jim in Haywards Heath.'

Sussex trainees in those days were also drafted out to reputable club sides to gain experience, and Peter Wales remembers a game at the Saffrons where 'Jim and I were playing for Southern Wanderers. He got a wonderful 100 while I scored 10 holding up the other end.' He also took two Eastbourne wickets with his leg-spinners. It was his first appearance on the Eastbourne ground, which would become one of his favourites.

His good form for club and ground – and possibly the reputation of out-county grounds for having sporting wickets – gained Jim his Championship call-up for the fixtures against Northamptonshire and Somerset at the end of July. At Rushden, Bartlett and the senior pros looked at the wicket and sagely opined, 'Oh, yes, it's definitely going to turn' – and played the young spinner. It seamed from the start, Jim Cornford took the first nine wickets – 'and I caught the tenth one off George Cox':[5] it was Rupert Webb's first Championship game with Jim. Neither distinguished himself – Jim got 6 'before Bob Clark, left-armer, did me', while Rupert was out for 10. A nine-wicket defeat there was reversed at Frome where the seamers were chosen on a green track,

> and it turned like a top from the word go. I was twelfth man there but I fielded for Chris Winn, who'd played for England at rugby. He had come down from Oxford University and was a flamboyant sort of cricketer, a magnificent fielder who used to fling himself around. He did that at Frome and ploughed through about three rows of chairs and did his knee in. So I fielded and caught Arthur Wellard in front of the sight-screen.

Jim held that catch but he dropped a clanger when he took the drinks out at the wrong moment. This mistake, born of inexperience, emphasised the value of this mini-tour in acclimatising the young professional to the atmosphere, the crowds and the grounds in county cricket.

In August Jim took 4 for 57 against Kent at Aylesford and was awarded his Second XI cap. Playing for the club and ground against Pevensey & Westham at Pevensey later that month, Jim met Raman Subba Row, later a Test colleague and still a firm friend. Subba Row, then at Whitgift School, was on holiday with his parents at Norman's Bay and playing for Pevensey on the recommendation of Frank Quaife, the coach at Eastbourne College.

At the end of this debut season Jim discussed with his father the fact that in first-class cricket, everything happened more quickly. 'That's quite a point,' said Jim senior, 'but you must also remember that the fellows you meet in top-class cricket can do nothing more with a ball than the chaps you face in club games, but they can do it better.'[6] Jim had had to fight for every one of his 26 runs that season and realised that he would improve only if he continued to play against better players.

It was a championship season for Jim that winter on the soccer field as Haywards Heath won the first of their two successive County League titles. It was also a winter of political activism. He worked for the Conservative agent, a man called Captain Williams, at East Grinstead for £5 a week. 'I was supposedly looking after the Young Conservatives but in the General Election I came back to work at the office in Haywards Heath. Churchill just lost that election but returned a few months later.'

After Jim's political winter it was appropriate that the 1950 season should open against the backdrop of one of those periodic bouts of internecine

politics which bedevil cricketing counties. Following a row about team selection, the captain, Hugh Bartlett, resigned before the season began. In March
the county's AGM at the Royal Pavilion was a stormy affair. The committee's
announcement that the captaincy would be shared between R.G. Hunt and
Hubert Doggart was howled down by the members, who felt that Bartlett
had been shabbily treated. When the meeting passed a vote of no confidence
in the committee, the president, the Duke of Norfolk, picked up his hat,
gloves and cane and strode imperiously from the chamber. Another meeting
a month later appointed Jim Langridge amid sustained applause. Sussex's first
professional captain, he was to hold the post with distinction for the next
three seasons. Highlighting accusations of autocracy and secrecy on the part
of the committee, along with inept man-management, the episode engen-
dered 'an uneasy peace and the rumblings continued through the 1950s and
into the next decade.'[7]

These unseemly happenings were of little interest to Jim. He was more
concerned with where the next run was coming from. 'I didn't get a great
start that season', he says, and by the end of May he had made 57 in 8 innings.
Despite a battling 23 not out against Tom Pritchard – the fastest bowler he'd
yet seen – as Warwickshire shot Sussex out for 97, he was dropped for the
attractive Whitsun match at Lord's. However, as Charlie Oakes was injured,
he was reprieved and he made his debut at headquarters. Thrilled to be playing at Lord's against Denis Compton, Jim recalls the sort of exchange which
characterised county cricket in the fifties: 'I got to the crease and took guard.
Les Compton was keeping wicket – he wished me good luck and moved
up to the stumps in the hope that Jim Sims' slows would draw me from the
crease.' Jim struck four boundaries in his 33 and kept his place for the next
game against Kent.

The experience at Lord's had given him renewed confidence and on a
turning wicket at Gillingham he scored his maiden first-class century. It was
'an innings that proved the old adage that whilst sheer talent will always
find its level, Lady Luck can help…. There was a lot of jammy Jimmy talk
amongst his peers.'[8] Dropped twice by Arthur Phebey, at 91 Jim found himself at the same end as Alan Oakman. 'I set off for the run. Derek Ufton, the
keeper, threw it to Ray Dovey who missed it. I made my ground and got
my first 100.' In the late forties Doug Wright was the leading leg-spinner in
the country, with an idiosyncratic approach to the wicket. Jim was unsure
whether to laugh or attack as, hopping like a kangaroo, Wright skipped up
to bowl. Rupert Webb was 'absolutely amazed because this eighteen-year-
old lad could pick Doug Wright's googly. He was a difficult bowler to deal
with… but Jim hit every google over square leg for four.' Jim hit 16 fours

and one six in his 159 not out, and Sussex won by ten wickets. The cricket
headlines that day were full of Jim Laker's 8 for 2 in the Test trial at Bradford
but this milestone could not be ignored:

> MAIDEN 100 BY PARKS V. KENT. After dismissing five Sussex batsmen for 188,
> Kent could not force home the advantage at Gillingham, mainly because of
> a great innings by J. Parks, the eighteen-year-old son of the former Sussex
> player, who was undefeated with 120 at the close. Wright worried the early
> batsmen and at first the only one to face him confidently was the left-hander,
> D.V. Smith, after whose dismissal this determined resistance was taken up by
> Parks. Although his stubborn defensive play brought ironical clapping and
> cheers from the crowd, Parks remained unperturbed and hit out only at loose
> deliveries. Going in at the fall of the fifth wicket, Parks reached his maiden
> century after 3 hours and 5 minutes. His previous highest score was 33 against
> Middlesex on Monday. So far he has hit 13 fours. He gave five chances.[9]

The innings secured Jim his place in the side and gave him the relaxed confidence to play his shots. He stayed in the team until mid-July when the
University amateurs, Sheppard and Doggart, arrived, and then went back
into the Second XI. 'I was tired, I'd had a good run and it was an enjoyable
education. I had begun to learn what the game was about at county level
– and I learnt that only the man who is willing to concentrate will succeed.'
The learning curve had been steep: Jim had batted brilliantly at Gillingham
but, still learning his trade, he lacked consistency and had bowled barely
eight overs in seventeen games. As for the county it had been an indifferent
season, finishing thirteenth in the Championship, but considering the turbu-
lent noises off in the spring, Jim Langridge had welded a happy side.

That winter Jim exchanged cricket whites for the blue serge as he was
called up for national service. He had managed a year's deferral, but on
12 December he reported to Padgate for his basic training. He became A/C
J.M. Parks, No.6 School of Recruit Training, K Flight, No.3 Squadron, No.2
Wing, RAF in the same training unit was Jim's former colleague and erst-
while house-guest Gordon 'Gilly' Potter, who had fond memories of the
place – 'I remember us peeling these mountains of carrots and potatoes.' Jim's
squarebashing memories are sketchy but 'I remember the fearsome corporals
Ball, Boobyer and Hyman and marching through the streets of Hereford to
the camp when we came out of the station.' Just before Christmas, owing
to a flu epidemic, the trainees travelled home and were later transferred to
Kirkham, near Blackpool. Ron Lack, who had joined up on the same day as
Jim, still has the leave forms – they were called '1250s'. He remembers that

when they got to London, Ron said he had just enough money for his bus fare back to Crystal Palace but Jim replied, 'We'll get a taxi – my dad will pay.' Ron didn't realise at the time that he was Jim Parks, the cricketer! Although Blackpool was not Sussex, for Jim and Gordon there were compensations – 'We were allowed out at weekends and Jim and I used to stay with his aunt Ivy and go dancing at the Tower Ballroom.'

British-born journalist Fred Cleary writes: 'Coastal Command HQ was situated in a stately home in Northwood, near Harrow. One February day in 1951 I was walking past the manor house when I saw an aircraftman walking towards me, laden down with luggage. "Hallo, my name is Parks. Can you direct me to the Adjutant's office?" he said. "I've been posted here."'[10] Basic training over, Jim had been posted to Northwood on the princely sum of 4s a day. On the Sussex committee was ex-Wing Commander Jimmy Lawson, who was a great friend of Air Chief Marshal Sir Charles Steel, the boss of Coastal Command and a member of MCC. Jim's posting to the Accounts and Pay department had been fixed before he went, though he knew nothing of this: 'I thought: "Coastal Command" – that'll be somewhere up in Scotland!'

One of the arguments advanced in the perennial debate about the value of National Service is that it makes boys and girls into men and women and teaches them discipline, team-work and self-respect. Jim would agree: ''51 was a good year. I think the RAF did me a bit of good and I matured as a person.' He certainly matured as a cricketer. His time in the RAF was the most carefree period of his life, for he had no responsibilities. In effect Jim was paid for playing cricket while he was in the RAF – and he made the most of the opportunity.

Over the next two seasons, Jim played for Coastal Command, the RAF, Combined Services and of course Sussex. He shared rooms with Ray Illingworth and widened his experience by playing in Europe: 'I can remember Fred Trueman coming over there with Roy Swetman and Alan Moss. We had a week in Germany and then in Holland on matting.' Although he did not play football for the RAF, he did represent the Command, and continued to turn out regularly for Haywards Heath in the County League. He was still courting Irene from a distance: they had become an item just before they had left school. Jim wangled enough leave that season to play seven Championship games. He also made his debut for the Combined Services at Pontypridd. Keeping wicket for the services was Corporal Keith Andrew, later an England colleague in the Caribbean and widely regarded (once Evans had retired) as technically the most accomplished wicketkeeper in the country. Andrew remembers the game well: 'It was my very first

first-class match and Jim was a star in the making as a batsman.' Keith Andrew
would not necessarily have formed that impression at Pontypridd – Jim
scored 0 and 19 – but he did later: 'In that Combined Services side, he was
a Compton himself – he played all the strokes and dominated the bowling
when he was in. Had he not become a wicketkeeper, I think Jim would have
been recognised as a great batsman.'

Fred Cleary was another of Jim's new acquaintances to have been
impressed with Northwood's acquisition. The base complement was only
300 officers and staff, yet every Wednesday it fielded three cricket teams.
Cleary was the umpire.

> Flight-Lieutenant Alan Shireff ran cricket affairs and told me that this fellow
> Parks was in the side for an away game. When he went in first wicket down,
> it was obvious he had been playing a lot lately. Showing excellent timing,
> confidence and footwork, he carved the opposition bowling to shreds with an
> impressive array of shots, hit a century-plus then, when we fielded, he grabbed
> a handful of wickets with his spin bowling. We were all in the NAAFI cel-
> ebrating in time to listen to the Derby on the radio.

That May was particularly bleak: ten days before the Epsom classic John
Langridge's unbeaten double century saved the game against Derbyshire
after Sussex had followed on 293 behind in 'arctic June weather'.[11] It was
unfortunate for Jim that he was not a betting man – the Derby was won by
Arctic Prince!

Jim's arrival on the county circuit as a precocious talent was confirmed
that June against the old enemy at Tunbridge Wells. Against a blooming
backdrop of rioting rhododendrons, Jim came of age as a professional player.
There was something symbolic in Jim's stand of 294 with Jim Langridge,
himself a link with Jim's father's cricketing past: Jim Langridge, who had
toured Australasia with Jim senior; Jim Langridge, who used to bowl at
young Jim in the Hove nets; Jim Langridge, for fifteen years a team-mate of
his dad's, with young Jim parks, the newest scion of the county's cricketing
dynasty, piled on the runs to within 4 of the Sussex third-wicket record. The
Kent Messenger conceded that the 'personal triumph of nineteen-year-old
Jim Parks was a popular one. He obtained special leave from the RAF for this
match and showed his partiality for Kent bowling by hitting a magnificent
188.'[12] Jim had joined John Langridge when Don Smith was out at 16, and he
promptly hit Doug Wright for a consecutive four and six. When at 58 John
Langridge was bagged by Arthur Fagg at slip, his brother joined young Jim
and they were there at the close, with Sussex on 325 for 2. Jim had reached

his hundred in three hours twenty-five minutes 'on a smallish ground and a beautiful wicket. I got quite a lot of runs off Doug – it wasn't turning much and he dropped a few short. I remember hitting Ray Dovey's off-spinners over the top into the railway.' With both Jims going well, the scoreboard men could not keep up. Quipped umpire Frank Chester to Alex Skelding: 'If they hit one more six they'll pack up altogether.' Young Jim promptly obliged and the scoreboard men sat back and just watched. In the end, after batting for just over six hours, Jim had hit 2 sixes and 13 fours in his 188.

Towards the end of his innings, Frank Chester asked Jim if he had got his county cap. 'No,' he said. 'It's about time you did,' replied Chester, 'I'll have a word with Jim Langridge.' When Oakman (5 for 34) and James (3 for 32) forced Kent to follow on 233 behind, the game was as good as over and Cornford and Wood had them 8 down at the close. 'In drenching rain on Tuesday morning Sussex finished off the Kent second innings for the addition of only 10 runs... The resumption... with all the formalities of first-class cricket to be observed, was rather farcical.'[13]

These obsequies having been duly fulfilled, the team travelled back to Hove and on the morning of the game against Essex Jim achieved his first major cricketing ambition. 'Congratulations,' said Jim Langridge. 'I've got something for you,' and presented Jim with his Sussex cap. There was no fanfare, no ceremony on the pitch, no pictures, no song and dance, yet:

> It was a tremendous moment, especially as I wasn't on the staff at the time. It had implications for money once I'd come out of the RAF – I was a capped player and it meant a secure job once I was demobbed. Not being capped meant you played only for expenses – the cap meant you had an automatic three-year contract.

True to tradition, the drinks were on Jim that night. Next day he batted with his new county cap perched proudly on his curly fair hair – and was bowled by Ken Preston for 1. The mists of the celebrations had cleared sufficiently three days later when he posted a half-century on a hard, fast Hove track against a Gloucestershire attack including George Lambert, who in those days 'was regarded as the fastest bowler in English cricket'.[14] County cap or no, the avuncular Langridges would still help out when the going got tough: 'George Lambert hit me under the heart and it hurt – there was no flesh on me in those days. Dear old John – he said, "We'll get a single," and he took all of George Lambert. I had Colin Scott's gentle medium pace.' An innings win was wrapped up thanks to 5 for 38 by eighteen-year-old Don Bates and a hundred from John Langridge.

The side then faced the long trek north to Hull, where the team 'rushed into the hotel just outside the station and went straight into the bar where we listened to Randolph Turpin winning the world title. Next day John Langridge and Don Smith put on 200-odd for the first wicket.' Jim's journey was scarcely necessary: Sussex's reply of 420 for 6 to Yorkshire's 318 included a second successive century from John Langridge but only three from Jim. Yorkshire batted out a dull draw and Aircraftman Parks returned to Northwood.

Three further solid performances for the RAF and Combined Services completed a season in which 'Parks, when on Service leave, maintained his earlier promise and received his county cap.'[15] Jim had matured as a batsman but had not bowled a ball for the county. Robin Marlar offers some perceptive thoughts on the reason why:

> Charlie Oakes, another of the great Sussex brotherhood, was then batting in the middle-order and taking wickets with leg-spinners that tended to deceive by holding course rather than deviating. In those days there were many wrist-spinners who lost the leg-break by stretching shoulder tendons as they offered a host of googlies. Jimmy's arrival rang bells of alarm with Charlie, who proceeded to turn in some of his best-ever performances. The result was that Jimmy barely bowled at a critical stage of his development. Considering that he had been such a prodigious all-round talent, this was an opportunity allowed to lapse. One feels that the lesson remains. It is often odious to compare, whether across generations or continents. Nonetheless it is impossible to think that such a talent would be allowed to wither in Australia, either then or now.[16]

In the RAF weekend leave was a matter of a 36- or 48-hour pass, so that winter he was able to pursue his increasingly serious courting of Irene, to whom he had become officially engaged. Jim's second winter in the service of king and country saw him play football regularly for The Heath. That season was to be their last in the County League at Victoria Park: it had been the club's ambition since before the war to move to a new ground with more congenial spectator facilities at Hanbury Park, off Allen Road. This move was accomplished at the end of the season, together with admission to the Metropolitan League.

Jim embarked on the 1952 season in that difficult position familiar to all new stars in the county firmament; no longer the fresh talent, presenting battle-hardened county bowlers with different problems, making care-free runs with almost naïve abandon, but a player whose honeymoon was coming to an end. By 1952, 'canny county bowlers instinctively knew how to bowl at him. Here was a stroke-maker, an off-side player. Therefore give him nothing. Bowl middle or middle and leg, just short of a length. Keep the nip-backer as the wicket-taking ball, hoping to go inside the full swing of the bat.'[17]

That summer Jim was able to play eighteen Championship games as Northwood was absurdly overmanned. For an establishment of a corporal and two clerks, the Pay Accounts department had two corporals and ten clerks:

> I didn't play a huge role in defending the country. All I had to do was to make sure I balanced the Pay Accounts books by 10 every morning, so I used to get a file and go and have a chat with Alan Moss. Our boss was Air Chief Marshal Sir Charles Steel, so when we had RAF matches Alan and myself used to travel with the Air Chief Marshal and arrive at grounds in his car! I was almost never on camp the whole of the summer – I used to go back and collect my pay about every six weeks.

Jim Langridge's last season as captain saw Sussex stand their traditional form on its head. Often Sussex had started a season well and tailed off in August. In 1952 it was the reverse and the county won seven of the last eleven games. Perhaps the arrivals in the long vacation of Sheppard and Marlar from Cambridge and Doggart from Winchester lifted a side which had won only three Championship games all summer. Sussex continued to entertain; while no bowler took 100 wickets, four batsmen made 1,000 runs – the Langridges, George Cox and Alan Oakman, who also took 62 wickets (including a hat-trick). The young bloods – Suttle, Oakman and Jim – showed consistent improvement and while the side finished thirteenth, Sussex became only the second county to beat the touring Indians, Jim Wood and debutant Ian Thomson taking fourteen wickets between them.

Wood and Thomson were only two of the very effective seam bowlers which Sussex could field that season. In this transitional period, between the passing of the old guard – the Langridges, George Cox and Charlie Oakes – and the maturing of the new wave – Oakman, Parks, Suttle and Thomson – Jim Cornford, himself in his last season, and Ted James, together with Wood and Thomson, were all capable of bowling a side out cheaply. 'Yes, a fine bowler, Cornford,' said Jim. 'Used to hit the seam a lot and about the same pace as Tommo.' He would be sadly missed – 'He could move the ball both ways, and, on anything resembling a green wicket, was extremely dangerous.'[18]

The next season's opener against Warwickshire at Hove was a real thriller, for at one point in the visitors' second innings Wood and Cornford had them at 13 for 5 and then 28 for 6 – and still Sussex couldn't win. Warwickshire opened with 138 and in Sussex's reply Charlie Grove, then forty, took 4 for 24 as John Langridge made 65 out of 123. When the visitors batted again, Wood (4 for 40) and Cornford (2 for 14) shared the first six wickets and a stroll to a 10-wicket victory seemed imminent. Sussex were left to chase 132 and once more Grove struck, taking 6 for 49. Jim failed against spin for once, holing out to Eric Hollies at square-leg, but at 116 for 6, a home win seemed certain. Rupert Webb remembers the edge-of-the-seat finish:

> It was an exciting game on an absolutely dead wicket. The finale came when I went in number eleven and we wanted 12 to win. Ted James and I plodded on getting ones, and then Eric Hollies did me with his googly, lbw, so that was that.

Ted James remembers it differently. In his rich bucolic brogue, he chuckled, 'Interesting! – I'd never known cricket go so slow in all my life. We kept prodding and one would go through the slips. They brought Eric Hollies on and Webby tried to sweep him. We had a tie. Talk about slow!' Lightning struck twice that year for Charlie Grove, as in the return fixture at Edgbaston he demolished Sussex for 86 in returning his career-best figures of 9 for 39.

The team of the decade was undoubtedly Surrey. County champions in seven successive seasons, they were the finest side that Jim played against in his early career. 'They had tremendous bowlers, Bedser, Stuart Surridge, who used to bowl away-swingers and then Lock and Laker, although in those days Locky hadn't started to bend the elbow and bowled flighty little left-handers.' Add in the name of Peter Loader, a tall, high-stepping bowler of genuine pace, and you have an ideally varied, Test-class attack. The batting was useful too – 1952 was Laurie Fishlock's last season, but David Fletcher was a stylish opener, often with Eric Bedser, and with players such as Peter May, Mickey Stewart, Ken Barrington, Bernie Constable and the reliable Tom Clark, not to mention Surridge himself, the line-up throughout the fifties was formidable. To complete the XI, wicketkeeper Arthur McIntyre was unlucky to play in the shadow of the great Godfrey Evans; in another era he would have made more than his three Test appearances. His successor, Roy Swetman, played eleven times for his country. Surridge, ordinary player though he was himself, was a shrewd and charismatic captain, imaginative in his field-placings and courageous in his almost suicidal short-leg position. With bowling of the highest quality, coupled with keen fielders cleverly marshalled and disposed, Surrey were a hard side to score off.

Jim had the desire – and the confidence – to compete with the best and so he was keen to play at the Oval early that season:

> On the first morning Jim Langridge and I were looking at the wicket and Stuart Surridge was there. Jim introduced me saying, 'He's going to get a lot of runs for us one day,' and Stuart replied, 'Well, I hope it's not today.'

Jim arrived at the crease at 93 for 3 and John Langridge greeted him with this advice: 'Never forget – good though they are, they can bowl only one ball at a time, and treat it on merit.' Laker made him play every ball, shrewdly using flight and change of pace and Alec Bedser gave the young player, in his first innings against him, no respite with his persistent accuracy. For once Jim got his head down. A partnership of 191 in which Langridge made 135 and Jim 138 enabled Sussex to declare at 365 for 9. David Fletcher made a century as the home side led by 67 and then Tony Lock (5 for 28) and Eric Bedser (3 for 32) bowled Sussex out for 136 – Jim being caught round the corner by Surridge off Lock for the second time in the match. Fletcher and Eric Bedser knocked off the runs for a ten-wicket win. Jim had had a taste of true Championship cricket.

There was time to reflect on the Oval experience as the express steamed west through Reading, Swindon and Bristol to Cardiff. The game for Combined Services against Glamorgan meant that Jim missed the debut of a cricketer from Essex who was to become a Sussex bowling legend, a close friend and, for a golden winter a dozen years later, a Test colleague. At Horsham, Ian Thomson claimed his first scalp when he bowled the prolific Australian Jock Livingston for 105. At the Arms Park, Jim was getting on with business: 'Parks, the young Sussex batsman, played delightful cricket, and his 63 included eleven 4s.'[19] The tiring return trip to Horsham was disappointing as Hampshire beat Sussex by eight wickets, despite Jim's 46 in 28 minutes, including 17 off one Shackleton over.

County bowlers – even those as uncannily accurate as Shackleton – were taking their time to work Jim out. Early in June Ronnie Bird, the Worcester captain, tried eight bowlers at New Road as Combined Services amassed 548 for 4 declared. David Heath, later the Warwickshire secretary, opened with 149, John Manners, a naval officer who played for Hampshire on either side of the war, made 103, as did A/C Parks. A young squaddie from Farsley, Ray Illingworth, chipped in with 42 not out, and the likes of Keith Andrew and John Mortimore, both future Test players, did not get a bat. Other men doing national service at the time, later Test players like Alan Moss, Roy Swetman, Fred Titmus and Fred Trueman were not even playing! This was

undoubtedly the time to which Peter Wales was referring when he said that
Jim was enjoying his happiest period in the game. The responsibilities of
being a leading batsman, then a senior professional, and later the captain, not
to mention the pressures of the competitive cauldron of the Test arena, and
still less those of family and mortgage, were all still to come. For now, for this
summer, Jim could bat freely, wheel away with his spinners and swoop about
in the covers with the grace of his uncle.

It helped that Sussex were winning at last. Against Somerset at Hove, with
the assistance of a hat-trick from Alan Oakman, Sussex achieved their first
win for almost a year – since July 1951 against Gloucester. In an extraordinary first innings, John Langridge scored 111 out of Sussex 's 191 – but let
Wisden take up the story:

> While most batsmen found the pace of the pitch disconcerting, John
> Langridge… proved a notable exception. Carrying his bat through an innings
> of three and a half hours, he put together his 69th century for Sussex, so
> eclipsing the record held by C.B. Fry since before the First World War…
> Sussex gained a lead of 28, for Oakman finished the innings by performing
> the first hat-trick of his career. Sussex established a strong position when Parks
> hit 52 in seventy-five minutes, but the last six wickets fell for 40… Against the
> bowling of Cornford, James and Oakman, Somerset never looked like getting
> the 174 necessary to win.[20]

Sussex clinched victory by 55 runs. They should have beaten Kent at
Tunbridge Wells, but needing only 44 with thirty minutes and four wickets
left, Ted James and his captain scored only 15 runs. Perhaps it was the legacy
of a side who had forgotten how to win, lacking the confidence that only
success can bring.

Jim missed that disappointing draw, appearing for the Combined Services
against the Indians and helping the RAF crush the Navy by 90 runs at Lord's,
but he returned to Championship cricket against top-of-the-table Surrey at
Hastings. The game was a personal triumph for Jim as he made his second
century of the season against the team destined to dominate English cricket
for most of the decade. The author's local paper, the *Hastings & St Leonards
Observer*, tells the story :

> In spite of a brilliant century by Jim Parks yesterday afternoon a depleted
> Surrey side beat Sussex by 64 runs… Sussex were nearly always struggling. The
> only time they were really on top was when Parks and Suttle shared in a grand
> partnership yesterday. There was a pleasant and entertaining day's cricket on

Wednesday… The talk was mostly of one of Sussex's promising young hopes, Jim Parks, who had been at the wicket only a few minutes. Why was this? Let one forget the first ball he received, about which he knew absolutely nothing. He took a single with a graceful cut and then, in the last but one over of the day, off-drove Surridge for four with a classically effortless stroke which was worth waiting all the day to see… All this with three wickets down and the light not all that it might have been.[21]

Then, when stumps were drawn, the dash for the train home. Not for the county yeomen of the fifties the sponsored Saab or the expenses-paid hotel. This was a home game. 'When play ended at Hastings,' Ted James recalls, 'we walked up Station Approach. Sometimes you played till seven and you only had half a hour to change and get the train. I lived at Lancing then. There was a fast train back to Brighton and we used to get the members ready with the door open so we could rush up and catch it.'

On the second morning,

Jim Parks' adventurous spirit even exceeded that of George Cox. Parks did not bat without blemish, but his style, range of strokes, and the confident, almost carefree, manner in which he made them, was ample justification of those who had been so warm in his praises the previous evening. *Loader finished off the innings in a spell of 4 for 1 in 2.2 overs. Sussex were left 321 at a run a minute. Ted James opened with John Langridge. They were out quickly and Oakman joined Jim.* The scoring rate at once quickened and again Parks scored effortlessly all round the wicket… Parks continued confidently to complete his 50 in 65 minutes. He found a congenial partner in the left-handed Suttle, and these two youthful batsmen pasted the Surrey attack.… In the last over before tea there was a tremendous cheer when Parks completed a brilliant century, celebrating by square-cutting Surridge for four in the same over… Parks' innings ended soon afterward when he was lbw playing forward to Lock. He hit 14 fours in his 2 hour 30 minute innings.[22]

After that defeat the side went through August unbeaten for the first time in fifty years. Four Championship victories and a notable win over the Indian tourists ended an eventful summer and enabled Jim Langridge to hand over to his successor a side with an agreeable mix of youth and experience. The most exciting finish came in the traditional Bank Holiday game against Middlesex at Hove. Sussex opened on the Saturday with 149, the visitors mustering only 83 in reply, Jim vividly remembering 'catching Denis Compton off Jim Wood at second slip for 1'. Bowling round the wicket, Wood achieved real nip off the pitch and took 7 for 31. Jim Wood was a true Sussex character. When he died in 1989, he had been living in the same house in Horsted Keynes for forty-two years. David Sheppard remembers that game: 'Jim Wood had extraordinary figures. He was a small man with a lively action and he could make the ball swing a bit into the bat. Every now and then he was very effective.' Sussex made 149 again and Middlesex, chasing 216 to win, were undone by Ian Thomson, who, with 5 for 52, had Jack Young caught at slip with only three balls left, sealing a thrilling win by 15 runs. The victory over the tourists featured Jim's first appearance behind the stumps for Sussex, deputising for 'Billy' Griffith, who needed three stitches in his forehead after being struck by Manjrekar's bat. Having lost the Test series 3–0, the Indian side lacked confidence and it was a relatively comfortable win. At the death, the two graduates from the class of '49, Ken Suttle and Jim, saw Sussex home to their target of 177 and a six-wicket win. Sandwiched between these two victories, a match at Lord's saw the Combined Services take on the Public Schools and Jim set eyes on two men who would loom large in his later career – E.R. Dexter of Radley and R.W. Barber of Ruthin.

The residue of the season belonged to Robin Marlar as he beat Glamorgan virtually single-handed on a turner at Swansea, taking 15 for 133, then did the same against Lancashire at Hove, returning 12 for 135. Jim made an undistinguished contribution in Jim Cornford's swan song against Derbyshire at Hove but, taking the season as a whole, he had made steady progress. As *Wisden* put it, in a comment on the Combined Services season, 'Undoubtedly the most impressive batting came from A/C J.M. Parks (Sussex). He was always looking for runs and, though some of his strokes were charged with risk, he seemed destined for the highest honours in the game.'[23]

For Jim the end of the season meant a return to the real world. His winter love, Haywards Heath FC, moved to their impressive new ground at the start of the football season. Opened by Sir Stanley Rous, Hanbury Park attracted about 3,000 spectators for the inaugural match against Horsham, who won 1–0. Jim passed his driving test in October, having been taught to drive by his father in his old Morris 8. His innate pragmatism surfaced once again: 'I was due to take my SAC exam on the same day as my driving test – and I thought, "Well, I know which is going to be more useful to me." Being a senior aircraftman would have meant a little bit more money but I was coming out to play cricket anyway.' Jim returned to civilian life on 11 December and as always spent Christmas at his grandmother's. In January the indoor school at Hove opened in the old chalet and he became the first coach, while still finding time to become the season's leading goal scorer for Haywards Heath.

Jim reckons it takes three full seasons to become a county cricketer. In a player's first season, he is sized up by the opposition and can get away with weaknesses in technique and attitude. In the second season, his limitations are better known and the average county bowler will have found ways to exploit them. The third year is the true test and examines whether a player has the ability, fitness, temperament and concentration to succeed as a professional cricketer. Jim had played seventeen games in 1950, seven only the following year and another seventeen in 1952. His apprenticeship was over. He had paid his dues and the Coronation summer, under a new captain, would provide a serious assessment of his mettle.

Chapter 4
Coming of Age

In 1953, when the Sussex committee appointed David Sheppard captain, they did so in the knowledge that he could offer them only one season as he intended to study for the ministry. In that summer of the Coronation, the Ashes win, the Matthews final, Gordon Richards' Derby and the conquest of Everest, there dawned a new Elizabethan age when it seemed one could dream impossible dreams and Sheppard, this 'most complete of modern captains',[1] led the county almost to the summit of its own Everest – the County Championship. His kindness and firm authority brought out the best in his players, for whom 'he was an inspirational leader. He had an aura about him – he led by example.'[2] Thus 'the Rev', as he became affectionately known, moulded the team into a side who 'used to go out and think, "We can beat this lot"'.[3] Not only did Sheppard have an outstanding season with the bat, hitting seven centuries in scoring nearly 2,000 runs at an average of 55, he took up the toughest fielding positions. For the first time in sixteen years, two bowlers – Ted James and Ian Thomson – took 100 wickets, many captured by the captain's brilliant catches in the gully, incidentally boosting Thomson's confidence in his first full season as a professional.

The Sussex side under 'the Rev' was a team in transition. The old guard – George Cox, the Langridges, Charlie Oakes and Jim Wood – were all in the twilight of great careers. The young bloods – Oakman, Parks, Suttle and Thomson – who would be the backbone of Sussex cricket over the next two decades were promising but inexperienced. Sheppard's achievement was to weld these disparate entities into a competitive and enterprising whole. Under his inspiring leadership the county mounted a credible challenge for Surrey's title, rising from thirteenth in the table to finish runners-up. Apart from the skipper, four other batsmen – Cox, John Langridge, Parks and Suttle – reached 1,000 runs, and despite the absence of a match-winner, all the bowlers contributed. Alan Oakman, with 63 wickets, Wood (79) and Marlar (56), down from Cambridge, had successful seasons.

This memorable campaign got off to a faltering start, however. May and early June were damp and gloomy; the defeat of Somerset at Taunton was the sole highlight and on Coronation Day, which was wet and watched by the nation in black and white, Sussex were playing out a colourless draw at Ilford. One win in six competitive attempts was hardly the stuff of champions and the team's indifferent form was reflected in Jim's own performances. After two games he had taken more wickets than he had scored runs. At Taunton Jim Langridge and Suttle both made hundreds, Wood and Thomson took fifteen wickets between them and Jim made a duck. A crushing victory for Lancashire on a wet wicket at Aigburth saw a slight improvement: he scored a battling 64 not out as Roy Tattersall, with 12 for 70, spun Sussex to an innings defeat.

The bank holiday game at Lord's was an entertaining affair. On the Saturday Jim watched his hero hit an undefeated 143. However, on Bank Holiday Monday, Suttle made 'a very good 100 – kept slogging them over long-on.' On the last day Sussex, left 202 to win, succumbed to the spin of Young and Compton to go down by an innings and 101. The aficionados who flocked to headquarters in their thousands that bank holiday certainly got their money's worth – an astonishing 387 overs were bowled in the three days!

All 'the Rev' had to show for a month's endeavour were three damp draws, a win over the side who had finished bottom the year before and a couple of innings defeats which emphasised the team's lack of match-winning bowling and its reliance on the captain and the Langridge brothers for runs. Jim showed some kind of return to form, making 97 at Ilford, but he failed to make any impression in what was virtually an exhibition game against the Australians at Hove. These were prestigious fixtures and counties fielded their strongest sides. Nevertheless, three tourists – McDonald, Hassett and Harvey – scored hundreds and against a bowling attack including Lindwall, Miller, Johnston and Davidson, Sussex, at 190 for 9, were holding on for a draw at the close.

It was a subdued side who made the train trip north that night to face Leicester. In the morning Maurice Tompkin, later to tour Pakistan with Jim, overcame a lively pitch to make a sound 150 before being caught by the captain off George Cox. The wily veteran 'was an occasional trundler, but he had plenty of brains and used to bowl little floaters at varying pace'.[4] John Woodcock suspects that 'he could have bowled respectable medium-pace as well. George Cox was a lovely cricketer – in a way he personified summer days at Hove.'

This was a different proposition. It was scarcely flaming June, Grace Road was scruffily urban and the home side had made a respectable 371. 'The Rev' was irritated: 'I put on 97 and was very cross at being caught and bowled by Jack Walsh. I thought I played those people quite well – I kept calm and

---

didn't panic as half Sussex seemed to do.' Apart from Jim's well-made 53, the rest showed more style than substance and were all out 109 runs behind. When Leicestershire batted again, the visitors' captain, this Corinthian cricketer, twenty-four years old, a Cambridge Blue and a man of God, showed a streak of steel and a shrewd cricket brain. Sheppard decided to force the Leicester skipper's hand:

> He took the new ball from the umpire and said to Woody, 'Take your time – don't take the ball out of its wrapper and I'll move the field round a bit.' Suddenly Charlie Palmer came tumbling down out of the pavilion and declared. As we walked off David said, 'I knew they couldn't afford a new ball.'[5]

Sussex needed 346 to win in a little over 70 overs – rapid scoring even by today's standards. The captain put on 153 for the first wicket and with characteristic modesty described it as 'a good day'. His match-winning 186 not out, including 20 fours, a six and a five, transformed the season.

Suddenly it was sunshine after the rain, Technicolor instead of monochrome. It was bunting and beer tents at the birthplace of the Oakes brothers for the farmers' festival week at Horsham's Cricketfield Road, where Jim had made his first-class debut almost exactly four years before. George Cox led the way against Warwickshire with Sussex's second century in successive days, scoring 127 out of 306. Wood took six wickets in Warwickshire's first innings and Oakman 6 for 91 in the second. Jim was still not at his fluent best but the team had won by 43 runs and he was fielding like a dream. In the opinion of Rupert Webb, 'he was certainly the best cover-point in the country'. John Woodcock saw him perpetuating a great tradition:

> Jim was a very fine natural cricketer – a lovely fielder. Jim could do anything on the cricket field. There was a great deal of George Cox about him – ideally suited to a lovely day at Hove, playing the most exquisite shots, fielding beautifully.

In the fifties Sussex appeared unable to play Glamorgan without a measure of rancour. During his long career with the Welsh club, Wilf Wooller and incidents seemed to go together 'like toast and marmalade'.[6] At Hove the year before, as Glamorgan pressed for victory, Wooller had provoked jeers by telling Rupert Webb not to waste time. This year at Horsham, the Sussex captain took Wooller apart in scoring a magnificent 174 and 'Wilf and David had words. When David played a ball back to Wilf he threw it at the stumps and it went for 4 overthrows. Everyone laughed in the pavilion, which riled him even more.' Jim and another eminent contemporary, Trevor Bailey, saw Wooller prowling the county scene 'rather in the fashion of a Captain Bligh striding the decks of the Bounty'.[7] He was a man of strong opinions and assertive personality, but both agree that 'off the field when you had a drink with him he was most charming'.[8]

It was a rainy June and on a drying wicket at Dudley Roly Jenkins, with 15 for 122, spun Sussex to their last defeat of the season. In a low-scoring game, the home side won with only six minutes to spare. Jim performed reasonably well on a tricky pitch and his steady improvement in form continued. Next morning, Jim caught the bus east to one of his favourite stamping-grounds at Tunbridge Wells, and back in the evening: this was classed as a *home* game! Sheppard scours his memory: 'It was a low-scoring match – I got a 100 and Jim made 50. It was the one stand which won us the match. Thomson and James swung the ball,' and Kent were dismissed for 116. Sussex had struggled to 43 for 2 in reply, when Jim joined his captain. They advanced the total to 169, Jim contributing a valuable 51 in a first-innings lead of 122. Then Ted James (4 for 38) and Jim Wood (3 for 35) hustled the hosts out for 133 and Sheppard and Langridge secured a comfortable ten-wicket win – the first of five in the next six games.

The team now had a respite from competitive cricket until the stern test of Surrey at Guildford. The leisurely loosener against Oxford University at Hove meandered to a light-hearted draw, but as a foretaste of the events which changed Jim's career five years later, the last afternoon threw up a delicious irony:

> The match was fizzling out into a draw at Hove and so the skipper said, 'Last session after tea – swap over'. Rupert bowled little leg-spinners and Charles Williams charged down the wicket, missed it by a mile and it was one of the easiest things to do.'[9]

So the scorecard read, 'C.C.P. Williams, stumped Parks bowled Webb 33'.

July opened at Guildford where just after lunch on the first day Surrey were cruising at 86 for 3. Then an astonishing spell by Ted James saw him dispose of Peter May, Eric Bedser, McIntyre and Surridge for 5 runs and, when Jim Wood had Ken Barrington lbw for 4, the champions had slumped to 93 for 8. Only a dogged 40 from Tony Lock enabled them to struggle to a respectable 145. In reply 'the Rev' made 105 and Jim 68 as Sussex achieved a first-innings lead of 108. The seamers shared the wickets, Alan Oakman chipped in with 3 for 14 'and we caught a whole lot of wonderful catches' – nine, in fact – as Surrey were dismissed for 213, leaving Sussex 106 to win.

When the captain and Cox fell to Stuart Surridge, Sussex were 3 for 2, but Kenny Suttle and Jim saw Sussex home to a seven-wicket win, a success of far more significance than the exciting run-chase at Leicester. The champions had been defeated on their own patch and Sussex were now serious title contenders.

Three more wins that month sustained the momentum. Two of them came on a poor wicket at Worthing. The Manor Ground had been allotments during the war and was now maintained by corporation groundsmen more accustomed to looking after bowling greens than a first-class cricket square. On a pitch shorn of grass, Hampshire were all out for 92 soon after lunch and Sussex gained a lead of 134, with the help of half-centuries from George Cox and Jim – only his second half-century in eleven innings that month. Thomson finished with nine wickets in the match and Oakman eight as Hampshire were skittled for 114, wrapping up an innings win before lunch on the second day.

Winning was now a habit. Against Worcestershire Sheppard pleased the Saturday crowd, scoring 129 out of Sussex's 333. Thomson and Oakman were again among the wickets as Worcester were forced to follow on 194 behind. A fighting 94 from Jim's future England colleague Peter Richardson helped take his side to 286, leaving Sussex 93 to win. The redoubtable George Cox made 61 and it was left to Jim and Alan Oakman to steer Sussex, not without alarms, to a 5-wicket win.

These three successive victories had taken Sussex almost to the top of the table. The team journeyed to Bournemouth full of confidence, expecting to beat a Hampshire side devoid of star batsmen but possessing opening bowlers in Shackleton and Cannings who were as accurate and effective as any in the country. The captain was aware of their potential to dictate the course of the match, as Rupert Webb recalls:

> When we won the toss he said 'We can't get bogged down by Shackleton and Cannings because they'll keep plonking them on a length, we'll finish the day on about 250 and we can't win from there.' So he played Shackleton's first couple of overs quite normally. Then in the following two overs he jumped down the wicket and hit Shack over his head for 17 and 20, something like that. They took him off and he didn't bowl again until after tea.

By then Sheppard had made 88, Ian Thomson a doughty 42, and Sussex ended at 221. The next morning the home side were in dire straits at 37 for 8 as Ted James bowled at his unplayable best. He returned figures of 6 for 19 as the home side were rushed out for 85 in only 43 overs. On the final morning

Sussex left Hampshire a target of 311 but it was beyond them. All the bowlers contributed to send Sussex home on the train as Championship leaders.

While the side basked in the euphoria of topping the table, Jim was in mediocre form and missed an intense game against Yorkshire at Hastings:

> I was disciplined by David Sheppard because I'd had a slog at Bournemouth which he didn't like. I was trying to win the match very quickly so I was sent to Heathfield and played for the club and ground.

Jim Wood was brought in on a ground where, depending on the state of the tide and the sea breeze, the wicket could seam around early on. Yorkshire, albeit a depleted side, with Hutton and Trueman on Test duty at Headingley and Close injured, were dismissed for 226, whereupon Sheppard played his highest innings at Hastings. He made 181 not out as Sussex replied with 387 for 3, thanks to a stand of 279 between the captain and George Cox, who made 144. The home side were close to victory on the last day as Yorkshire were only 51 ahead with three wickets left. Robin Marlar famously blames an incident in this game for the loss of the title: 'Our wicketkeeper, dear old soul, dropped Vic Wilson in the Yorkshire match, and that was it.' He was still going on about it years later; 'There may be an element of bias here since I was bowling at the time and had turned the ball away from the left-hander.'[10]

In all probability, of much more significance in the destination of the title was the blow suffered by Alan Oakman earlier in the day. His description encapsulates the dry humour and stoicism of the county pro in the days before physios, medics and back-up teams:

> I missed August with a compound dislocation and fracture of the thumb. Ted Lester edged one and it hit my hand – the bone was sticking out. Sam Cowan, our masseur, said 'I'll put it back.' I think he'd done his qualification by correspondence course so I decided to go up the hospital. I got in the car – it was a bit difficult trying to change gear and drive, but in Casualty there was a Hungarian doctor I'd dealt with before who looked at my thumb and got his hands round it. I didn't feel it go back. He said, 'You'll be in plaster for about a month.'[11]

The loss of this influential all-rounder seriously unbalanced the side at a crucial time. With a draw inevitable, Marlar's eccentricity came to the fore, as he changed over to bowl the last ball of the match left-handed to Johnny Wardle, a left-handed batsman who completed the joke by turning round and batting right-handed.

The County Week at Hastings was a frustrating one. Twice the side were within sight of wins which would have cemented their leadership in the title race. Jim was back in reasonable form for the traditional clash with Kent. George Cox's chanceless 145 charmed the Saturday crowd, including the author in short trousers, with paste sandwiches, Penguin bar, lemonade, Smith's crisps with salt in blue twists, sixpence for an ice-cream – and the obligatory autograph book. Sussex made 267 with Jim's 39 second top score. On the Monday Peter Hearn with 114 and Arthur Phebey dug in, and just after lunch Kent were 221 for 1. By tea they were all out for 265. Bowling his medium-fast off-breaks on a damp wicket, Ted James took 5 for 23 and when Sheppard declared at 177 for 9, Kent were left to score 180 to win. With Sussex pressing for a crucial victory, Sheppard had men all round the bat as Geoff Smith and Ray Dovey held on to finish at 154 for 8.

Just as Jim was regaining some of the old fluency, the Championship push was beginning to falter. At Northampton Jock Livingston and Des Barrick both made big hundreds, Kenny Suttle followed suit and rain on the third day washed a result down the drain. Jim compiled a sound 81 not out against Middlesex at Hove as Alan Moss's 7 for 35 shot out the title leaders for 118. Compton and Edrich had made hay and it was left to Hubert Doggart with a patient 104 and Jim to bat out time. Then Sussex 'had an extraordinary run – we were top of the table in July and went three matches – Derbyshire at home, then Gloucestershire and Warwickshire away – where we followed on every time and then played wonderful cricket to draw, by which time the Championship had gone beyond our reach.'[12] Jim's return to form continued as the side followed on at Hove. Les Jackson and Cliff Gladwin, as hostile an opening pair as any in the Championship, shared the wickets as Sussex conceded a first innings lead of 241. In the follow-on Jim scored 124, his first century for over a year. The visitors, left 85 to win, finished three runs short at 82 for 7. 'The Rev' had asked Thomson and Wood to bowl outside the leg stump, 'because it was a home match, they were hitting furiously and it was very exciting. We shouldn't have done it but England would have lost that match at Leeds when Trevor bowled down the leg-side.'

Sheppard's version of 'leg theory' reached its apotheosis at the Cheltenham Festival over the next three days. It was David Allen's debut: 'I'm seventeen, I've come straight from school. Mortimore and Wells were in the services so I got in the side. It was a super game and it got very close.' George Emmett entertained the festival crowd with a big hundred and Sussex had to follow on for the second successive match. Ken Suttle (108) and George Cox (95) gave the visitors a fighting chance of forcing an unlikely win and Gloucestershire set off in pursuit of 169. Jim brought a rumbustious partnership between George Lambert and Jack Crapp to an end when he dropped Lambert at deep mid wicket, retrieved the ball and ran Jack Crapp out. Allen remembers:

> We wanted about 40 and we claimed the extra half hour. Suddenly the game changed. David Sheppard got Jim Wood to bowl left-arm over and Ian Thomson right-arm round and they bowled it wide.' For the second match running, Sheppard resorted to bowling leg-theory to stop his opponents winning: 'It was a hard-nosed cricket decision, but I was ashamed of it.
>
> These tactics effectively shut the game up for about 10 minutes. Jack Crapp walked out in front of a huge Cheltenham crowd, who were anticipating what they thought was going to be an exciting finish and he told the umpires, 'The match is over', which they accepted. Sheppard said, 'Hold on − if one of the captains wants the extra half hour he can claim it.' Jack retorted, 'Only if you're trying to win. You're not so I'm calling the sides off.' There was a tremendous hoo-ha on the pitch and David said, 'I apologise − and we'll go back to a proper game of cricket for the last twenty minutes,' but it was too late.

Gloucester members vented their feelings against Ted James: 'I was fielding fine leg and the members behind me were giving me awful stick. If we'd won I reckon we'd have been attacked.' Crapp was furious − and not only at Sussex. His side had come perilously close to losing. Within sight of victory, three wickets fell at the same score and it was left to young David Allen to bat out time:

> I'm a young lad from school, very proud of myself and thinking myself bloody clever. When we were fifteen runs short somebody got out and I walked out for the last five minutes quite slowly. We played out a draw and Sheppard was full of apologies.
>
> Jack Crapp quietly came over to me and said, 'I suppose after what they did you were quite pleased, walking out like that.' 'Well, I don't know, skipper,' I muttered. 'Don't you ever do that again. People like Sheppard might play that kind of cricket but we in Gloucestershire never will.

Here was the professional captain, upholding the etiquette of the game and the amateur, the Cambridge Blue destined for the Anglican ministry, showing his teeth. 'David was a hard-nosed cricketer', says Suttle, 'and he didn't like to lose.'

In cricket, as in life, things tend to come in threes, and after following on twice in succession, at Edgbaston the pattern was bizarrely familiar − opponents bat first, get a big score, Sussex fall 170 or 180 short, recover well and there is something of a finish. Jim battled to 57 in the second attempt and at the end Rupert Webb and Jim Wood were hanging on at 239 for 9, to deny the home side a chance of a chase to victory.

After a soggy and amazingly incident-free draw with Glamorgan at the Arms Park, Jim was back on the south coast after ten days away. Sussex's sojourn to the west had curtailed his involvement with wedding preparations. He and Irene were to be married the week after the season ended and he had left all the details in the capable hands of Fred Titmus, his best man. It was Eastbourne Week, on a wicket at the Saffrons which was one of the flattest in the country. Many seaside pitches, however good, could misbehave in a sea-fret or just after a shower – and Eastbourne was no exception. Given the right conditions, the Saffrons was usually a result pitch. The holiday-makers in the deckchairs had rich entertainment that week. They saw the elegant Reg Simpson and the classically upright Joe Hardstaff make fifties as the visitors totalled 252. Local favourite George Cox responded with a half-century as Sheppard declared two runs ahead. Then the visitors collapsed to 101 all out as, not for the only time against Nottinghamshire at the Saffrons, Ian Thomson bowled an inspired spell, taking 6 for 37. Sussex made heavy weather of getting the runs. There had been a shower and Sussex had struggled to 71 for 5, with Jim trying to steady the ship:

> With Bruce Dooland bowling, it was turning so much that he couldn't control it, and the ball was literally going straight to slip. Robin came in when we were 74 for 7 and managed to get bat to ball. It was going here, there and everywhere but we got away with it – wet wickets were interesting.[13]

Kenny Suttle had got a pair and although he had been chosen for the West Indies, 'I was left out for the next game and then came in the game after', which began his extraordinary sequence, unlikely ever to be beaten, of 423 consecutive games for the county. The diminutive chatterbox from Worthing therefore sat out the season's most shattering victory – over Gloucestershire. Before the game Sheppard apologised once again to Jack Crapp for the Cheltenham farrago. That was as far as he took his magnanimity. 'Eastbourne was very funny. Most people would say that when the wicket was very wet it was a slow pudding. I knew that it wasn't.' Robin Marlar took 7 for 42, exploiting the turn to perfection, and by mid-afternoon Gloucester were all out for 84. When Sussex batted, John Langridge was caught behind and Sussex did not lose another wicket in the match. Sheppard's share of the home side's 181 for 1 was an undefeated 128. 'I declared long before I would have done if I hadn't the local knowledge. It rained again, you see.' What Gloucestershire didn't know was that 'if you bowled medium-pace on it the ball stopped and went straight up in the air. Ted James got a lot of wickets.' Although not many Sussex bowlers relished bowling at the Saffrons, James did: 'it was hard work bowling at Eastbourne. If it rained you had to take advantage of the wicket before it dried out.' This under rated swinger from Buckinghamshire employed his leg-cutters to devastating effect and returned 6 for 19, leaving Sussex only 17 to win. Two wins by the seaside had come too late. 'That was in August, when we'd really lost our chance of winning the Championship.'[14]

Yet when Surrey came to Hove at the end of the month, a victory for Sussex could have brought them their first title. They started encouragingly. On a pitch damp after early rain, three Surrey wickets fell quickly to Thomson and James, but Fletcher's dogged 81 took Surrey to 220. Sheppard, trying to push for a result, declared a run ahead, whereupon Surrey were content to play out time. The last rites of what might have been an epic game were brightened for the members by 136 from Peter May. Ted James was injured, but every other Sussex player apart from Rupert Webb bowled. The champions had come for a draw and Surrey's pragmatism ensured that the title returned to the Oval.

The final game at Hove had a vaguely celebratory air as an innings victory over Lancashire clinched the runners-up spot. Bowling with impeccable consistency, Robin Marlar took 10 for 129 as Lancashire were all out for 152 and 176. Sussex declared at 340, Hubert Doggart making a hundred, George Cox 96 and Suttle a bustling 89. The win by an innings and 12 runs was a heartening climax to a memorable summer. Jim had come of age and, despite a mid-season slump, hit 1,227 runs at 34.08, receiving the approbation of *Wisden*:

> Suttle… with six centuries to his credit, showed a great advance, and like the free-hitting Parks, exceeded 1,000 runs in his first full season. This young pair, too, played a full part in making Sussex one of the best fielding combinations in the country.

Sheppard's charismatic, almost mystical leadership had brought out the best in Jim and his colleagues, who bade farewell to him with a mixture of sadness and respect, feeling that 'a wonderful man has given his services to a better cause than even the game we love.'[15]

Jim wound up his season with a romp for the South of England against the Rest of England in the Hastings Festival. The same boy with autograph

book and short trousers saw Jim bowl his old friend Subba Row. Four days
later at St Wilfrid's, Irene Young, private secretary to an architect, became
Mrs James Parks. 'For £2,700 we had a house built called Nursery End,
which had nothing to do with Lord's; it was on the edge of an old nursery
that my dad used to work on when he was a young man.'The happy couple
honeymooned at Bude and a fortnight later returned from Cornwall to start
married life.

Jim had always loved football. As a Parks you played most ball games; from
time to time you would be injured. When Jim went to Southwick on a blus-
tery Wednesday evening at the end of September he was looking forward to
his first game of the season in his familiar berth at inside-left. Shortly after half-
time, 'I went down low to head the ball and was kicked on the skull. Everyone
on the ground, except me, heard a crack, and with my wife watching me play
my first game of football after our honeymoon, it was a moment the Parks
family will not easily forget.'After the magic sponge, Jim was apparently none
the worse:'I came to and thought I was fine' and 'after 19 minutes... Parks
[gave] Haywards Heath the lead from some distance out.'[16] Jim had hit the
winner but he knew little about it – he had suffered concussion and double
vision.Three days later at Newhaven, in front of 1,000 spectators and despite
having a headache, Jim was having a good game but just before the end, 'I
remember going up to head the ball, blacked out and ended up at Hurstwood
Park hospital. I was frightened to death actually because I had double vision
– I thought 'Will I be able to see the ball next year ?''' Acutely interested no
doubt in Jim's injury was the Newhaven right-half – Jim's county colleague
Ian Thomson.

The diagnosis was delayed concussion, but soon Jim was back and scoring
goals. In late November, against Gravesend and Northfleet 'A', 'Haywards
Heath took the lead after four minutes. Keith Elphick centred the ball from
the left... Jim Parks fastened on to it and fired a first-time drive into the
net.'[17] After Christmas Jim travelled to north Kent for the return:'Accepting
a neat pass by Keith Elphick, Jim Parks atoned for a missed goal a minute
previously by equalising with a well-aimed drive which kept low,'[18] and
midway through the second half'Denys O'Brien deftly slipped the ball to
Parks, who caught the opposition at sea with a clever lob shot which sailed
over Wright's head into the net.'[19]

The Metropolitan League in the mid-fifties featured some illustrious
names.The week before,The Heath had journeyed to face Chelsea 'A', but
not at Stamford Bridge. Chelsea's third team played at the Welsh Harp and
the *Middy* gives us a flavour of non-league soccer half a century ago:

There is no stand; no programmes were available; and the playing pitch faces a large lake. A mere handful of spectators were present and there was but little atmosphere. A cold wind was blowing and the playing surface was muddy and exhausting.'[20]

A season which had begun with a potentially worrying head injury ended on a happy note as in late March, against Dunstable Town, 'Peter Hyslop fired over a beautiful centre for Jim Parks to head a grand equaliser,'[21] whereupon it was time to get the train south – and to meet the new skipper.

A man of immense charm and infinite bonhomie, Hubert Doggart suffered from not being David Sheppard. Rupert Webb describes an early season exchange with Ian Thomson: 'Hubert was in a normal gully position. Tommy walked up and he said, "Will you come in from third man, Hubert, please, into the gully?" Hubert walked forward a bit and stopped. Tommy said, "I want you to stand where David Sheppard stood."'

He meant it literally, but he might also have been speaking metaphorically. Doggart, a Cambridge Blue and, briefly in 1950, a Test player, was a naturally gifted sportsman, whose attitude to the game was directly in tune with the Sussex tradition. While it was taken seriously enough, Sussex cricket was traditionally played with a smile on the face and an expansive spirit, and there was in that depressingly damp summer of 1954 'the faint suggestion of sand-shoes, of a breeze off the sea, and of people inordinately enjoying themselves.'[22] Jim enjoyed the season despite the drab weather, although Sussex were never in contention for the title. He found Hubert a happy-go-lucky character, as did Ted James, a newly-wed like Jim: 'We had good fun – socially he was absolutely marvellous. He'd get us tickets for the theatre and as his father was chairman of the FA we went to Wembley for the cup final.' Doggart was competent enough and popular, but although the team won more matches than it lost, Sussex slid to ninth.

Despite the grey skies and wet wickets, Jim hit the ground running. By the Whitsun bank holiday game he had already scored 611 runs. There had been no sign of his football injury as he hit 61 and 70 off a Northampton attack including Test bowlers Frank Tyson and George Tribe, and 120 in a seven-wicket defeat at Edgbaston. Jim was in form but the team was not winning. Surrey had won an exciting game at Hove by one wicket just on time, where in a match of three declarations George Cox made 167 and Ted Clark 101 in Surrey's reply. Doggart's declaration at 270 for 5 left Surrey 240 to win, and Jim Laker, batting at number eight, made 53 not out to see the champions home.

Jim's vein of fluent form continued, via a well-crafted 46 against the Pakistan; tourists at Hove and a few runs in what must be called 'Wardle's match' at Hull. The clever left-armer took 16 for 112 in the game and for good measure made 66 not out as the hosts crushed Sussex by an innings and 20 runs. Jim was becoming known as one of the finest players of spin in the country, yet he would not have had much experience of left-arm wrist spinners. 'There weren't that many left-armers of Wardle's type around then, apart from George Tribe and Jack Walsh', says Ted James. 'Yorkshire were a hard side and we got well beaten.' It was also virtually a Test side – Wardle, Hutton, Lowson, Watson, Yardley, Close, Illingworth, Trueman and Appleyard – plus Roy Booth and Vic Wilson, experienced county pros. If Sussex had suffered on a spinner's track on Humberside, then the tide turned for Leslie Compton's benefit match – the bank holiday fixture against Middlesex. On the Saturday Jim was 8 runs short of a century when Doggart declared at 263 for 8. A shower had forced the captain's hand, and as *Wisden* put it, 'Middlesex were caught on a drying pitch and only a masterly innings by D. Compton enabled them to avoid a follow-on.' In fact Jim's hero made exactly half his side's runs as they struggled to 144. Further rain on the Tuesday precluded any hope of a result.

In the dismally wet June of 1954, Sussex were winning at last. Jim made his customary runs, scoring 64 at Tunbridge Wells, and in Hugo Yarnold's benefit at New Road Doggart's side won by an innings and 14 runs. Matches in July showed the free-wheeling nature of his captaincy. The side tumbled to a 76-run defeat in a bizarre game against Derbyshire at Horsham. Each innings was smaller than the one before, Les Jackson and Cliff Gladwin taking 14 wickets between them. Licking their wounds, the side entrained at Paddington for Taunton, where Ian Thomson bowled magnificently in the home side's second innings, taking 7 for 31. Only 28 were required and Jim and Ken Suttle knocked off the runs needed for victory after Sussex had contrived to lose Langridge and Sheppard. 'The Rev' was back for a few games, and in fact was recalled to skipper England in the Second Test at Trent Bridge as Len Hutton continued to convalesce. He had come to Taunton straight from the trouncing of Pakistan, in which Compton made his highest Test score – 278.

County Week at Hastings was a microcosm of Doggart's season. Coming to the Central Ground after totalling only 26 in four innings, Jim hit a chanceless 135 as Sussex reached 350 for 8 declared on the first day. A sporting declaration by Doggart left Nottinghamshire to make 264 to win. Playing enterprising cricket, they reached their target just before the close. Jim missed the next game as his first representative call-up took him to Lord's to play for the Players in the quintessentially English fixture against the Gentlemen, but he missed all the fun by the seaside. The tide must have been in that Wednesday morning as Jack Flavell steamed in from the Town Hall End. He took the first nine Sussex wickets, as Doggart recalls:

> I remember John Flavell being kept on by Reg Perks for a last precious three-quarters of an hour while those two stalwarts, Ted James and Jim Wood, had a stirring unbroken last-wicket partnership that paved the way for a great nine-wicket victory.[23]

At Lord's Jim made only a modest contribution, but clearly he was in the selectors' minds, and when Frank Lowson, chosen to open the batting in place of the still indisposed Hutton, had an injury scare the weekend before the Third Test, Jim was called up as twelfth man. 'I was reading the paper at my mother-in-law's when the team was announced at 2 o'clock. I was amazed.' Not so Irene. When she came home from work Jim told her he was in the Test team. 'Are you?', she said, 'Good show' – and she put the kettle on. It may have helped having 'the Rev' in the corridors of power: 'I think I met with the selectors for that Test. Since I was captain somebody must have asked me what I thought of Jim and I would have given a very positive account.'[24] Jim Swanton was rather more dubious:

> Now Parks on achievement is very lucky to get an England cap. He has made only two hundreds this year. Nevertheless, the market being so bare it will be refreshing to watch a new young cricketer and moreover a stylish striker of the ball, in the Test environment, and to judge, if we can, whether he plays right behind the line of whatever pace Pakistan can muster. Parks's appearance is welcome because he is a fine mover in the field with a deadly throw.[25]

Certainly the door was open for Jim to claim a place on the Ashes tour that winter. While eight places were secure, 'of the others, Sheppard is a candidate as a batsman and perhaps as vice-captain as well; Parks may clinch the one place usually reserved for a player of more promise than achievement.'[26]

Jim left Hove and packed. The telegram arrived the next day: he had to travel up on the Wednesday and report by lunchtime.

> I didn't have my first car until '57/58 and I can always remember walking up to the bus stop with my cricket bag and hold-all. While I was waiting for the bus to the station, grandma told me that I was playing as Lowson was injured. I'd never been to Old Trafford before, so I travelled up on the train with Sheppard and May. We stayed at Altrincham – or Mere – and I shared a room with Jim McConnon, the Glamorgan off-spinner, another debutant. We

got to bed about 10.30 – and we nattered about cricket for an hour or more. Well, you did talk cricket in those days – we'd talk through the day's play in the pub afterwards. The opposition weren't your enemy then.

The next morning, Trevor Bailey gave the debutants a lift to the ground and Jim was immediately impressed by the quality of the light at Old Trafford. Jim senior, coaching at Trent Bridge, was thrilled at Jim's Test debut and was on the phone with advice: 'Treat it as a game of cricket, Jim. Don't be overawed by the occasion.' Sheppard won the toss and batted. On a typical Manchester midsummer's day, the Pakistan bowling was steady and defensive. 'I couldn't quite believe I was playing Test cricket with Compton, my boyhood hero. It had come out of the blue so I didn't have time to worry about it – we were just out there playing a game of cricket. There was no hype at all about it.' Jim, due in at six, went through his ritual of putting on first his left sock, boot, pad and glove. If he had to remove his right glove, he always took off the left glove so he could put it back on first again. Compton had made 93 when at 4.55 p.m. he was caught at the wicket: Jim arrived to join Tom Graveney – and the new ball was due. He had felt nervous for the first time before going in to bat, but the adrenalin banished that empty feeling as soon as he hit the turf.

He soon realised that this was no sunny Saturday in front of the deck-chairs at Hove with the seagulls wheeling away in a cloudless sky. Test cricket had a different atmosphere, with none of the banter of the county game. The Pakistanis were treating the match as a serious moment in their lives. Nevertheless, 'Treat it as a game of cricket', his dad had told him, so he did.

'I got off the mark against Ghazali, the off-spinner with one of my favour-ite off-the-mark shots, turning it to square leg: in the next over they took the new ball.' Fazal Mahmood was then one of the most effective fast-medium seamers in world cricket. Like Alec Bedser and Brian Statham, he bowled an immaculate length and was naggingly accurate. Against this skilful swing bowler, 'Parks began well, and his first two scoring strokes against the new ball were four for an off-drive and four for a fine leg-glance, both strokes of quality.'[27] After half an hour he had made 15, but he was being frustrated by Fazal. Straining at the leash, 'he aimed another leg-glance, moved across too far, and was bowled leg-stump behind his pads.'[28]

Friday's play succumbed to the Manchester monsoon, and after Sheppard had declared early on the Saturday, Pakistan collapsed dramatically from 63 for 2 to 90 all out. Jim McConnon took 3 for 12 in six overs and the visitors

were 24 for 5 second whack. Then it rained for three days. In the second innings I can remember catching Wazir Mohammed at gully off Bedser. I don't know what I was doing fielding there, but I was. I would have loved to have had that second knock – Colin Cowdrey and I were both having reasonable seasons. It was a toss-up who would go to Australia in the winter. Well, they chose him, he had a successful tour and that set him up.

It had been a valuable experience: Pakistan, themselves starting a Test career, taught Jim that a Test batsman had to work for his runs. As his captain said, 'Getting runs in Test cricket is quite rough.' *Wisden* gave him a favourable review: 'In his first Test, Parks lived up to his reputation as a young batsman of much promise who, with more experience, might be a regular Test cricketer of the future.'

After his first taste of international limelight, Jim came back down to earth the following day. He made the short trip to Blackpool, where Auntie Ivy saw him top score with 37 as Tattersall and Hilton bowled Sussex out for 105. Fortune smiled on Doggart's men, however, as the dreadful Lancashire weather which had washed out the Test gave them a draw.

Jim reflected as he travelled south that night: he had become a Test player, but he had been away for ten days and it was good to be going home. Besides, it was August Bank Holiday, Middlesex at Hove, a big crowd, the flavour of Brighton rock, candy-floss and the whiff of the briny as you strolled out to bat. Not that Jim strolled:

> The arms flailed like a windmill as he marched out on to the field. The bat was raised aloft like a spear and the slim, boyish figure gave an extra hitch to his flannels. Chocks away. This was a cricketer who meant business.[29]

Holiday or no holiday, Jim was back to business. A regulation opening day saw Middlesex reach 271 and John Warr's 5 for 21 brought Sussex up 25 runs short. Alan Oakman then took 4 for 19 to leave Sussex 173 to win, and they lost only Sheppard and Langridge as the captain and Jim saw them home.

Jim had made his Test debut at the expense of Frank Lowson, and the Yorkshire opener exacted ample revenge in Charlie Oakes' benefit game, another match in this dreary season ruined by the weather. Yorkshire made 334 for 9, Lowson scoring 165, and Sussex, following on 217 behind, were 233 for 5 when rain set in for the next five days, annihilating the Kent game as well. Jim made 85 in that second innings and such were the vagaries of fortune and the weather that he made only one run in the next twelve days. For Jim, the long trip to Swansea was hardly worth it. 'I'll always recall the occasion. At Swansea there are seventy-six steps from the pavilion down to the field. First ball I got a nick off Alan Watkins and Haydn Davies caught it.

"This can never happen again," I thought. When we batted again I couldn't
get off mark for half an hour. Then I got a single and I was so relieved at not
getting a pair I played down the wrong line to Wilf Wooller next ball and
went up those 76 steps again.' The game was dominated by the bowlers, the
weather closed in and after the inevitable draw the teams got the same train
back to Sussex that night for the return match. Jim was out of touch – but
at least it was the benign featherbed of the Saffrons which beckoned, the
traditional haven for batsmen scarcely able to put bat on ball:

> In the old days Eastbourne was the best batting wicket in the country and
> they used to say that dear old Wilf[30] slept under the covers at night to make
> sure nobody could damage the wicket! If you were out of form you went to
> the Saffrons to get back into form and if you didn't get a couple of hundred
> runs that week in four innings there was something radically wrong. I used to
> love playing there.[31]

Glamorgan didn't – at least not that year. In their first innings, apart from
Bernard Hedges' determined 62 they had no answer to Alan Oakman's off-
spin and managed only 142. Jim returned to form with a fluent 74 when the
home side replied, but the innings was dominated by a forceful 133 from
George Cox. Ted James saw it from the middle:

> George played a brilliant innings. He kept talking to Wilf, and playing and
> missing and as soon as he pushed one wide, he went down on one knee and
> smashed it through the covers. This was banter, not sledging. Wilf wouldn't
> take himself off even when George kept on hitting him because he was after
> his 100th wicket. The Glamorgan boys wanted him to change, because he'd
> got old Len Muncer and Jim McConnon there. It was so funny.

Needing to bat with more resolution the second time around, the Welshmen's
response was equally pusillanimous. They crumbled to 132 all out, giving
Sussex a handsome victory by an innings and 97 runs. According to Rupert
Webb, they described it as the worst week they had ever had. 'They played us
in a drawn match at Swansea, travelled all the way to Sussex with us on the
train, then we beat them by an innings!'

Equally convincing wins over Somerset in the second game in Eastbourne
Week and against Hampshire at Bournemouth gave Doggart's men a pleasing hat-trick at the end of a happy but inconsistent season. At the Saffrons
Jim was back to his stroke-playing best, delighting the Saturday holiday mak-
ers with 88 in Sussex's 314. A century from David Sheppard enabled Doggart

to set Somerset 236 to win: they caved in to Thomson's swing and James' cutters to go down by 122. It was a similar story at Dean Park. Hampshire faced a first-innings deficit of 74 and after Shackleton had claimed 5 for 42 in Sussex's second knock, Hampshire, set 288 to win, could only reach 178, Thomson doing the damage with 4 for 29. Back at Hove, England all-rounder Trevor Bailey very nearly beat Sussex single-handedly in Doggart's penultimate game in charge. He made 83 as Essex posted 272 in the first innings and took four wickets as Sussex fell 44 runs short. The home side were then set 230 to win after Bailey hit 79 and Jim bowled Mike Bear for 33 in Essex's 185 all out. Kenny Suttle led the charge with 78, and Don Smith (48) and Jim (38) kept the momentum going, but wickets fell at crucial times and, in a close finish, Ted James and Rupert Webb were left clinging to the wreckage at 214 for 9, a tantalising 16 runs shy of a fourth win in succession. Hubert Doggart's final game as captain exhibited the features which had come to characterise his whole season – an entertaining but irritating blend of high promise and, if not low farce, then amiable underachievement. After conceding a first-innings lead of 129 to Lancashire at Hove when Roy Tattersall again bowled well, Ian Thomson took 4 for 27 when the visitors were all out for 104, Cyril Washbrook accounting for 57 of them. Sussex, chasing 234 for victory, stood encouragingly at 94 for 2, when Jim, Kenny Suttle and George Cox were dismissed for two runs. With the cream of the batting gone, the last five wickets fell for 54 and Lancashire ran out winners by 83 runs.

Jim had a breezily enjoyable end-of-season caper by the sea at the Scarborough Festival, watching an attractive hundred by Peter May for the Gentlemen and making 57 in a 50-run victory for the Players. Despite Sussex's indifferent performance in the Championship, it was a season of noteworthy individual achievements. Ian Thomson took 127 wickets, more than any other Sussex bowler for twenty years, and Alan Oakman failed by just one to reach his 100 for the season. David Sheppard headed the averages, scoring 1,265 in 16 games, Jim scored 1,478 runs at 36.95, and the captain had made over 1,600 runs. Once again, *Wisden* noted Jim's progress: 'Parks and Cox proved the most reliable run-getters. Sounder than hitherto, Parks retained his attractiveness and he fielded splendidly, especially at cover.'

Jim had now matured as a professional. Under the tutelage of George Cox he had become possibly the outstanding cover-point in England. He had made his mark on the county scene as a fluent, attacking batsman, one of the finest players of spin-bowling in the country. In somewhat fortunate circumstances he had made his Test debut and may have been unlucky to miss the tour to Australia. Now a married man with domestic responsibilities, he could look forward to the full blossoming of his talent under a new captain, a Cambridge man like his two predecessors, but a very different animal. If Jim and his team-mates had followed Sheppard out of loyalty and Doggart for the fun of it, they were to follow Robin Marlar out of sheer curiosity, for here was a leader more eccentric than most, a man of decided opinions 'which he was prepared to defend and maintain with all the passion of a Calvinistic Minister at the time of the Reformation'.[32] 1955 would be an interesting year.

Chapter 5
Broadening the Mind

At the beginning of October Jim was back at inside-left against West Ham 'A' – a welcome return as the Blues had suffered six defeats in a row. Having opened the scoring 'with a delightful cross shot which sailed just under the bar',[1] Jim completed a first-half hat-trick when he 'rounded off a lovely solo run from the halfway line.'[2] He also created a goal for player-manager Ronnie Rooke, who in 1939 had scored six for Fulham in a cup tie and two seasons after the war netted 33 times for the Arsenal – an achievement equalled only in 2003/04 by Thierry Henry. Jim was a local celebrity and even though Rooke's better days were behind him, 'we probably got 500–600 for that game, but in Victoria Park in the County League we got 2,000. In those days there wasn't much else to do. Families came into town on the Saturday, the wives would go shopping and the husbands would come to the football. We used to get trainloads from Lewes and Eastbourne.'[3] Regular football kept Jim fit throughout the winter and in February a team representing Sussex CCC won the first indoor five-a-side tournament sponsored by the *Evening Argus* at the Brighton Stadium. It was a useful side – along with Jim were Kenny Suttle, Ian Thomson, Gordon Potter and Don Bates, by then on the books of Brighton and Hove Albion. Sussex could boast a wealth of footballing talent at that time – Denis Foreman played on the left-wing for Brighton, and George Cox, for whom 1955 would be his last season before retiring to coach at Winchester, had played for Arsenal, Fulham and Luton Town. When Doggart returned to the groves of academe at Winchester, Cox was a possible interim candidate to succeed him. According to a senior player, when the rumour was put about that Robin Marlar was going to be the next captain, 'John Langridge and George Cox begged the committee not to appoint him. Instead they suggested that George should captain the side. He would have been a brilliant captain but,' he said, 'they wouldn't have it',[4] for the committee was certain in its collective wisdom that Marlar fulfilled its criteria for a captain of Sussex. After all, he was a Cambridge Blue and an amateur.

The committee saw Marlar as the archetypal Sussex captain, but in that golden summer, under dazzling skies of cerulean splendour, he showed a strain of such quixotic whimsy that the committee worthies must at times have scratched their heads and asked themselves what they had done. For Jim these considerations were an irrelevance. His attitude to the game and its more esoteric ramifications was always one of 'the dogs bark and the caravan moves on.' He reported for duty in early April with his characteristic affable enthusiasm: he was looking forward to going to work. He was however in woeful form, scoring 174 in seven first-class innings. Despite this poor run, he was chosen twice for the MCC, against the champion county and against the touring South Africans. This recognition by Lord's was for Jim a silver lining in a heavy low cloud: 'When I was chosen for the MCC, it was similar to being chosen for the Test team – it meant they'd noticed you.' Jim was a realist, however: a total of 59 runs in four innings was unlikely to earn him a Test recall.

A week later Jim was back at Lord's for the bank holiday fixture with Middlesex. On a green wicket Marlar asked the hosts to bat and Jim witnessed one of the finest innings he ever saw:

When we went out to field Denis wasn't there – he never arrived on time. Then we suddenly saw him on the balcony in his civvies. A couple of overs later, they were 4 for 2 and we had to wait for Denis to come out to bat. We got them all out for 206 and Denis got 150-odd. He was last man out: Ken Suttle caught him in front of the stand. I was at cover in those days and he just stroked it one side and then the other all along the ground. I don't think he played and missed although it was seaming all over the place – he just played perfect shots. Second highest score was John Warr with 13.

This was a masterclass by Compton on what Suttle called 'a dodgy wicket – but then he was a fine player on all wickets. I caught him on the boundary off Marlar, when he was down to the tail and he was crashing it about. He was a genius, and a very nice fellow.' Rain on the last day put paid to a result, but it had been an innings to remember.

Jim was struggling for runs but the team's fortunes were beginning to improve. Against Yorkshire at Hove Ted James took a career-best 9 for 60 'on a wicket which was just going a bit. I used to like bowling from the Cromwell Road end because of my short run – all the big guns used to come up the hill. Freddie Trueman used to have a problem down the hill because of overstepping.' Jim was bowled by Brian Close for a duck in Sussex's 138 and the visitors were left 156 to win. Thomson (6 for 55) and James with another couple dismissed Yorkshire for 135 for the season's first win.

Jim was still not in touch. 'I had started very badly, and I normally didn't play against the Varsities, because it was the only chance of having a rest, but I decided to hit myself out of trouble against Cambridge University' – hardly a risk-free approach, but it was not like Jim to graft his way through a sticky patch. Mike Smith saw that: 'I don't think Jim could play defensively – it wasn't in the bloke's nature.' On this occasion, fortune favoured the brave and he hit 175 not out. For good measure, Jim took 3 for 23 and 1 for 36 – the best bowling figures of his career. His 61 at Dudley against Worcestershire confirmed his return to form but set against George Cox's whirlwind hitting in the second innings it was small beer. In thirty-eight minutes Cox hit 63 not out, put on 46 in twelve minutes with Marlar for the eighth wicket and in one over dispatched Reg Perks for 26. Once again Thomson won the match with 5 for 57 and the home side went down by 108 runs. After a fluent 118 against the South Africans at Hove Jim felt jubilant:

> I thought nothing but happy days were ahead. I was soon to have a rude awakening. Once more a gremlin perched itself on the handle of my bat and I found myself making errors which, to say the least, were bad ones.[5]

Then, at Aigburth, on a wet wicket overlooking the Mersey, Roy Tattersall bowled Sussex out, and in one of his best innings of the year Jim made 63. he felt better. After all, Eastbourne Week was coming up and he always made runs there – didn't he? Unusually, however, in this sunshine summer 'there had been a bit of rain, and the wicket wasn't the usual flat one.' Conditions were ideal for medium-pacers and Hampshire had two bowlers supremely equipped to exploit them. Sussex were limited to 172 in their first innings, Shackleton and Cannings taking four each. Thomson and James ensured that Hampshire replied with a similarly moderate 153. The contest sprang to life when Sussex could scrape together only 120 leaving the visitors to make 140 to win. With the ball nipping off the seam, Ted James' outswingers had Hampshire struggling at 84 for 8 when Vic Cannings joined Peter Sainsbury. He was not known for his batting, but the pair reached 139 before Sainsbury edged James through Oakman's legs at slip to bring the scores level. Rupert Webb takes up the story:

> Ted James bowled Sainsbury with the last ball of the next over and Mervyn Burden came out as white as a sheet, having smoked about 150 fags in the previous two hours! Actually Burden never faced a ball – in the next over Vic tried to turn Tommy to leg for the winning run, missed and was bowled. It was a tie.

It was only the third tie in all Sussex matches; Ted James thought Hampshire might have won; 'Another amusing thing – one ball went through slip and went over the line by a whisker. If it had been short, they would have run five easily.'

The abundance of characters who played county cricket in the fifties with such generosity of spirit and immense camaraderie gave rise to many comical incidents. Vic Cannings, the Hampshire seamer and 'a bit of a wag',[6] had borrowed a 1924 Rolls-Royce from a Mr Price, a Hampshire committee member, and as he drove into the Saffrons

> I shouted to some of the Sussex lads, 'Get away from my car!', never dreaming they would think it was mine. I drove it right round the ground and put the word out that I had won the football pools. All the Sussex players believed it apart from Robin Marlar, who at mealtimes in the pavilion would talk about the affluent young professional who had the Rolls-Royce.[7]

If it had been part of Cannings' prank to impress Marlar, the Old Harrovian, he had certainly succeeded.

The win over Gloucestershire rounded off a thoroughly satisfactory week at the Saffrons. Jim's 54 in that game presaged a brief flurry of form as he journeyed up to Sheffield: 'I got some runs there – 69 and 86 not out – and Willie Watson got the most beautiful 100 against us. At Bramall Lane, yes – funnily enough I played the last match they ever played there, with Somerset in '73 because I remember sitting next to Herbert Sutcliffe for dinner.' Sheffield was a false dawn, for over the next month Jim amassed, if that is the word, 195 runs for the county at just over 24.

There was no doubt that Jim was depressed about his form, and by the time Sussex arrived at Chelmsford at the beginning of August 'I could see little daylight.' He decided to have a chat with John Langridge.

Jim asked the seasoned opener, 'What do you think has gone wrong with my game?' Langridge gave a careful reply, 'In my view, your stance is too closed. That's the first thing you've got to put right.' Jim saw that this was an accurate summing-up – he had almost become an off-side player. During Jim's innings at Chelmsford John Langridge coached him, which proved invaluable: so much so that Jim saw a century before lunch looming, opened his shoulders to the last ball and was bowled by Roy Ralph for 98. 'It was a silly shot but it was the way I played.' On a sporting wicket Essex left Sussex to score 56 in six overs and at the end it was agonisingly close. Sussex had failed by 2 runs and Jim remained, 17 not out, with Alan Oakman at the other end.

Jim's *tête-à-tête* with the old master bore fruit later in August – 'the new stance suggested by John Langridge resulted in my hitting the ball hard once again all around the wicket.' Jim's steadily increasing confidence brought him 714 runs in little more than three weeks as the side won five of its last seven games. The captain was leading by example. His 15 for 119 against Lancashire at Hove is one of the great bowling performances in Sussex's annals. Their 87-run win had a definite Light Blue tinge as Sheppard and Doggart shared a stand of 110 in the first innings. Nottinghamshire were thrashed by ten wickets and in the next eleven days Jim made 117, 68, 7, 63, 101 not out and 205 not out. It was almost the halcyon era of his career. The customary defeat by Surrey at the Oval was followed by the demolition of Derbyshire by 94 runs, and to go with Jim's 101 not out, Alan Oakman made his debut hundred and the skipper weighed in with another twelve wickets.

The last game of that memorable summer dripped with nostalgia, the swan song for a trio of players who between them had given seventy-five years of service to the county. John Langridge, George Cox and Jim Wood bowed out against Somerset at Hove amid tributes and memories. It was carnival cricket as 530 runs were scored on the first day, Doggart declaring at about twenty past five with Sussex 464 for 9. Jim had scored his only double century at a run a minute, hitting 5 sixes and 25 fours – 'the type of innings that can be played at the end of the season with nothing at stake.' After Smith and Oakman had laid the foundations with a solid start, Jim made his highest first-class score. Against the seam bowling of Lomax, Yawar Saeed and Lobb, and the spin of Lawrence and McMahon (hardly the most penetrative of county attacks) he hit 205 in three and a half hours. Somerset were forced to follow on and 'we won very easily in the end – it was a nice way for John and George Cox to finish'. Sussex, left 18 to win, sent out the old warhorses, yoked together for their last hurrah. There was the inevitable anti-climax. 'Cox was caught in the deep from what would have been the winning hit and it was left to Marlar to make it.' In the September twilight the captain bade farewell to the three stalwarts, all of whom responded, most notably George Cox, who spoke with wit and sentiment.

As a climax to Marlar's first season in charge it could hardly have been better orchestrated. The county's thirteenth win enabled them to finish fourth, six batsmen – Jim, Ken Suttle, Alan Oakman, George Cox, John Langridge and Don Smith – made 1,000 runs, and, while the captain led the way with 129 wickets, Ted James and the inevitable Ian Thomson also took 100. With sixty-five victims Rupert Webb had his best summer:

I got a lot of stumpings that season – mainly off the quick bowlers. I used to stand up to them all the time – that was a tradition of Sussex wicketkeepers. Maurice Tate wouldn't bowl unless Tich Cornford was standing up. Although the wicketkeeper never got any credit he was attacking the batsman every ball because they couldn't move forward. Anyway Marlar went softly-softly catchee-monkey at everything and George Cox and John Langridge kept him pretty much under control, as they were very senior players. We had a good season – it never occurred to me then what was going to happen in the future.

The future for Jim was another country. Indeed, *in* another country, for his brilliant August form, his season's 2,054 runs and his outstanding fielding earned him a place on the MCC 'A' tour to Pakistan that winter. In the last game of the season he crossed swords with one of his tour colleagues for the Rest against the champion county. Jim signed off his scintillating summer with 96 against a strong Surrey attack at the Oval, where Doug Insole was bowled by Tony Lock. As he passed on the way back to the pavilion he enquired, '"How was I out – run out?' Locky really was throwing in those days.' Thrower or not, Lock would be joining Jim in a party travelling to the sub-continent with a dual purpose: to ensure that the cricket-playing nations saw English teams at regular intervals and to give the more promising of England's younger players the experience of playing international cricket overseas free from any attendant stress. With Jim in the party were his old RAF team-mates Alan Moss and Roy Swetman, his best man Fred Titmus and another colleague from the Combined Services, Brian Close.

Captained by Donald Carr and managed by Geoffrey Howard of Lancashire, the party gathered at a London hotel three weeks before Christmas. The MCC president, Lord Alexander of Tunis, outlined briefly the implications of touring Pakistan over the next three months; bearing in mind subsequent events it might be thought that his Lordship's counsel entered one ear and exited the other. However Jim's mind may well have been on more domestic matters. He had just learnt that his first winter away would coincide with Irene's pregnancy, for their first child was due the following May.

As the Anchor Line's SS *Circassia* left Liverpool, the first day's serene voyaging gave no hint of the rough seas ahead. The immediate priority was for the players to get to know one another:

Every morning we took part in PT under the supervision of Peter Richardson who, as a former PTI in the Army, was soon picking out the 'non-benders'. We also enjoyed several by no means fruitless attempts at batting, bowling and fielding practice in an impromptu net rigged up on the forward deck. The game could be costly in the expenditure of balls, and I remember one morning when Brian Close made such good use of the sea breeze that he swung a bright new ball clean into the Mediterranean.[8]

The four unofficial 'Tests' did not begin for a month. A lengthy period of acclimatisation began over Christmas in Karachi where, against the Karachi Cricket Association, Jim and others 'all made runs brightly and impressively'.[9] Jim sat out the game against Sind at Hyderabad, where he remembers 'staying in two ramshackle guest-houses. It was only seven years after partition and the tourist industry was only just getting on its feet. There wasn't a lot to do – there were no bars and you couldn't drink anyway.' Bahawalpur at least had the excitement of a genuine turf wicket and, although Jim made only 4, MCC won by an innings, after which the party visited the Emir's palace and took tea on the lawn as the household cavalry put on a display.

A long and dusty train journey through the desert brought the party to the Punjab capital Lahore, once the home of Rudyard Kipling, in the crisp, sunny air of late January. Jim was struggling for form, but not all of it was of his own making:

> Jim was given out to three appalling decisions but he suffered in silence which took some doing, I can assure you … both sides suffered from bad decisions. I would say that over the series Waqar Hassan was no less unfortunate than the majority of MCC's slighted victims. Yet even he was not as badly off as Jim.[10]

So Jim missed the first Test in Lahore, which was drawn, after Hanif and Alimuddin had crawled through two days at little more than 15 an hour. He was recalled for the second Test in Dacca, having made 78 against the Combined Schools, and took the field knowing that he would soon be joined by his Sussex room-mate Ian Thomson. Mike Cowan, having ricked his back in Karachi, had broken down again and would miss the rest of the tour. Sad though it was for Cowan, the news might have cheered Jim, but it did nothing to improve his fortune. Two poor lbw decisions and a defeat by an innings meant he was left out of the next international at Peshawar.

Before leaving Dacca, Brian Close, later an avid aficionado of the turf, organised a cycle rickshaw race along the 150-yard track between the hotel and a nearby club. With rupees wagered on the outcome, the players hired a rickshaw each. In the mêlée, one of the machines had a single spoke damaged, which was paid for. The locals treated the affair in good fun yet this trivial escapade was to return to haunt the team three weeks later in

Peshawar, venue of the third Test and capital of the North-West Frontier Province, near the Khyber Pass — names evoking echoes of an imperial past.

On arriving there, the party was dismayed to discover that the umpires for the game were Shujauddin and Idris Begh, a rich Karachi jeweller and natty dresser whom all the locals called 'the Peacock'. His umpiring had already given cause for concern and thus it was, in Tony Lock's memorable phrase, that 'Peshawar became an appealing match which could not have appealed to anyone.' A fighting 40 from Roy Swetman after the first innings had slumped to 88 for 6 and accurate seam bowling from Titmus and Moss gave MCC an unexpected lead of 36. This was immediately thrown away as Khan Mohammed and Kardar shot the tourists out for 111, and by the end of the third day Pakistan needed only 8 to win.

The next day was a rest day and the English players were in the mood for some fun: 'we wanted to throw off the cares of the cricket and celebrate the fact that we would be home in three weeks' time.'[11] In short, they were 'demob-happy', which may explain why water-pistols were bought in the bazaar and mock Western-style duels were fought out to the theme of *High Noon*. After dinner, which both sides attended in dinner-jackets, Jim and a few team-mates 'decided to invite Idris Begh, who'd been the main culprit as umpire, to one of the hotel rooms and we would do something about it.' Almost everybody in the team had had the water treatment, says Brian Close: 'we'd just catch them unawares and soak them. We all took it with a laugh and a smile.'

Accordingly Begh was invited but had left the hotel, 'so we had a bit of fun "kidnapping" him. We put him on one of those horse-drawn vehicles and I was holding him with my knees — he didn't come freely but we didn't hurt him at all. We got him to the captain's room and sat him down.'[12] Jim describes being on the door with Donald Carr when 'We offered Idris scotch. As you know Muslims don't drink, but Idris liked a scotch. He said, "I must have some water." Closey was hiding in one corner, Roy Swetman in another.' Cut to Close:

> So Donald Carr comes in — 'Here's your water, Idris' — and that's when we poured the two cauldrons of water over him. He was always spick and span and he was a bit upset at being drenched, but we quietened him down a little, saying 'We do this to all the best umpires in the world', and he warmed to the occasion. The unfortunate thing was that two of the Pakistan players had heard something about it and they walked in and saw the dishevelled Idris Begh. Regrettably they laughed at him and he took the huff and dashed off.

That was the problem. The Pakistani players had seen Begh's dignity lowered, and when he returned to his hotel, he gave the Pakistani press a passionate account of the humiliation he had suffered. 'The press claimed that we'd kidnapped him, dragged him through the streets and forced alcohol down him.'[13] The 'vandalism' to the rickshaw in Dacca was thrown in for good measure and as a result there was a near-riot that night, with angry students besieging the team hotel. News of the incident reached Lord's and Jim thought 'at one time we were going to be sent home'. Lord Alexander, whose guide to etiquette on the sub-continent had seemingly fallen on deaf ears, fired off cables to the President of the Pakistan Board of Control and the Governor-General of Pakistan, expressing concern, regret and apology, and it was later revealed that he had indeed on one occasion offered to cancel the tour.

On the rest day, Jim took the advice of the management and headed out of town: 'Some Australian took Fred Titmus and myself off into the Khyber Pass and we had a marvellous day.' Brian Close, a single-handicap golfer with either hand, got his clubs out: 'The next day was the off day, and some of us played golf. Fifty yards behind us we had a troop of soldiers just in case. Peshawar is a very dangerous place – everybody carries guns.'

The last rites in the match came as an anti-climax: for the record, *Wisden* describes early morning rain, a resumption at about 2.30 p.m. and a Pakistani victory by seven wickets in little over half an hour. The traumas of Peshawar were soon forgotten however, as in early March the team moved on to Sarghoda, the headquarters of the Pakistan Air Force, where Jim opened for MCC with Brian Close and joined him in an impromptu football match against the RPAF College. Jim thought it was the highlight of the tour and after the side had wrapped up an innings win over the exotically named Combined Railways and Baluchistan XI at Multan, a soccer gauntlet was thrown down which Donald Carr picked up with alacrity. The MCC party could call on some accomplished players:

Maurice Tompkin, Alan Watkins and Brian Close had played professionally; Don Carr, Freddie Titmus and Harold Stephenson had played in top-class amateur football, and Jim Parks and Roy Swetman were above average. We fielded the side which had done duty in Sarghoda, namely: Barrington, Thomson, Parks, Stephenson, Close, Watkins, Lock, Tompkin, Swetman, Carr, Titmus. Nets were rigged and a pitch marked out on the cricket field… The afternoon was hot, with temperatures high in the 80s, and a crowd of 20,000 were present. The Multan side were area champions, but we beat them fair and square, by 2 goals to nil. Don Carr and Roy Swetman were the scorers. The half-back line was unwavering, Jim Parks was irrepressible at full-back, 'Sam' put on a show worthy of Bartram himself, and Maurice Tompkin sent out some lovely passes from inside-right.[14]

A fractious tour ended on a sour note at Karachi. On the third morning, MCC were 141 for 6, 37 behind, and the match was delicately poised. Jim cut a ball from Fazal which wicketkeeper Imtiaz Ahmed seemed to catch on the half-volley. There was an appeal and umpire Shujauddin, who failed to consult Idris Begh, gave Jim out. The Pakistanis apologised for the dubious verdict and, typically, Jim did not complain, but his team-mates were infuriated at this latest example of idiosyncratic umpiring. These pent-up frustrations came to the boil when an lbw appeal against Imtiaz Ahmed was refused and two or three players gave vent to their feelings in traditional Anglo-Saxon expletives. Unfortunately Imtiaz overheard them and complained to the square-leg umpire and Donald Carr. The Press reported the story in lurid detail the next day and in a statement the Pakistan Board of Control urged both sides to play the rest of the game in the best possible spirit. Happily, they did, and in the end the Surrey pair of Lock and Swetman, riding their luck, saw the tourists home by two wickets.

Jim's trip home was not without excitement. The party's Argonaut was delayed six hours in Rangoon by fog and eventually took off from Karachi at 3 a.m. Then there was a delay at Baghdad because of engine trouble, and there was an earth tremor during refuelling in Beirut. There was no serious damage, but the team were glad to get back to London – albeit thirty-six hours late and with the music still to face when they arrived at Lord's. Geoffrey Howard issued a statement at Heathrow stating that 'the folly of the Peshawar incident has been fully realised', that 'the young team are bitterly sorry about it' and that the incident 'was actuated by nothing more than high spirits and a sense of fun'. He added 'it had no connection whatsoever with umpiring decisions made by Mr Idris Begh.' Given the views of Jim, Tony Lock and Brian Close, this last remark seems somewhat disingenuous. Three days later the team were lectured by Lord Alexander at Lord's and 'Donald Carr got it particularly as captain.'[15]

In cricketing terms, Jim's three months in Pakistan had been a rapid learning curve. Jim felt that the Pakistani crowds were inclined to take their cricket too seriously and 'the tension in which we found ourselves was not always good for young players.'[16] For Richardson, Barrington, Close and Lock, who took 81 wickets, the tour enhanced their reputations, but Jim enjoyed a modest tour, scoring 198 runs in 15 innings. While he felt the tour had not been a social success, it had been an invaluable experience in the development of a professional player.

Fatherhood beckoned for Jim as he reported to Hove for pre-season nets. Although his tour had been a disappointing one, fifteen innings in the heat of battle were preferable to a winter in the indoor school: he was match-fit and his eye was in. A solid pipe-opener for the MCC against Yorkshire at Lord's launched a prosperous May, during which he and Irene anxiously awaited the arrival of their first-born. Jim had a sensational start. By the end of the first week he had two centuries and two wickets: 'I got a hundred at Edgbaston and did Bert Walton with my swinger, loosening up, and then Dick Spooner with my google, first ball.' His 114 there in an eight-wicket win was followed by 106 not out against Worcester at Hove, 'when we won by 1 wicket – Ted James was with me at the end, and he was no mug with the bat. Roly Jenkins bowled me a googly, which turned like a top and went over the middle stump – how it missed I don't know, but it won us the match.'

Jim usually avoided the university fixtures, yet in 1956 he played in what was one of the most significant of Sussex's long history of games against the universities. He made 66 and took 3 for 44 and 1 for 57 to boot. He also saw Ted Dexter's maiden first-class hundred. 'I remember Ted smashing us around. It's a very big ground – you have to walk miles from the pavilion before you get to the square.' Big ground or not, Dexter hit Marlar 'for such an enormous, straight six that the ball had still not pitched when it struck the wall'[17] thirty feet beyond the playing area. Robin Marlar remembers it well: 'I was fielding at cover when Dexter hit one off the back foot. I was like a statue as it went past me to the boundary, and that was enough to convince me.' Negotiations were opened for Dexter, who had been born in Milan, to play for Sussex. Although Jim was not party to the talks, 'Robin convinced Ted to play for Sussex by telling him that Hove was about as close to Milan as he would get if he wanted to play county cricket.'

Marlar could have done with Dexter when the team travelled to Portsmouth. His batsmen gave the side a decent enough start as Don Smith (60), Alan Oakman (67) and Jim (71) contributed to a first innings of 315. The captain continued the good work taking 6 for 50 and by the Monday afternoon Sussex had a lead of 84. Then the pitch at the United Services ground bit back. It must have had something for lunch which disagreed with it, for only Ken Suttle reached double figures, scoring 17 out of an abysmal 55 all out, and despite Don Smith's 4 for 34, Hampshire tottered home by 4 wickets.

The 1956 skirmish in the county's long-running spat with Glamorgan featured the first confrontation as opposing captains between Marlar and Wooller, either of whom on his own was perfectly capable of starting a fight in an empty room. At Hove Wooller misjudged the wicket and gave Sussex first use of the track – and how they used it! Alan Oakman (178) and Don Smith (142) piled on 241 for the first wicket, whereupon 'Glamorgan set themselves to defend from the start of their innings, but Smith, with 6 for 29... was mainly responsible for them following on 315 behind.'[18] All out for 64, the visitors followed on and Wooller stayed six and a half hours for 79, he and Parkhouse taking five hours over an opening stand of 135, as Jim recalls: 'Wilf just dug in, wouldn't play a shot – we couldn't get 'em out second whack.' All the Sussex team had a bowl as 'Wooller bored for a draw,' says Suttle. 'He'd get a long-hop and just pat it down.' Glamorgan eventually averted defeat, but their tedious methods incurred some harsh criticism. 'He wouldn't play on until the crowd were quiet,' says Ted James. 'I mean, you didn't get a lot of noise at Hove anyway.' The game petered out into a very tame draw with Marlar bowling an over under-arm at the end.

After this distasteful episode, the rest of May was for Jim almost uncon-ditionally euphoric. 'At Lord's in the bank holiday match, we won by an innings – I got 92, and we couldn't get the last two out, so I came on and got two lbws'. He had the luxury of a few days off with Irene, before returning to Worthing for a peculiar game against Essex. Sussex, batting first on a pitch like 'a cart-track',[19] did well to reach 315. Jim suffered a double indignity as he got a duck and a top-edge off leg-spinner Bill Greensmith which split his lip. On the Sunday morning, looking as if he'd just taken on Rocky Marciano, he arrived at Cuckfield Hospital to see his wife and baby son Andrew Michael. Essex replied with 320 and when Trevor Bailey and Ken Preston rolled Sussex over for 126 Essex needed only 122 to win. At 75 for 5 they seemed unassailable; but one run later they were all out. Thomson (4 for 13) and Smith (4 for 15) had bowled Sussex to a 43-run victory – and to the top of the championship table. In those days, the council gave a dinner for both teams and Doug Insole, replying on behalf of the visitors, made the classic crack, 'It's lovely to come down to the beach but we didn't expect to play on it.'

In the second game of the week, the wartime allotments took their revenge as, despite half-centuries from Don Smith and Jim, the side went down to a heavy defeat by Gloucestershire, 'Bomber' Wells taking 7 for 73. Still, May had produced for Jim 541 runs at 54 and it was still as championship leaders that the county welcomed the Australians at Hove. The game was limited by rain to one innings a side, a disappointment for the spectators, who were ignorant of the less than harmonious atmosphere in the pavilion. With the first Test at Nottingham a few days away, the Aussie captain Ian Johnson had one eye on the wounded; for him, 'the value of this match meant little'.[20]

For Marlar, who did not want to frustrate a sizeable crowd, the last straw was that Johnson wanted play to end early on the last afternoon so his team could get away. As to the match the story is quickly told. The Australians made a modest 231 and in reply Sussex totalled 298 for 9, David Sheppard celebrating one of his rare appearances by stroking a graceful 97. Jim contributed 35 but it was the captain who gave the crowd the most to applaud, making 64, his highest score for the county, and reaching a half-century in 33 minutes. In a highly-charged atmosphere he was giving vent to his feelings and Ted James was at the other end: 'Robin came out and suddenly they started bouncing him down that end. "It's him we're after," they said, "not you."'

Jim followed the Aussies to Trent Bridge as that weekend he was summoned to be twelfth man. Sussex were playing Oxford University and it made sense for MCC to send for arguably the best cover fielder in the country. He arrived at Nottingham via Bradford where he made 87 battling against Trueman. Jim liked batting in Yorkshire, 'especially against Fred. He was the greatest bowler I ever saw because he was at you all the time.' The Test had ended in a rain-affected draw, but Jim was mentioned in dispatches: 'Burke came out of his self-built cage to pull Laker to leg for three, thus giving Parks the opportunity to throw from near the boundary to right over the bails, Evans never moving his gloves.'[21]

A week at Horsham, the traditional visit to Tunbridge Wells and two games at Hove gave Jim a rare opportunity to spend some time with his young family. In a career where men are inevitably away from home for long periods, these oases of domesticity were welcome breaks. Their absence often exerted considerable strains on the marriages of county players, and for men on Test duty for whole winters, international tours often spelt marital disaster.

The rain had followed Jim from the Midlands. Horsham had been a happy venue for Jim in the past, but not this season.

It was a disastrous week – 63 all out against Northants and 81 all out against Warwickshire. It was the last time we played there for a period. We'd lost the support – it used to be Farmers' Week and they used to get in the marquees and the bar and really enjoy it. Times were changing and the support fell off – it was purely a financial thing.

The team had conceded the lead in the title race to Surrey but Jim continued to make runs. A 40 at Tunbridge Wells was followed by 48 against Leicester at Hove, 129 against Cambridge, 46 at Old Trafford and 80 at Derby. The team wasn't winning though, a crushing 141-run victory over Kent at Hastings being the only success since Worthing. There was a false dawn at Trent Bridge where Jim saw eighteen-year old Derek Semmence get his 'maiden – and only – century. I remember him slogging Bruce Dooland to the top of the stand.' Semmence, now coaching at Hurstpierpoint College, looked a real talent but failed, in racing parlance, to 'train on' and was lost to the game for an academic career. Meanwhile Alan Oakman was being bowled by Ron Archer and taking two vital catches as, in the Third Test, Australia went down by an innings.

At Worcester, Sussex opened the batting with Gordon Potter, a steady player who had never established a regular place, and wicketkeeper Rupert Webb, who could hold a bat but was not many people's idea of a county opening batsman. Webb made 42 but Oakman returned for the defeat of Kent. This traditional local derby was distinguished by Ian Thomson's all-round performance. His 5 for 29 was largely responsible for Sussex's first-innings lead, and his then career-best 72 in a partnership of 112 with Denis Foreman left Kent to chase 310. Marlar's 5 for 44 ensured they fell 141 runs short.

Surrey, champions and top of the table, were the next visitors to the Central Ground, and even without May, Lock and Laker, at Old Trafford with Alan Oakman and David Sheppard, they were a formidable side. Once more Potter and Webb, sounding more than ever like a firm of provincial drapers, opened the batting, which looked distinctly thin, with Semmence, Foreman and Ron Willson in the middle order and only Jim, Kenny Suttle and Don Smith of any substance. In the end they made a reasonable fist of it but the exasperatingly dreamy skipper was continuing to win friends and influence people, as Gordon Potter recalls:

> I played for three years under Robin. I don't think anyone liked him as a captain. I like him now, he's a very funny man, great company. Against Surrey at Hastings it was a beautiful sunny day and Robin seemed to bowl all the afternoon. Don Smith said, 'Don't you think you ought to come off, skipper?' I think he'd forgotten he was captain and he was waiting for someone to take him off!

The Bedser twins shared the wickets as Sussex ended 62 shy of the target, Jim top-scoring with 54.

While his county team-mates were succumbing to the Champions in his home town, 'Oaky' was performing heroics in Laker's historic match at Old Trafford, snaffling five catches in his nineteen wickets. He was in the selectors' minds for the winter tour of South Africa as cover both for Bailey as opener and Laker as a spinner, as well as for his outstanding close catching. The touring party was about to be announced, the cricketing public were awaiting news of Compton's knee, and all the while Jim was making runs in a side struggling for form. He made nearly 500 runs in August, including

102 in a ten-wicket win over Gloucestershire at Cheltenham: 'it was probably one of the slowest hundreds I ever got, on a slow turner against Cook
and Morty.' He had come to the College Ground after having induced
Leicester's Gerald Smithson to hit his wicket at Grace Road – Jim's most
unusual dismissal. Smithson was an interesting cricketer. A Yorkshireman,
born in Spofforth – an apposite village for a cricketer[22] – he was a 'Bevin
Boy'[23] in 1947 when he was selected to tour the West Indies with MCC and
it was only after his case had been debated in the House of Commons that
the Government granted him permission to take part in the tour.

Another half-century in the customary loss to Surrey at the Oval, the
withdrawal of David Sheppard from the tour on the grounds of his moral
objections to apartheid and doubts about whether Compton's knee would
stand up to a long tour on hard wickets led to a public address announcement at the Saffrons. 'I was fielding when it was announced that two further
names had been issued by the MCC for the South African tour, "they are
Denis Compton and Jim Parks of Sussex".' MCC had been waiting on the
fitness of Compton's knee; it was thrilling for Jim that in effect he had been
picked as cover for his idol. Irene too was at Eastbourne and 'like me got
quite a thrill when the news was announced'.

Sussex were 82 without loss over the weekend in reply to Derbyshire's
187. There were heavy showers on the Monday morning, and no play was
possible before lunch. Jim recalls the joy of uncovered wickets:

> It was virtually unplayable – we lost two quick wickets in the first over. I went in
> at 99 for 3 and Kenny was at the other end. I was fighting off Les Jackson; he had
> Cliff Gladwin and was getting runs off him. I said to Kenny, 'Come on, let's get a
> single, get down the other end.' So we did and Cliff's first ball hit me straight under
> the chin! It didn't do me much harm, but for a minute or two I felt a bit groggy.

Despite this Jim made yet another half-century as he took Sussex home to a
six-wicket win. Les Jackson ascribes Derby's defeat to an invitation the team
received when it rained on the Monday – a classic and cautionary tale of
county cricket at the time:

> We felt there was not likely to be any more play that day, so when the local
> Star Brewery invited the visiting team to a tour, we readily agreed. We sampled
> all the goods and wares of the brewery and eventually arrived back at the
> ground, where we found out play was due to start again. We were a bit under
> the weather by then and resumed but never quite recovered![24]

Suddenly the pace of Jim's cricketing life had quickened with a new frisson. Once back at Nursery End, he had to pack for the sunshine tour. There was some unfinished business, however. Although Sussex lost to Hampshire by 48 runs, Jim scored his third 50 in as many games and then entrained for the Oval to act as twelfth man in the final Test. A couple of soggy draws saw the side finish a respectable if slightly disappointing ninth, after heading the table in June.

For Jim it had been a season of progress after the stresses of the sub-continent. He topped the Sussex averages with 1,825 runs at 42.44 and as *Wisden* put it, 'Parks, after his unhappy tour of Pakistan, took time to settle down and during the closing weeks of the season became the most consistent batsman in the side as well as being an outstanding cover-point.'[25] He would, it seemed, sail off in early October for the sunshine of the Cape and the beaches of Durban, to resume a Test career full of promise and expectation.

Jim shared a cabin on the *Edinburgh Castle* with Essex's Brian Taylor, something of a character and the deputy wicketkeeper. He felt fit and almost inevitably won the ship's table tennis title, beating his cabin-mate in the final in a howling gale. For Alan Oakman and Doug Insole, this would be their only tour. Otherwise, the party comprised the illustrious men who had trounced the Aussies in the summer:

Tyson, Loader, Bailey, Lock, Laker, Wardle, Compo, Kipper [Cowdrey], Peter May, Brian Statham – Godfrey was first choice wicketkeeper – and Peter Richardson, who'd been with me in Pakistan. The two weeks on the boat were marvellous. We were travelling first-class of course and changed for dinner. I shall never forget coming into Table Bay at 6 o'clock in the morning. Everyone said you've got to see it. So I don't think we went to bed that night – and indeed it was a memorable experience.

After a two-day sojourn in Paarl, where the MCC easily beat Boland, Jim's tour opened with a warm-up game in Cape Town against Western Province. A day or so later the tourists were putting in slip-fielding practice at Newlands when disaster struck. Jim was on the end of a line when a spectator came and stood beside him. He didn't give him much thought at the time – but when Jim missed the ball, the spectator stuck out a hand, and Jim's dream of a sunlit winter suddenly took on a rather darker hue.

Chapter 6
Donning the Gloves

The bystander was only trying to be helpful, but had he not deflected the ball,

it would have missed me. I got this whack in the back of the head, which triggered the old football injury. I felt sick and dizzy and the doctor told me to go to bed. When I resumed nets I discovered with horror that I was suffering from double vision again. A specialist examined me in Cape Town and after further tests in Johannesburg I flew home for treatment. I was very worried at the time; one eye had gone adrift and I was boss-eyed, so to speak. I was dashing to London nearly every day for a month having electrical treatment to refocus the eye, looking into a contraption like a big pair of electrically controlled binoculars. If the treatment worked the plan was for me to rejoin the tour early in the new year. I was in hospital for about a fortnight and they let me go home for Christmas.

I had to get fit though, so I used to run around the streets in the winter weather. Inevitably I caught a heavy cold and felt woozy for some days before I got on the plane but I thought, 'I'm all right – it's just a cold. Once I get in the sun I'll be OK.' At Heathrow, the excitement at returning to the cricket and my cold, which had worsened, made me feel pretty ill, so I thought a brandy and an Aspro would sort me out before the flight. I passed out in the plane on the tarmac – Irene said I turned green – and ended up in Westminster Hospital suffering from pneumonia. When I came home I wasn't allowed to do anything and convalesced till March. In fact I put a lot of weight on until we started again in the spring – but the eyes were OK.

Jim's own description sets out the plain facts of this critical episode which at the time gave rise to unkind questions. Accusations appeared in the cricket columns that he was daunted by the South Africans' 'fearsome' pace attack of Adcock and Heine.

It didn't bother me what people said about my not going – *I* knew I wanted to get back and play cricket. They had a reasonable attack – Adcock and Heine, and Hugh Tayfield – but nothing to be afraid of. My not being there meant that Alan Oakman got a lot more batting on that tour but of course poor old Alan did his back in and missed virtually the whole of the next season.

It has been suggested that though he was a superb player of spin, Jim's technique was questionable against real pace, that he somehow lacked the 'bottle'. John Murray, the Middlesex and England wicketkeeper, told me 'the theory was that he didn't play the quick bowlers too well, that he was never quite in line.' Trevor Bailey, as shrewd a judge of a player as any since the war, said 'I would have thought he was a tiny bit suspect against pace.' Ray Illingworth, a room-mate from his RAF days and later a Test colleague, thought that 'Jim had his limitations against genuinely quick bowling. That's probably because he was always looking to attack and his defence wasn't quite as solid as it should be' – and Alan Oakman, Jim's close friend and county colleague for nearly twenty years, said 'he was a good player of spinners but he didn't have much confidence against the quick bowlers.'

Set against that, John Woodcock, for half a century the *Times* cricket correspondent, who covered virtually all Jim's Test matches, did not think he was 'especially vulnerable against pace. He could play anything when he got in.' Ted Dexter provides perhaps the most balanced view:

> If there was a weakness with Jim it was that sometimes he seemed to get quite unsettled by the faster bowlers and I couldn't make out why. There were other times when they were bloody fast and he would play them very bravely. In those days there were no helmets, no protection whatsoever, and playing on uncovered pitches only the fearless survived. You still have to be courageous today to walk out to bat, but there are players who play fast bowling pretty poorly and get hit because their footwork's not very good. In those days they just wouldn't have come to the fore. I remember a game against Derbyshire at Derby – they always had lovely green pitches there. Harold Rhodes was starting and Les Jackson was still very hostile and mean, and on a pitch which had everybody else really hopping around, Jim just stood there and pinged them all round the park. He was a very accomplished player.

The critics who suggested that in 1956/57 he would rather have spent his winter pounding the foggy streets of sleepy Haywards Heath instead of playing the game he loved in the sun, representing his country with men whom he admired and respected, did not know him. Jim was a cricketing animal – it was in his blood. As the old saw has it, he would have given his right arm

to have batted on that tour. As he was to show three years later in the cauldron of the Caribbean, he had the technique and the temperament to face
the quickest and the best. The alarming scare which he suffered that winter
only made him more determined 'I am going to start the season match-fit
and prove that the business has not affected me at all.'[1]

His tally of 453 runs by the end of May proved his point, although the
124 at Fenner's was overshadowed by a whirlwind innings by Don Smith at
Hove. Gloucestershire had set Sussex 267 to win in three and three-quarter
hours. The more venerable members searched faded memories of Alletson's
189 in ninety minutes for Nottinghamshire forty-six years before, as Smith
scored 166 in 175 minutes. He hit 9 sixes and 11 fours, taking Sussex to
within 15 of eventual victory. The most electrifying passage of play was after
tea, when he smashed 74 in 27 minutes, hitting 8 sixes and 4 fours off 34
balls he received. Jim points out that the square at Hove is a small one and
'because so many matches were played there, we started on the outside and
worked in, so by the time bank holiday came you were right in the middle
and you started all over again. The boundary was no more than fifty yards
and Don kept lapping the off-spinners into the members and the press box.'
It was such a fierce onslaught that Jim and Kenny Suttle both remember
'some old boy going on with his umbrella appealing to the umpires that it
was too dangerous. He was right – there were no sightscreens for the spectators.' One six struck Mr Ernest Williams of Worthing on the jaw, but this
stoical enthusiast said from his hospital bed, as soon as his jaw would allow, 'it
was a marvellous innings'.

Jim, then, was in confident form as he travelled to the picturesque
St Helens ground at Swansea, making 70 in a trouble-free draw. However,
underlying this run-of-the-mill county game was the embryo of a disagreement which a year later had a significant long-term effect on Jim's career.
Rupert Webb took no catches against Glamorgan but had made doughty
runs as a nightwatchman. He felt that:

Marlar was sort of anti-me. I don't know why but he was. For instance, one of
Glamorgan's openers was a notorious edger. Robin bowled without a slip so I
said 'Rob, let's have a slip. He's an edger.' 'No, no,' he said. 'I'll have Oaky round
the corner.' So, three or four balls later the fellow got a thick edge where Oaky
would have caught it at slip and at the end of the over Marlar said to me, 'You
should have caught that, you know.' I said, 'You're not serious, are you?' 'Oh,
yes, you should have caught it.' It was the last time I gave him any advice. That
sort of thing started happening in '57.'

These exchanges passed Jim by he tended to avoid dressing-room intrigue. Of equable demeanour himself, he would not have imputed base motives to a team-mate nor sought to intervene in an essentially private quarrel.

He was too busy at work for such things anyway. Recalled to the MCC side at Old Trafford to celebrate Lancashire's centenary, he hit 132 not out, followed by 93 not out at Portsmouth. In between he had made only 6 and 13 against the West Indies at Hove, a game more noteworthy for the latest episode in the Webb/Marlar soap-opera. Cue Rupert Webb: 'We came back from Northampton to play the West Indies and he dropped me for the Second XI keeper, David Mantell', who recognised that he 'stepped in at a bad time for Rupert, who was naturally upset that he wasn't given the West Indies game. I was picked for three games at a time after that.' Graham Doggart, Hubert's father, was the chairman of the Cricket Committee and 'about the third week of July he said "We're not going to have any more of this wicketkeeping nonsense, Robin. I've got at the top of my list: R. Webb, wicketkeeper." Robin never said a word. I came back in and played the rest of the season.'

Webb's recollection was accurate, but he missed some fascinating cricket, such as Ted James opening the batting at Tunbridge Wells, where Jim got 74: 'We beat Kent and Tommo got thirteen wickets. It was usually a good track, but he used to swing it, which depends more on the atmosphere than the pitch.' From Tunbridge Wells to Eastbourne; in the fifties an idyllic ride by steam trail from the Kentish Weald through the Downs, through Eridge and Crowborough, Mayfield and Heathfield, Hailsham and Polegate, and for Jim his two favourite wickets. The week at the Saffrons brought him 248 runs at an average of 83, and for his side a defeat by Warwickshire and an extraordinary game against Worcestershire. For the lovers of esoteric cricketing trivia, on 2 July, under the new rules of 1953, Worcester became the first county to get 6 points as the side batting in the fourth innings of a drawn match with the scores level. The visitors had been set 209 in 130 minutes, and for the holidaymakers, and Kenny Suttle, 'it was very exciting. They needed two off the last ball, and Bob Broadbent was run out. Facing Thomson, he hoicked it into the outfield. I wanted to get it in quickly from the boundary because they were running a second; Jim backed up and threw it in. The ball brushed Bob's leg and hit the stumps.'

Over the next month David Mantell, Webb's replacement, had a Cook's tour of county cricket grounds, from Edgbaston to Hove, via Old Trafford, Ashby de la Zouch, Colchester, Peterborough and Hastings, seeing Jim score half a dozen half-centuries, winning only two matches and losing three. Perhaps the most unlikely venue was Ashby de la Zouch, where although 'the ground was small it didn't have a village atmosphere. There were tents and you could imagine the knights in shining armour charging around on their horses rather than playing cricket.' Although Jim never ate lunch, he remembers the catering provisions being fairly primitive: 'cold fish and chips for lunch usually – they'd nip down the shop to get them.' Mantell had tonsillitis in Colchester but thought 'if I told anybody this I wouldn't get picked, so the doctor there gave me some tablets.' They did the trick, as he stumped Bear off Thomson, but the team's performance was less healthy. Left 241 to win, they had reached 50 for 2 when Trevor Bailey captured 5 for 14 as Sussex plummeted to 56 all out, Jim top-scoring with 21.

Sussex's cricketing caravan then pitched camp on the Town Ground at Peterborough, which boasted an equally sporting wicket – and 'the Rev' was back. David Sheppard said:

> We used to talk about the pitches and if it was going to swing. The easiest batting in 1957 was in the two Test matches against the West Indies because we played on flat pitches. All the rest were as green as grass and at Peterborough it was swinging about. From the moment Jim came in – he was batting with me – the ball flowed effortlessly off his bat and there was great fluency about his play.

Jim scored 72 in a tame draw, but 'it was a wet wicket. Pompom Fellows-Smith was batting against Tommy, who made this leg-cutter go. He lunged forward and it hit him straight between the eyes – didn't do any harm, he just shook his head.'

The venue for the 1957 episode in the Sussex/Glamorgan saga was the Central Ground in Hastings. On an easy-paced pitch the batting was the dreariest ever seen there and 'at the end of the second day W. Wooller in protest bowled five underarm deliveries to his rival captain Robin Marlar. There had been some ill-feeling in the previous year's match at Hove.'[2] David Mantell, for whom championship cricket was an exciting new world, felt as if he had inadvertently stumbled upon a family quarrel: 'the feeling between the sides wasn't going to die, it was going to rumble on'. The medium-pacer from Cardiff, Frank Clarke, who perhaps appropriately had turned up for the fixture in his Army uniform, recalls the tension of that last over: 'Wooller stationed us all round the boundary and bowled an over of under-arm. There was a bit of bad feeling there. Willy Jones got a cut across his eye – it was more like a football match.'

Two draws at Hastings, where Kenny Suttle made 165 against Kent, and a defeat by Yorkshire at Hove were followed by a welcome win in the bank holiday game with Middlesex. This was the last match Denis Compton ever played at Hove and Jim caught his hero at cover off Ted James – 'I've never been so disappointed.' The great man took 5 for 40 in Sussex's first innings but the home side ran out winners by 99 runs.

The Cricket Committee had deliberated and the edict went forth – Mantell was out and Webb was back:'I always remember it because we went down to Weston-super-Mare for the first match of my recall.' In a victory by an innings and 44 runs Jim made 92 'and I got a stumping and four catches and about 30-odd and the tail put on about 100. We got a big score and it all got a mention in the papers next morning:"Webb on his return held the tail together".'

Jim's August now had a momentum, and after his 93 at Worthing he was selected for the twelve for the last Test against the West Indies.

It was a true Oval wicket in those days – it turned like a top so the selectors took one look at it and said – 'Right, we play all the spinners.' I remember that Jim Laker did Everton Weekes for a pair. It was a cart-track, honestly, and I've never felt so sorry for anyone. I watched two days and rejoined Sussex at Worcester. The New Road wicket was lovely to bat on in those days. I was very fortunate. Jack Flavell bowled me a beauty early on which nipped back, and as it hit me, I thought, 'Oh, no – lbw', but Dai Davies was umpiring and he said, in his broad Welsh accent, 'Not out – he hit it.' I hadn't hit it, I knew that, but lbws you didn't argue with. It was Pataudi's debut – he was 16. He got 0 in the first whack, and I was batting when he came in second innings. Jack Flavell steamed in and bowled Tiger the bouncer. He bent down and it went off the back of the bat for four down to fine-leg – his first runs for Sussex.

Wisden records that Jim,

released from his twelfth man duties in the Test, hit a century in each innings for the first time. His second hundred, which took only two and a half hours, came at an opportune time, for Sussex were 76 for 5 and only 78 runs on. Parks hit 14 fours in his first innings, during which he retired hurt after being struck on the knee. Suttle, who helped to add 100 runs in ninety minutes for the seventh wicket, also reached three figures.[3]

After the prosperous harvest in August, culminating in his 101 and 100 not out at New Road, Jim ended the season with a run famine. He scraped together just 20 in his last four innings. Luckily for Sussex someone was getting runs and Les Lenham, who in only his second match earlier in the season had been awarded his county cap, made his maiden century and was to become one of Jim's closest colleagues over the next fourteen years.

When Don Smith gained his Test cap during the summer, Sussex could now boast six batsmen at the top of the order who had played for England, yet the county finished ninth for the second consecutive season. Ian Thomson had taken his customary 100 wickets, but only three batsmen had reached 1,000 runs. Jim finished second in the Sussex averages, having scored 2,004 runs at 43.56. As *Wisden* noted: 'Parks, showing no sign of the indisposition which compelled his early return from the MCC tour of South Africa, was again the chief run-getter.'[4]

In the last two winters, the Pakistan tour and the South African injury had curtailed his football career, and the demands of a young family, coupled with the increased travelling now that the Heath were in the Metropolitan League, were instrumental in a break with the Blues.

> We travelled to Bedford, Dunstable, Newbury, Gravesend, which was a lot of travelling in those days, and we got rather fed up with it. In the end we decided it was too much, so the goalkeeper, Jimmy Revell, Danny O'Brien and myself left Haywards Heath and went to Hove Town.

Jim played for Hove Town in the *Evening Argus* five-a-side football tournament at Brighton Ice Rink in February. Left-arm spinner Ronnie Bell played for Hove Town too, and Kenny Suttle for Arundel. On the same bill the County Cricket Club – Thomson, Mantell, Cooper, Oakman, and Lenham – were playing a special challenge match against Brighton Tigers ice hockey team. They weren't in the main draw: 'We'd won it two years running. Then they banned us!'

The 1958 season was memorable for two main reasons – both of which were pivotal in Jim's career. Firstly, the five-year-long feud between Webb and Marlar erupted into open schism, and when the dust had settled Jim was left holding the gloves. Secondly, Ted Dexter played six innings for the county in the long vacation and made his Test debut. From that season on he was to exert an increasingly powerful influence on Sussex cricket as his batting of unparalleled majesty 'sometimes turned Hove into an Elysian field'.[5] He scored 114 in the opening game at Fenner's to follow his maiden first-class hundred against much the same attack in 1956. Jim made a modest start to his season – a century against Leicester at Hove being the only real highlight of a damp and gloomy May – and as early as this in the season Oakman and Mantell, could see that 'Marlar was trying to get another batter in the side'.

The winds which swirled around at Lord's that bank holiday and later at Tunbridge Wells held straws which pointed the way to Jim's future. The captain spelt out his thinking:

In those years [1955–58] Rupert Webb stood behind the stumps as keeper. He had come into the game late, from the Kodak factory in Harrow. He was a superb stylist, excellent standing up to the stumps. From time to time his understudies were given an opportunity but none was able to win the place for reasons of talent and temperament. Standing back, Rupert was not as mobile as the new generation of keepers whose style was notably changing. Keith Andrew, for instance, was Godfrey Evans' understudy and stood back with his hands outside his knees. His ability to cover the ground was akin to today's keepers whose area of control is almost five yards across. The leading bowler for Sussex was the incomparable Ian Thomson, whose consistent ability to swing the ball into the batsman and cut it away, whilst varying his pace all the way from medium to distinctly sharp meant that his keeper had to hop about sideways and even forwards if he was to pick up all the edges. In short, an athlete was needed.[6]

In that extract lie the seeds of Jim's fulfilment as a Test player. As Marlar says, 'Here indeed was a chance for Jim Parks, now an extinct bowling talent, to revive a Test match career frosted in the Heathrow waiting lounge.' It seems that the concept of a wicketkeeping all-rounder was born around then and Jim felt that 'the thought behind the suggestion was that one of the amateur batsmen [Dexter, possibly?] could then be included in the holidays.' The fact that an experienced professional (Oakman) and the Second XI wicketkeeper (Mantell) were both convinced that the captain wanted to strengthen the batting lends credence to that belief. It also supports the notion that the origins of this change of keeper were in Marlar's head and that he would have sold it to the Cricket Committee as being a good idea: 'I would put money on the fact that nobody was party to any discussion, except of course the captain and the Cricket Committee, who never made themselves obvious to me or appeared. It was no secret that Robin and Rupert weren't getting on.'[7] The first signs of clouds on the horizon appeared against Middlesex, as Alan Oakman recalls: 'I think the change-over started at Lord's. We had about half an hour of the game left so Jim said, "I'll keep wicket" and they let Rupert have a bowl. Parkser caught one standing back and it all sort of went on from there really.' Middlesex needed only 33 to win, and Jim did indeed catch Bob Gale in Don Bates's first over – and the seed was sown in Marlar's mind.

For the moment, however, for Jim, catching the ball behind the stumps was a pleasant diversion. He began to score heavily – 84 not out at Worcester 'and at the beginning of anything but flaming June',[8] 92 not out in an exciting game at Taunton. Sussex had been set 164 to win in a shade under two hours and had staggered to 86 for 6, whereupon Ian Thomson laid about him to such good effect that he scored 60 in 40 minutes in a partnership of 56 with Les Lenham. Eventually Geoff Lomax parted them and Sussex went down by 8 runs with four minutes left. The screw was further tightened when at Tunbridge Wells Jim made 56 and a dashing 127 – 'we had them on a wet wicket and it was flying about a bit. Rupert was getting towards retirement and he didn't have a great match there – one or two things went wrong.' At the Nevill, Marlar came up to him and suggested he take the gloves for the next game, and Webb's fate was effectively sealed.

It has entered into Sussex folklore and has become part of received wisdom in the wider cricketing fraternity that Jim was thrust into the wicketkeeping role 'in an emergency', when the long-serving Rupert Webb was 'injured'. This has no basis in fact. David Mantell maintains that 'Rupert wasn't injured, that's for sure' – and even if he was, Mantell had kept in a number of games the year before and could have been called upon in an emergency. It seems that the team arrived at Brentwood to play against Essex and as Jim was changing, 'Robin simply said to me, "It's all yours – you're keeping today." I had no gloves, so I borrowed Brian Taylor's. Unbeknown to us, Robin had told Rupert he wasn't playing.'

Webb himself is adamant:

I was never injured – *never* – that was a Marlarism because it would look better if it was put about I was injured. He'd lost the toss and I'd actually started to put my pads on when he came in and said, 'Oh, by the way, you're not playing.' So I said, 'Who's keeping wicket?' 'Well, Jim is.'

Jim did not believe Webb was injured, but he thought

Robin was a bit desperate, looking for somebody to take over from Rupert anyway. We'd tried two youngsters – David Mantell and David Manville – but they weren't going to make county cricketers. I kept all the third day and did reasonably well – I caught Trevor Bailey off Ronnie Bell, and Robin said, 'Fine – you're keeping tomorrow against the New Zealanders at Hove'.

Marlar's best-laid plans barely lasted overnight. Jim couldn't get out of bed the next morning. 'My stomach muscles and the backs of my legs were in agony – and in fact I didn't keep wicket until we went to Worthing.'[9] The New Zealanders were at Hove and for such a prestigious game it seemed almost as if Marlar had written the team on the back of an envelope and made up the batting order more or less as he went along. At the start of play Jim was on the scorecard, as Webb discovered:

I walked in at about half past ten – after all, you're contracted to turn up, snow or sunshine. The first person I saw said, 'Oh, you're not playing, Rupert.' I wasn't surprised. Somebody gave me a scorecard and it read 'Parks, wicket-keeper'. I went into lunch with them. Marlar never said anything to me at all, never spoke to me. I went off for a cup of tea and a member said, 'Oh, I see you're playing then, Rupert. You're on the second print of scorecards.' I thought – 'Right, he's not going to catch me.' I watched the wickets fall and when there were about seven wickets down I got changed and put my pads on so when he went out to bat at no.10, I was in my position at no.11. There was a big shout and a wicket fell; I walked through the dressing room on to the steps and I got out there before I realised he'd declared. I got my wicketkeeping gloves out because Jim was in the other room and he wasn't ready.

Ted James liked Webb to stand up to him, for:

> that was his strength, and in my second over, we noticed that when I put one down the leg-side the opener, D'Arcy, changed feet. Webby came up to me and said, 'Try that again – I think we can do him.' I did and Webby had the bails off; he hadn't got a price, it was that quick. Oaky said, 'Would you have done that, then, Jim?' Jim said 'No, I don't think so.'

That was the nub. Oakman felt that 'Rupert was good standing up but he was hopeless standing back. I know the way things are done in cricket clubs. It happens in all walks of life. You get stuffed sometimes but you have to put up with that, don't you ?'

Although the writing was on the dressing-room wall, for six weeks the future had to be postponed. Jim was still physically suffering from his Brentwood experience and though Marlar was convinced in his own mind of the right-ness of his case, 'he had a certain amount of opposition from the Committee, from the members and from several players because a lot of people could see that Jim was a brilliant batsman and cover-point and was going to get tired.'[10] Webb and Mantell boxed and coxed their way through the next half-dozen games. They began in Hastings, where Sussex were all out for 62, Les Jackson, the round arm bowler, taking lots of wickets and Marlar getting 'very annoyed and grumbling at everyone'.[11] They then journeyed to Kettering, Liverpool, Bradford and Portsmouth, before the merry-go-round eventually arrived at Worthing. Although Jim did not make runs, 'Rupert had an indifferent match against Glamorgan', and the game was up for the genial Webb. Jim took the gloves for the Yorkshire match and kept from then on. 'Rupert,' says Jim with a knowing smile, 'has expressed to me his views about Robin as a captain.'

The game against the Tykes was Jim's first real experience of keeping wicket and he came face to face with the full extent of the responsibilities of the job. He realised that he did not have the necessary ability to concentrate on every ball and learnt only too rapidly that the role was mentally tiring and physically demanding. 'After my first full day at the wicket my colleagues had literally to carry me back to the pavilion.' Webb knew why: 'He was an amateur wicketkeeper. He was only doing it because he was good with the ball. He would probably have admitted as much at that point.'

Mantell, too, saw the way the wind was blowing:

It made some kind of logic that Jim, being a natural ball-player and catcher, could make a wicketkeeper. I'm still not sure that he actually wanted to be keeper, but there was the cauldron, with three people thrown in it, Rupert, Jim and myself. When something like that happens – hearing that Parks was going to get the gloves – how *do* you think? I could see the end of the road because if Robin or the Cricket Committee said that I was the one for the future *I* would have been in those games, not him. Quite clearly, it was a turning point, whether it was successful or not. There was a move away from pure wicketkeepers, whom we always had in England, to players who were or could become batsmen. I think that was the birth of that era.

Webb and Mantell had fallen foul of the air of feudal hierarchy which passed for man-management in Sussex cricket in the fifties. Mantell felt:

the administrators were trying to deal with the future without consulting the people who were directly involved. That was the way things were done at the time. Later in the year Colonel Grimston, the Secretary, said to me, 'We think you are better against slow bowling,' and while he never said that Jim was going to keep wicket, he was really saying that this was the end of the line.

That summer was effectively the end of the line for Rupert Webb, too: 'I could have played probably another five seasons if that hadn't happened, but I never had a cross word with Jim – about the wicketkeeping or about him.' As David Mantell said:

Jim was Jim – you couldn't think he was trying to undermine you or steal something from you. He was just a pleasant guy who got on and did the job. When somebody said 'Put the gloves on', he'd have said 'OK' and you would have expected him to. There was nothing to say he shouldn't have done it. You could perhaps point fingers at the people behind him. When you're travelling a lot and staying in hotels, you get to know people and I have only happy memories of Jim as a person. Kenny Suttle was the archetypal chatterer, and though Jim didn't have Kenny's personality he had a wonderful smoothness and warmth with people. He wouldn't sit at the bar reeling off funny stories but he'd be there to chat to – he wasn't a withdrawn individual.

It was lucky for Jim that he had a new role to worry about as over the next month he scored just 213 runs in fourteen visits to the crease. He did however notch up nine catches and four stumpings as he settled into life as 'a long-stop with gloves on'.[12] The summer had been dull and damp and August was no different. Six of the ten games were draws, but Sussex achieved three wins, including a close finish at the Saffrons, with the weather again playing a major role. Sussex were dismissed for 175 on the first day, Shackleton taking five wickets. Overnight there was a storm of such tropical intensity that the ground was saturated and on a remarkable second day, nineteen wickets fell for 180 runs. 'If it rained at Eastbourne it was a very nasty wicket to bat on.'[13] Thomson and Bates made the most of the moist sea air to move the ball about to great effect. Another Sussex collapse for 83 (Shackleton again the main destroyer) left the visitors 180 to win. At 22 for 4 they looked dead and buried, but they were within 32 runs of victory 'when left-arm spinner Ronnie Bell took centre stage. In an atmosphere of high drama, with a thundercloud that had flooded streets less than a mile away looming over the ground',[14] he took 3 for 6 in seven overs to clinch a stunning victory. Another win at Trent Bridge – by an innings and 73 runs – and a rain-affected draw against Worcester at Hove brought the recently crowned seven-times champions to Eaton Road for the final match of this crucial season for Jim. On one of the few bright days in a dreary, soggy summer the author remembers sitting at the Sea End with a schoolmate, eager to see Peter May play an innings of grace and timing, full of fluent driving and confident power. Except that he didn't. He nicked a ball from Don Bates to Smith in the slips and was out for a duck. The most powerful county side of the twentieth century were all out soon after lunch for only 83, Ted James polishing the innings off with 4 for 5. By the close Sussex had mustered only two runs more and twenty wickets had fallen on one summer's day. Over the weekend the hesitant sun worked on the uncovered pitch and Robin Marlar, with 5 for 39, spun Surrey out for 89. What was good for him, though, was equally beneficial to Bedser and Laker, and Sussex, needing only 88 to win, were bowled out for 70 – the fourth innings under 90 in this astonishing game. Kenny Suttle has no excuses: 'It wasn't too bad a wicket. There'd been no rain – it was some good bowling and some indifferent batting.'

Sussex supporters must have an affinity with those of West Ham United, forever blowing bubbles during the post-war decades, only to see their dreams fade and die. The side, 'rich in tried talent and young promise',[15] slid from ninth to thirteenth in the Championship and won only six of twenty-eight games, losing seven, with the rest falling victim to the dismally poor weather. Jim could look back on a season in which he had made his customary 1,000 runs – 1,255 at 32.17 – and had taken a significant step in a new career direction; not that he saw it as such:

> When I took up keeping I was just doing a stop-gap job for Sussex till the end of 1958, and there was no mention that I was going to keep wicket in '59. I didn't practise in the winter. After the South African disappointment, I didn't really think much about getting back into the Test reckoning.

Jim could therefore throw himself into his last full season as an amateur footballer – and look forward to an addition to his family, for Irene was expecting another child in the summer.

It was an undistinguished swansong. With Jim as captain, the brief life of Hove Town FC came to an inglorious end at the bottom of the Sussex County League. The club's record that last season was a sad one: played 30, won 0, drawn 4, lost 26, goals for 29, against 128. In May, in a room above a pub, cup final tickets were raffled and the last rites pronounced, presided over by John Vinicombe, then the football reporter for the *Evening Argus*. By then Jim was in the nets. He was still inexperienced with the gloves, yet 'suddenly the team went up for the first match and I was wicketkeeper. I realised I had better start working at it.'

Jim also had a new and secret weapon. That was the month that

> I first used the bat with the sloping shoulders. John Newbery made all my bats. His father Len ran Gray-Nicholls at the time and John suddenly appeared with this thing in April at practice and said 'Will you give it a try ?'

Apparently the theory was that with the shoulders shelved in a more traditional shape, for the equivalent weight the player got more 'punch' in the meat of the bat where Jim seemed to hit most of his shots. Jim gave the new blade a run at Lord's for the MCC against Surrey, 'got a 100 there and used it for the rest of my career.'

Jim, often a slow starter, hit the ground running, with the result that '1959 was my golden year really.' By the end of May Jim had made 628 runs and taken 25 catches. The weather was persistently sublime, a memorably halcyon summer of stifling seaside days, ice-cream, Tizer and glorious cricket. Jim's batting was equally brilliant. Set to get 320 by Glamorgan, Sussex got home with twenty minutes to spare, and Frank Clarke, now a Sussex resident, was there:

> We left Sussex 300-odd and Jim got them. I remember that as if it was last week because the skipper said that there's a good chance of us winning. The train was all arranged and by tea-time the bags would have been packed. But when Jim came in the whole game changed. I was fielding down by the pavilion gates and I can remember chasing round that blinking boundary. He just came in and flayed everything.

Jim, whose all-round hitting brought him 4 sixes and 16 fours, made 157 in 170 minutes and he and Graham Cooper took Sussex to victory with 137 in seventy minutes. Jim had scored 242 runs without being dismissed, as *Wisden* records: 'Apart from Parks, who hit firmly all round, the Sussex batsmen did not shine against accurate bowling and fine fielding.'[16] Indeed, in Glamorgan's bowling attack were Jim McConnon, Alan Watkins and Peter Walker, who all played for England, and Don Shepherd, who perhaps should have done.

Jim's express start hit the buffers in the Whitsun match at Lord's as Sussex, needing 229 to win, lost by 1 run. Les Lenham had been sent home over the weekend, having twisted his ankle falling over the boundary boards chasing a catch. In the box seat at 209 for 5, Sussex collapsed, leaving the skipper and Don Bates to secure victory.

> When I went in at number 10, we wanted about 10 to win. We had a discussion at the end of an over and he said, 'Right – if I call for two, you come' because we wanted to keep the bowling. He played one down to long-leg so I rushed off and turned without looking as he said he was going to run two. I got halfway down and he said, 'Wooah!' It was a bit moist so I ended up flat on my back, got run out and we lost by one run. Les could have come and stood at one end and we might have scraped home. Robin sat in the dressing-room for a long time afterwards, head in hands, because we hadn't beaten Middlesex at Lord's for ages.'[17]

The Tipton Road ground in Dudley is an unlikely setting for any kind of record. Yet on a rare cold and windy afternoon in late May 1959 that unprepossessing ground in the heart of the Black Country saw Duggie Slade slash at a long hop from Don Bates, giving Jim a simple catch to equal Harry

Butt's Sussex record of six in an innings in 1900. One more and he would have equalled the world record. 'It wasn't anything heroic really – they were all nice little catches standing back. It was the greatest moment of my career at that point because I had discovered a new avenue in the game plus the fact that at that time I was still getting runs. It was always my worry that it would affect the batting, which it did to a certain extent' – but not yet.

Back at Hove, 121 (and seven more catches) in a 9-wicket win over Gloucester was followed by 87 against Lancashire, for whom Alan Wharton hit a career-best score before being run out for 199. Jim had a ringside seat for this calamity: 'Alan Wharton tried to get a run to Ronnie Bell in the gully. Ronnie flicked it back to me and he dived full-length. His bat was about an inch short of the line. I was looking down at him as I took the bails off.' Irene was now very pregnant; fortunately in the next month Jim had only two longish trips away, to Newport and Bradford, and Robert James, like the good cricketer he was to become, had the sense of timing to arrive while Dad was playing Hampshire at Hove. His birth, in Cuckfield on 15 June 1959, was about the only silver lining in an otherwise dismal month.

'We didn't have a good June. We lost five matches that month.' Glamorgan, Hampshire, Worcester, Yorkshire and Surrey all inflicted sizable defeats and only when the side reached the haven of the Saffrons did the tide begin to turn. Against Somerset Jim took six more catches and on the last day, set to get 221 at 90 an hour, 'Sussex fell behind the clock, and 136 were needed in 85 minutes, but Parks, batting with a broken left thumb, and Dexter took them to victory with seventeen minutes to spare.'[18] The injury kept him out of the game against the Indian tourists, then 'I came back in and played as a batsman. Sam Cowan, our masseur, made me a steel thumb-piece but it was still painful when I got one on it.'

Painful or not, it did not prevent Jim storming to the end of the season, plundering attacks all over the country for 964 runs in six weeks at an average of 64. 'In those days you played at some lovely old grounds,' and he kicked off with 130 at the charmingly named Rutland Recreation Ground at Ilkeston, where he 'got another top edge in the mouth – Derek Morgan was bowling fast off-cutters.' He was working well behind the stumps too – by the end of August twenty-eight catches, including seven at Old Trafford against Lancashire, made him the leading keeper in the country, but it was his innings there which gained him another prestigious award.

In their second innings, when Ted Dexter was out after a magnificent 112, Sussex were 201 for 3 with the new ball due. As Jim passed him, Ted was contrite. 'I'm sorry, Jim.' 'So am I', Jim replied – Statham and Higgs were as menacing as any new ball attack in the country. However, Jim was facing

Colin Hilton, fast but less accurate. He scored 7 off him and then took a boundary and single off Statham's first over.

Jim had started quickly, as his dad had taught him. 'I like if possible to score off the first ball I receive, but instead of hitting this with the full flow of the bat, I simply push the ball with very little backlift, and play like this for the first few overs.' Jim senior had told him, in the back garden at Western Road, 'If you drive at an away-swinger, especially off the new ball, you will almost certainly hit it late and get caught at second slip. But when you are pushing, instead of hitting the ball, you are there a bit sooner so the ball will go square of gully.' After looking at the bowling and getting the pace of the wicket Jim liked 'to open my shoulders and have a go. The harder you hit the less likely you are to get caught out.'

So he did – and the runs flowed: 48 in just under thirty minutes. Statham said, 'Eee, I reckon you can easily get the quickest 100 of the season. You've only been in six overs.' Jim replied,' I certainly can't with you bowling' for he knew he couldn't take liberties with the world's most accurate pace bowler. He realised however that he was in with a chance of the 100 guineas award and the Lawrence Trophy for the fastest hundred; in the next over he tried to drive Statham and his bat broke. Three minutes were wasted getting a new one and then the well-informed Lancashire crowd joined in Jim's race to the quickest hundred. As he hit boundary after boundary, they raced to return the ball. When Jim hit a six over the pavilion he settled in to wait for the ball to be fetched – but a spectator had rushed to retrieve it. At 91, he knew he was well inside Maurice Hallam's 71 minutes and he took two more boundaries before Wharton bowled a full toss on the leg stump. Jim took a single.

He had reached the fastest and most memorable 100 of his career to date:

> It was a low-scoring match really. We were both bowled out on the first day. It just happened. The new ball was due and I took 35 off Ken Higgs' first two overs. Hubert [Doggart] did a marvellous job because he kept bellowing for singles and giving me the bowling. The lads were on the balcony giving me a count-down of the time. I still have the cups – I don't think they're very clean though.

Jim's record knock left Lancashire 359 to win and, after Ian Thomson had taken three wickets in one over to finish with 5 for 36, they never recovered and were all out for 134.

This brilliant summer had a magnificent crescendo: at Worthing, with his dad standing as umpire, he scored another century against Derby, and so to

Hove, where the season reached a stirring climax against top-of-the-table Yorkshire, who needed to win to keep their championship chances alive. They began well enough on the Saturday, having Sussex 76 for 6 soon after lunch, whereafter only Pataudi's 52 offered much resistance to Ken Taylor's medium pace and Sussex were bowled out for 210. Yorkshire fared little better. At the close Dexter and Thomson had reduced the leaders to a fragile 89 for 5.

A holiday crowd settled into deckchairs on the Monday, trains having decanted 'people with baskets, litter and opinions, the seaside's staple ingredients'.[19] What they saw was a fight-back by the Yorkshiremen, and Ray Illingworth make 'a hundred in the first innings. We were in trouble actually – we'd lost four wickets very quickly.' Don Wilson kept him solid company for an hour then hit briskly at the end for his maiden fifty, giving the visitors an unlikely lead of 97. When Sussex replied, wrote E. W. Swanton, 'Dexter and Parks took the war into the other camp and we saw some fine driving by both to end the long day,… Parks… hitting Illingworth successively for six and four.' Tony Goodridge of the *Guardian* felt even more lyrical. 'As the slanting rays of the sun gave way to a foreboding autumn chill, Dexter and Parks went briskly about the getting of runs. There is still a lot to play for today.' And there was. On that Monday morning, as September opened, it seemed that only time could thwart a perfect finish. A spirit of adventure imbued Sussex's approach, and as Robin Marlar wrote later in the *Brighton Gazette*, 'Parks launched himself into one of those bursts of hitting which are at once delightful and infuriating. He tried to hit Wilson for a series of sixes and in the end fell, as he was almost bound to do, to a catch at deep extra.' Jim had made 85 and at lunch Sussex were 280 for 7, a lead of 183.

When would Marlar declare? Jim remembers 'Hubert trying to talk Robin into declaring earlier, because we all thought Robin had gone on too long to make a game of it, to give us a chance. I don't think he wanted to give Yorkshire anything. That was his attitude.' Taylor recalls that Marlar 'didn't like the north. He didn't like the Yorkies in particular.' He made it patently clear that he was not going to declare at all, since the championship was at issue. The Yorkshire team were livid, although as Bryan Stott admits, 'if we'd been in his position we wouldn't have either'. But, 'in the end Ian Thomson had a deliberate slog and holed out. If he'd hung for another two or three overs it might have been too late.'[20] When the captain was caught first ball by Jack Birkenshaw on the square-leg boundary, Yorkshire had to score 215 in 103 minutes to take the title.

Jim sums up the *dénouement*: 'It was an incredible victory for Yorkshire. They just came in and smashed it to all parts.' The visitors reached their target

with seven minutes, five wickets and three runs to spare. Thomson criticised
Marlar 'for his odd field placing in Yorkshire's second innings. I had asked for
defensive field support, but Marlar was down at long-off in a dream, even
after Stott had taken 15 off my first over.' Stott drove him straight for six and
Close hooked him out the ground for another in his second, at the end of
which Thomson found that he had taken no wickets for 32 runs – rough
treatment indeed for an opening bowler. Jim sympathises with him:

> I agree with Tommo. Marlar had gone walkabout mentally, and he seemed to
> lose control completely. He disappeared to the boundary and we didn't see
> him again. We just carried on without him.

Marlar explained his reasoning in the *Brighton Gazette*. 'With a right and
left-hander batting it would have meant an immense field change with every
ball and would, I think, have been hardly sporting.' Illingworth was watching with mounting excitement: 'Stotty and Padge ran them to death. Those
were the days before one-day cricket and they were playing tip and run all
the time. It wasn't easy to place a field when two blokes were going well.'
Stott and Padgett added 141 in 60 minutes when 'Tiger' Pataudi appeared to
have made a legitimate catch on the long-on boundary before going over
the ropes; Pataudi himself chivalrously signalled a six. At 181 for 3 Stott was
legally caught by 'Tiger' and Fred Trueman was promoted to throw the bat,
only to be stumped by Jim. 'He hit over the top, and he dragged a little. I was
quite pleased with that one.'

Alan Oakman had 'never experienced anything like it – it was like 20-
20 really. Closey smashed a few – we were spread to all parts. I was down
at long-off for a while. I think Marlar was off at fine-leg or something at
the north end of the ground and he just kept signalling. It was chaotic.'
Illingworth recalls that 'Brian Bolus and I were able to take us time for the
last 15 or 16 runs, which was unbelievable really.' Yorkshire had scored 218
in 28.3 overs and when Bolus glanced the winning boundary at 4.23 p.m.
Yorkshire had wrested the pennant from the Oval. Today Jim looks at *Wisden*
and shakes his head. 'Tommy, 87 off ten. Unbelievable. You didn't often see
Tommo slogged.'

The author wishes he had been there but a Boys' Brigade camp near
Folkestone seemed to take precedence. He was, however, at the Central
Ground to see Jim play for an England XI against a Commonwealth XI in
what was George Tribe's last first-class match in England. Jim enjoyed these
light-hearted end-of-season games, played in cavalier spirit for the holiday
crowds – 'they were good fun and I played quite often.'

It was the cheerful coda to a superlative summer, in which Jim scored more runs – 2,091 – than in any other and topped the Sussex averages with 53.61. *Wisden* records his golden year:

> Tried as a wicketkeeper, Parks proved a pronounced success, helping in the dismissals of 93 batsmen and, with 86 catches, establishing a record for any player in a season in first-class cricket… Parks supplemented his wicketkeeping success with attractive and forceful run-getting. He exceeded 2,000 runs for the third time in his career and put together five centuries for the county. From the Lancashire attack at Old Trafford in August, he scored 100 in 61 minutes, so winning the award for the fastest century of the season.[21]

Typically, Jim gives the credit to Ian Thomson. 'He had a good year and they just kept nicking them. He was great to keep to, especially left-handers as it swung away from them.'

Equally typical was Jim's conviction that he still had a lot to learn about his new position 'and I remember talking to Godfrey.' This jovial and warm-hearted man, acknowledged throughout the game as the pre-eminent wicketkeeper in the country during the fifties and widely regarded as one of the greatest of all time, had not been chosen for the MCC tour to the West Indies. Keith Andrew, technically proficient, and Roy Swetman, neat, compact and confident, were the men selected to travel – and Jim was bitterly disappointed. He believes that Evans should have gone and feels that he should have been his understudy. However, that was cricket – 'after the season I'd had, all the press were saying I should go but I wasn't picked.'

Jim would still be in the Caribbean, though. Learie Constantine had met Jim senior during the war when playing for a West Indies XI at Imber Court, and young Jim watched in awe as the great all-rounder hit a rapid 44. Fifteen years later Constantine, through the MCC, 'was the instigator of my appointment as coach to the Trinidad Cricket Council, which was arranged before the end of the season.' After a Christmas at home with his young family, Jim left Heathrow on 4 January 1960, bound for Port of Spain. He would be away from his wife and toddlers for the best part of the winter: 'I had a twelve-week contract. It was my job and the money was good out there. We weren't getting paid much over here.'

As he flew off from Heathrow, Jim never dreamt that as events were to turn out he was about to be given the biggest opportunity of his career.

Chapter 7

The Right Place
at the Right Time

Jim had signed a contract to coach in Trinidad, based for six weeks at the Texaco refinery in Pointe à Pierre, then six weeks in Port of Spain. He coached lads up to the age of twelve in the morning and youngsters between seventeen and twenty in the evenings. He loved it. They were the most enthusiastic cricketers he had ever met, their lives revolving around cricket, carnivals and calypsos.

At the end of January, with the touring party in town for the Second Test, there was no coaching and Jim found himself in the MCC dressing-room at the Queen's Park Oval. England were now accustomed to the fast pitches and the light, and were coming to terms with short-pitched bowling. On the opening morning the English batsmen faced a terrific onslaught from Watson and Hall. Barrington was hit over the heart and later laid out with a blow to the head but, showing the doughty resolve and pugilistic demeanour which characterised his England career, he ended the day 93 not out and went on to complete a gritty 121. With Mike Smith also making a 'studious, logical, determined'[1] century and Dexter 77, England posted a respectable first innings total of 382.

Overnight, West Indies were 22 without loss and Smith remembers the carnival atmosphere on the Saturday: 'this was the day they were going to smash us about.' By lunch the innings was in tatters. Keeping the ball pitched up and varying their pace, Trueman and Statham had reduced the West Indies to 45 for 5. In the afternoon the captain, Alexander, and Butcher strove to stop the rot but as the shadows began to creep across the square, the locals were not happy. Their heroes were 98 for 7, and Trueman had taken 4 for 32. Trinidad had been 'struggling for a major cricketing name because Sonny Ramadhin, a Trinidadian, had lived in the UK for many years so they played Charan Singh, a slow left-armer, in the match. Near the end of the day there was a cock-up between Ramadhin and Singh.'[2] Dexter recalls that he 'ran out their local boy', and from where David Allen stood 'it wasn't a close decision. Dexter threw from cover-point and he was two or three yards out.'

Jim was in the dressing-room with his ciné-camera when Charan Singh was given run out. 'Alan Moss rushed in and said "Come and look at this little lot, Jim." The game had been halted by what the Trinidad Prime Minister later described euphemistically as "a disruption of play", in which "a hail of bottles, beer tins and other refuse suddenly descended on to the field from the popular corner of the ground".'[3]

Ted Dexter felt they 'were getting beaten, they'd had too much beer and got over-excited.' As the crowd poured on to the field Jim went out with his camera – 'I didn't feel my safety was threatened' – unlike David Allen, who did feel in danger 'when all hell broke loose, but as a young man you take these things in your stride.' Ray Illingworth, the phlegmatic Yorkshireman, stayed on the field but

> we were surrounded by about 4,000 people. Brian Statham and Fred Trueman both took a stump out because it looked like we were going to have to fight us way through the bloody crowd, they looked that dodgy. Bottles were raining down on us and some of them blokes had bloody good arms.

Mike Smith saw 'a fella stagger as he lifted this bloody great rock. Statham yelled, "Grab a stump", which I didn't think was great advice. A bloke flew past me shouting, "We're not after you, man, we're after them umpires!" but they'd gone like rockets.'

The crowd's rum-fuelled frustration was aimed not only at their team and the umpires; a window was shattered in the Radio Trinidad box. Unfortunately there were only a handful of police on duty and the public address system was not used for twenty minutes. Eventually, the riot squad, equipped with helmets, batons and fire hoses, arrived and the hoses were turned on the crowd. The Governor of Trinidad, Edward Beetham, joined the police and when Learie Constantine, the Minister of Works, appeared they turned on him as well. Luckily, the old all-rounder was still spry enough to catch a stray bottle. The royal yacht was in port and the sailors from HMS *Britannia* made a passageway for the players into the pavilion. The mayhem gradually subsided and the teams sat drinking together, but as the 'flocks of white pigeons on their endless, undeterred circuits, took the late sun on their wings as they dipped against the hills',[4] after all the scuffles and minor casualties, play was abandoned for the day.

The crowd had been dumbfounded by the astonishing turn of the game. In Swanton's memorable prose, 'It was a mixture of sun, rum, disappointment and sheer evil mischief.' Mike Smith agrees: 'As you know they gamble quite a lot and they drink their share and Fred and Brian bowled them out. These things happen some days.'

Whatever the well-springs of the riot, there was some feeling in the English camp of 'Let's go home.' Jim was not with the team all the time but did not believe that the majority wanted to abandon the tour. Walter Robins' view was that MCC would play on. After a day's negotiations, common sense and good leadership prevailed and it was decided to make up the ninety minutes lost by adding half an hour to the next three days' play. 'We were lucky that the next day was a rest day. If it hadn't been, we couldn't have started on time because there was that much bloody glass on the field.'[5]

The West Indian authorities were thoroughly embarrassed by what the Trinidad premier Dr Eric Williams described as 'one of the most disgraceful episodes I have ever seen... on a cricket field.' There was no antagonism between the players and 'all Peter insisted on was that the time lost should be made up – which it was. In their second innings the bloke who got the runs was Kanhai. That was the big wicket.'[6] With an hour and three-quarters to spare, West Indies still needed 256 to win when Watson, last man in, played 'a leaping kind of aboriginal stroke to his first ball'[7] and Allen, lying deep at mid-off, took it safely. The bowlers had shared the wickets but the real threat had always come from the pace men. 'On this flat, bare, brown wicket', Allen recalls, 'Statham and Trueman were swinging the ball a little bit, getting movement off the pitch. I think it was one the greatest fast-bowling feats I've seen. Almost at their peak then, they had perhaps lost their outright pace but the skill was tremendous and the work-rate huge.'

After the heady excitement of the riot and the crushing victory Jim returned south and by the end of February he had moved to Port of Spain for his six-week stint in the capital:

> I'd made a lot of friends in Trinidad, particularly 'Sammy' Guillen, who kept
> wicket for the West Indies and later New Zealand. We enjoyed the carnival
> and went round with one of the bands. On one memorable night we saw
> Louis Armstrong play in Port of Spain.

Via a fluctuating and ultimately tense draw in Jamaica, MCC had arrived in Georgetown for the colony game and the Fourth Test. It was the final day of the game against British Guiana, and Jim, back in Pointe à Pierre, was about to set off to the east coast for the weekend. 'I called in at the local store to collect some groceries when Max Marshall, the West Indies assistant manager, appeared. "Jim! Walter Robins has asked if you could fly over to Georgetown to join the MCC. Several players are on the sick list, and he needs your help."' Alan Ross records that 'Trueman had ricked his back batting and... Barrington, who'd had flu earlier in the week, had a relapse and went to a nursing home with bronchial asthma… Our resources had suddenly grown very slender.'

It was therefore a somewhat beleaguered Robins who announced that May, who had been suffering for some time with a reopening of his operation scar, would not play for two weeks and that Cowdrey would captain the side in the Fourth Test starting the following Wednesday. The absence of May meant there was now no reserve batsman and that the choice would be Jim. 'MCC were fortunate', in Swanton's view, 'to have so close at hand a substitute whom many people, myself included, thought an obvious choice for the team in the first place.'

Jim had to be out of Trinidad as soon as he could. Max Marshall arranged for him to be on the midnight flight and for his release from the Trinidad CA.

> I had stuff at the laundry all over the place so it meant I had to get up to Port of Spain. I rushed up there and back in an old borrowed Morris Minor and collected as much as I could. Inside eleven hours I was aboard Pan Am for Georgetown, where I arrived at 4 a.m. fast asleep – two glasses of champagne saw to that. I arrived at the Tower Hotel in a power failure and went straight to bed. I was sharing with Illy, who wasn't enjoying the tour very much as they'd been playing on very good wickets.

Jim was up at 10 a.m. and after his habitual good breakfast was off to the ground. Robins explained that Ken Barrington was doubtful for the Test, which was two days away. Jim tried to get accustomed to the light, which was brighter than in Trinidad, but was soon back at the Tower and fast asleep. On the Monday, 'they got me up at 1 to have a net. I hadn't got much gear. I didn't even have a bat. I borrowed Keith Andrew's bat and his pads, which was a generous gesture.' Jim very much appreciated the valuable friendship of the amiable Northants keeper: 'When Jim arrived in Georgetown from Trinidad he had little kit. I lent him some and he got a hundred with my bat in Berbice. Funnily enough it was a Gray-Nicholls with the sloping shoulder.' In the nets he faced Moss and Statham, who gave him a few bouncers. As usual, Jim hit it hard and a yorker from Statham broke the only bat he had. He was exhausted. He had lost nearly six pounds in the session and felt that his thirty-five minutes work had equated to a three-and-a-half hour innings. Colin Cowdrey had a long talk with him about Hall and Watson. The captain's advice was to '"take middle stump". He thought they were playable then and he was right. You had a better chance of getting into line more quickly.' Jim also spent time keeping to Moss, Greenhough and Andrew, and found that he had to crouch lower than in England as the ball was liable to slip through, especially with the spinners.

As the week wore on, it seemed that Jim had a sporting chance of play-ing for Barrington, who was still in hospital. Jim went to see him on the eve of the Test and though 'he looked far from well when I was shown into his ward,' when Thursday came he had improved a little. Though many har-boured doubts, ten minutes before the teams were due to take the field the tough little Surrey man decided he was fit enough to play. Jim had not played a first-class match for six months, and as Swanton put it, 'Parks, who is an admirable all-round fielder, will be twelfth man, and I have no doubt he will be tried in the next match at Berbice with two possibilities in mind for the Fifth Test, either as batsman, supposing May does not consider himself fit, or as wicketkeeper/batsman if his form merits it.' Subba Row, Jim's friend from Pevensey a decade before, came in for Peter May. For Cowdrey, it was quite a responsibility to take over the captaincy for the last two Test matches and he:

> found a close manager/captain relationship difficult and once Peter May had returned home I was distinctly vulnerable. The team enjoyed listening to him [Robins] telling his stories but were puzzled by his determination to admin-ister military-style discipline. To be deprived of May and Statham was asking a lot, but there was no doubt that the team united and were in the most deter-mined frame of mind to give everything they had.

The Bourda ground in Georgetown afforded Jim a return to the Test match arena, when Subba Row was hit by Hall and chipped a bone in his right hand. Jim spent two and a half days as a sub watching West Indies grind out 402 – a first-innings lead of 107. The pitch was slow and flat, the cricket moderate and the over rates funereal. On an easy pitch, England crawled to 295, Allen making his first Test fifty, 'against the short-pitched stuff – mind you, they had two chuckers – Watson and Griffith. Wes was a super athlete and a very fair bowler, though as it climbed past your face he would shout, 'Up, up, man!' By the fifth day it was stalemate and although England were under some pressure, Pullar and Dexter wiped off the arrears before stumps. On day six England's second innings shone Light Blue as Dexter and Subba Row made match-saving centuries and the match petered out into a boring draw, although in the view of Alan Ross, 'it had been a better match than the scores suggest.'

Down on the Berbice river against Berbice County Jim kept wicket for the MCC for the first time, using Andrew's bat and pads, Cowdrey's gloves, Illingworth's trousers, Statham's cap and Dexter's thigh pad.[8] According to Allen:

Joe Solomon, their skipper, agreed that they would bat for a day and then we'd bat for a day and we'd slog it out in a declaration match. At the end of the first day we said 'Thank you very much' and Joe said, 'I've got 87 not out and my supporters would want to see me get my hundred.' So we virtually gave him his hundred next morning and said, 'How about that?' 'Well, Basil Butcher's now got 87 and we are from different backgrounds, one Indian and one African; politically it wouldn't be right to declare now.' So they batted for a day and half but we got our own back. Colin said, 'Right, we'll just bat till the close' – and we did. They got 350 in a day and a half and we got 650 in a day and a half. Although it was an awful game Jim had made runs superbly in very quick time and it got him his Test place.

In fact seven MCC batsmen made fifties and Jim, Barrington and Illingworth scored hundreds:

Parks, in his first innings, made 183, driving tremendously hard and hitting 5 sixes and 21 fours in a stay of four hours twenty minutes. He and Barrington put MCC ahead with two men out, their stand producing 283, the highest of the tour.[9]

In addition to his century, Jim's keeping 'went well. I remember keeping to Tommy Greenhough – the only time I ever did. Roy Swetman had not had a very good tour.' Mike Smith agreed: 'Roy had struggled for runs and Jim was in the front-line as a straight batter in England.' The main keeper in the party, Keith Andrew, laid low early in the tour with a debilitatingly high temperature, was now fully fit but Illingworth felt 'they played Roy Swetman because they thought he'd make runs, but every time a quickie ran up his pole went out. In fact he had a 'mare behind the wicket.'

The party then flew back to Trinidad and on the Thursday, the day before the final Test was due to start, Cowdrey offered his congratulations and told Jim that he would keep wicket. Jim mumbled his thanks but was staggered. He had kept in only forty games; one of the first to shake hands was Roy Swetman. A few days earlier, while Jim was twelfth man in the Test, his son Andrew had been very ill in hospital. 'It was panic stations at the time. I remember talking to Rene on the BBC phone and she said, "Well, he's OK." I got a telegram of good wishes just before the Test started saying that he was due to leave hospital next morning.'

The match was potentially a strict examination of his international credentials but 'it set my career up, as I was in the right place at the right time.' While the MCC were fortunate to have Jim on the doorstep, a lot was being asked of him 'on such slender preparation, and he may conceivably make 0 and drop a crucial catch or two.'[10]

Cowdrey won the toss, the fifth out of five, batted and on the first day made 256 for 3 – more runs than either side had scored in a day during the entire series. Cowdrey 'led the way with an innings of 119, one of my best. Robins appeared to be quite pleased with our approach.' He played beautifully, as if the 'cautious old owl of Georgetown fluttered his plumage and emerged rather as a soaring eagle.'[11] In the afternoon Cowdrey and Dexter shared a stand of 191 in just over three hours and although Sobers dismissed them in successive overs after tea, it had been an excellent day's cricket.

On day two there was some skilful bowling by Ramadhin and, for the first time in the series, 'the England tail, even with Parks there to strengthen the lower middle, failed to hold up the enemy.'[12] At lunch England were 308 for 4, runs coming at better than 50 an hour. England were batting to a plan, 'and in this Parks played his part as to the manner born.'[13] Beaten twice for pace early on, he gradually settled in and was not troubled by Hall or Watson, 'a fearsome pair, although Frank Tyson was still the quickest I'd faced.' It was a unique experience and although Watson averaged three bumpers an over 'you could get inside them most of the time. Chester Watson was another chucker, but Wes was particularly awesome.'

Jim had had a good look at Ramadhin when he had bowled at Hove in 1950 on a wet wicket. Here in Trinidad on a perfect wicket and in great light Jim saw him more clearly. 'It was the first time I'd faced Sonny since he bowled me out for 0 and 1. I'd never seen anything like him at that time. You could read Sonny's leg-spinner only because you could see the hand.' In the afternoon Ramadhin came into his own, taking 4 for 25 in 15 overs, and though Jim bolstered the tail who could stay with him? He lay back and hooked Ramadhin into the trees at mid-wicket then moved down the pitch to drive twice in one over, once over extra-cover and once on to the sight-screen. 'I made 43 in the first innings, caught and bowled Sobers. I was smashing him and didn't quite hit it.' This was a revelation to the locals. 'Knowledgeable West Indians were soon asking why he had been passed over when the team was picked. How could the selectors ignore Parks' obvious class and his outstanding form of last summer?'[14] England had reached a solid 393 and West Indies were 49 for 1 at the close, having lost McMorris, run out when Trueman deflected a straight drive by Alexander on to the stumps.

As in most cricket matches, the chief factor over the next two days in the outcome of the game was the pitch, affected by the rain that curtailed play on the third day. On the fourth morning, at 150 for 2, Sobers wanted to accelerate but found the pitch unresponsive. England bowled only 13.3 overs an hour, and it seemed that the captain had lost the plot. Needing to bring in the field to deny Sobers the strike, Cowdrey exerted too gentle a grip on the game and West Indies scored 65 before lunch for the loss of Walcott. Missed by Jim when he nicked a bouncer from Trueman, he was beaten by Allen in the air and Jim stumped him for his first Test victim. After lunch, Worrell, Kanhai and Sobers were bowled, Alan Moss capturing the latter two scalps in five balls. Then Allen bowled the captain, playing down the wrong line: 'it might just have turned a bit, nothing to get excited about. I remember Ray Illingworth's comment at the end of that match – "If tours are like this, they can keep 'em, lad."'

Tea was taken at 302 for 7 and when Hall, after a flamboyant 29, was yorked by Trueman, Alexander declared 55 behind to see if they could bowl England out. Just before the end England lost Cowdrey. Hall, bowling with a strained side, offered the England skipper a slow-medium half-volley third ball, which Cowdrey popped into Worrell's hands at short leg. David Allen went in as nightwatchman: 'Kipper had looked at me and said, "You haven't batted much recently. I want you to do nightwatchman tonight. You'd better go and have a net." So off I went for about a quarter of an hour, got padded up and lo and behold Cowdrey's out. We survived that night', and at stumps England were 18 for 1.

If England could bat with sufficient enterprise and cohesion there was a real possibility of winning a series in the Caribbean for the first time. Yet when Jim joined Mike Smith in mid-afternoon the West Indies were one wicket away from a crucial breakthrough. The day began and ended well but wavered in the middle. Allen was run out after an hour:

> We were doing so well – I kick myself now but we all make mistakes. Noddy hit this slow one to mid-off and called for a quick single. He caught me ball-watching. We'd put on 59 and I got a hell of a rocket from Kipper.

Before lunch England made 84, losing Pullar caught and bowled by Sobers 3 balls before the break, and after lunch Subba Row was lbw to Ramadhin. At 3 p.m. England led by 200 when Barrington played an off-break from Sobers to short-leg and Dexter was thrillingly run out when Hunte threw down the wicket from a fierce cover-drive. At 148 for 6 Jim joined Mike Smith, and with England only 203 ahead with four wickets left the West Indies would have been favourites had they broken through then. Jim relished this challenge to his ability. It was a difficult moment but as Ted Dexter said to me wryly, 'Tell me a time when it isn't difficult to come in in a Test match!'

> Jim took the fight to them, as he would, especially when the spinners came on. Ramadhin was still a threat but Jim took him apart. He had a long-on and

a long-off only thirty or forty yards apart and Jim got down the wicket and hit it almost between them! It was a superb innings – typical of Jim playing spinners.'[15]

At tea England led by 223, with four sessions left and the new ball seven overs away. Rain after tea curtailed play and despite the damp outfield, when Alexander decided to take the new ball the situation changed completely. Jim edged a four off Griffith through the slips, but then unleashed some handsome strokes, notably a scintillating back foot drive off Watson. The pair added sixty in forty-five minutes together, but the captain took a pessimistic view: 'We were in trouble, only 200 runs ahead and six wickets down. It was a bad night to live through as defeat stared us in the face.'[16] If it was a bad night for Cowdrey, it was a good one for Jim:

> Some friends had come up from Pointe à Pierre. We went out that night and I was well away. I returned to the hotel at about one in the morning, which you couldn't do nowadays, and the press, who were still in the bar, beckoned me over for a drink! They were still our friends in those days; they weren't out to do you down.[17]

The stand-in skipper need not have lost any sleep. On the last day Jim and MJK took the stand to 197, a record for England's seventh wicket. Though the West Indies bowling was half-hearted and the fielding careless, the Englishmen fought bravely; batting out of character Jim crawled towards his 100. He was becalmed on 94 for half an hour and when he was on 98 Watson came back for more bouncers. At last Jim got two off him for 'a handsome, if latterly languid, century'.[18] This milestone in his career had taken three and a half hours and Allen thinks Jim 'must take more credit than any batter for turning the match round.' It was one of Jim's greatest experiences in first-class cricket. When Hunte's bustling medium pace had MJK caught behind for 96, Cowdrey declared at 350 for 7, Jim remaining undefeated on 101.

The captain had refused an altruistic declaration: 'We were out of trouble but there was no time to bowl the West Indies out and win the match. There was no point in risking all with a quixotic declaration.' After sweating it out through five hard Tests, 'we didn't want to give it away on a whim.'[19] There had been a dispute on that last morning between captain and manager:

> Colin, quite reasonably, said 'I'm going to bat on,' because we were on our knees, really. We'd got no May, no Statham, Barrington and Ted had taken a real battering from their quicks... Quite frankly if we'd declared they couldn't lose.[20]

Cowdrey points out that

> Robins was not there in the morning to watch our magnificent show of bat-
> ting. His bustling arrival by taxi and public dressing down of his captain in the
> dressing room only served to spoil what I thought had been a successful day
> for English cricket. At the end of the match we were joint hosts at a happy
> party for our many West Indian friends. It is to my regret that apart from a few
> formal greetings over the next few years he had little time for me.[21]

When he did arrive, feelings became heated:

> Fred almost lifted Robins out of the dressing-room. I was sitting on the side
> very quietly and thought, 'Is that what you do to team managers?' The boys
> were very upset. It was a tremendous series on very difficult wickets in stifling
> heat and we were a young side. We'd worked terribly hard and there was no
> chance on this flat wicket with our depleted attack and their batting line-up
> of us bowling them out. It was typical of Robins on that tour – he had very
> little to do with the players and everything to do with the press. In Australia
> the year before the side had had a difficult tour with the press: he was there to
> quell any problems from that score, and this he did.[22]

After Cowdrey's declaration the West Indies played out time, Jim stumping Hunte off Illingworth and catching Walcott off Barrington. Worrell and
Sobers played some glorious strokes in what became pure carnival at the
end. So England won the series, 'one of the most remarkable and praiseworthy victories of the recent past'.[23] *Wisden* declared:

> Cowdrey and Dexter were the best batsmen and good support came from
> Pullar, Barrington, Subba Row, Smith and Parks, who joined the side on the
> return of May and played an important part in the fifth Test…. Parks kept in
> two matches, did all that was necessary behind the stumps and his fine batting
> helped to strengthen the side considerably.[24]

Keith Andrew agreed that 'Jim's century [in Trinidad] was instrumental in his
being in the side for a long spell, but whether it benefited England is another
point – I think he should have played as a batsman.' Alan Ross, a Sussex supporter and long-term admirer of Jim, felt vindicated by Jim's return to the
Test scene: 'Parks, without help from the selectors, had made his point (and
mine, I'm glad to say) as finally as anyone could. An England side with him at
no.7 was not going to be beaten easily, by the Australians or anyone else.'[25]

Jim went to Trinidad a county batsman who kept wicket and came back an international cricketer with a Test hundred to his name – and he carried his Caribbean form into the new season. 'I got 3 hundreds in May – 140 at Taunton against Somerset, 131 off Glamorgan at Hove and 155 against Surrey' – and by the end of that May he had made 771 runs at 77. For many spectators around the county grounds in 1960, Sussex were the most exciting side to watch. Under Dexter's captaincy the team was encouraged to play attacking, enterprising cricket, and they had the ammunition to do it. 'Dexter, Parks, the new England wicketkeeper, Oakman, the left-handers, Suttle and Smith, all of whom passed 1,000 runs, and Lenham constituted a run-getting combination of such strength that Sussex totalled more than 300 on eleven occasions.'[26] With a bowling attack of Thomson and Bates, now seasoned performers, the young Tony Buss, Ronnie Bell, Robin Marlar and, in his last year at Hove, Ted James, there were the makings of a formidable side, especially when three of the batsmen were capable of turning in match-winning performances with the ball.

Dexter's men won five of the first six matches. After a six-wicket win at Edgbaston and a gratifying victory over the new Champions Yorkshire at Hove, against Glamorgan on a turner at Eaton Road, Jim hit a century which Peter Walker recalls with admiration:

> Jim Parks had made a hundred against us on an unpredictable wicket... It was the speed and precision of his footwork that had kept us, and Don Shepherd in particular, at bay.

A swashbuckling 151 by the skipper set the Welshmen 272 to win and four wickets each for Bates and Buss gave Sussex a victory by 133 runs.

After crushing Nottinghamshire by ten wickets at Hove, Dexter's 104 and 60 from Jim enabled Sussex to reach 327 at the Oval, but rain on the last two days washed out both the rest of the match and Sussex's opportunity to force a rare win over Surrey. Ten days later on a green wicket at Hove, Surrey were struggling at 58 for 6 when Eric Bedser, Tony Lock and David Gibson helped the visitors to a respectable if unconvincing 158.

> Then Dexter and Parks gave a delightful exhibition, continuing their big stand on the second day until it had yielded 222 runs... Parks hit one six over the sightscreen and 15 fours, getting to his dazzling 155 in four hours.[27]

The captain weighed in with 135: 'Ted got a very good hundred. I remember him picking up a good-length ball from Alec Bedser and putting it through a window of one the houses on the east side of the ground.' Sussex were able to declare at a huge 451 for 5, and in their second innings only a stand of 128 between Parsons and Swetman gave Surrey any hope of making Dexter's side bat again. At 243 for 5 they were within 50 of their target, but five wickets fell for 11 runs as Bates and Tony Buss, with 5 for 55, clinched a resounding victory. Jim took 'great delight in winning that one after being hammered for the last seven years.' In Sussex's substantial first innings Tony Lock went for 1 for 113, as Jim recalls: 'Locky had had to change his action that winter. He used to chuck from twenty yards because he had this enormous drag. ICC suddenly decided they'd got to come down on chuckers – they'd been to Australia and seen Meckiff, Rorke and all the rest.'

In that summer, three months after the Sharpeville massacre had brought the racial divisions within South African society to world attention, England's cricket fields played host to the Dominion's cricketers, and to one of the most palpable 'chuckers' in the game. Jim first saw Geoff Griffin when he played for the MCC against the touring South Africans at Lord's, where Frank Lee and John Langridge both called him for throwing. England won the First Test at Edgbaston by 100 runs in a tedious game notable for the debut, as a leg-spinner, of Bob Barber. Jim had an undistinguished game after the heroics of Port of Spain, but remembers 'Griffin coming outside the sightscreen with his bent elbow. The South Africans very carefully kept him away from Sid Buller by bowling him from Buller's end.'

The real moment of truth came at Lord's, where:

The no-balling of Geoffrey Griffin, a twenty-year old opening bowler from Natal... scarred the memory of the game as well as convincing the South African authorities at long last that to continue to expose him to the umpire's scrutiny was unfair and unkind both to the English umpires and to the young man himself. No overseas bowler had ever before been called in England. Yet before the Second Test no fewer than six umpires had no-balled Griffin. D.J. McGlew, the captain and the tour manager, Dudley Nourse... decided on a showdown at headquarters where Sid Buller, the leading umpire, was standing with Frank Lee. McGlew avoided putting Griffin on at the end at which Buller would judge him at square leg. Lee however no-balled him eleven times.[28]

He had a kink in his bowling arm as a result of a riding accident as a boy and Jim found him a 'nice bloke but a blatant chucker'. Chucker or not, at the end of the second day 'Griffin had M.J.K. Smith caught behind for 99 off the last ball of one over, and with England throwing the bat in the knowledge of a weekend declaration, he picked up Walker and Trueman from the first two balls of his next',[29] thus becoming the first South African to grab a Test hat-trick – the only man to get one in a Lord's Test till Dominic Cork in 1995 – yet his achievement passed relatively unnoticed. MJK 'was Geoff Griffin's first hat-trick victim and Fred Trueman was his third. It was very sad about his action, but quite frankly I don't think he ever *bowled* a ball. It was a most embarrassing summer.' He never 'bowled' another ball on the tour.

England wrapped up an innings win soon after lunch on the fourth day, Brian Statham achieving the best Test match figures of his career – 11 for 97. It was a good match for Jim too; he had had six chances and had taken six catches, with no byes at all, which he attributes to the accuracy of Trueman, Statham and Moss.

After his meteoric May Jim was finding runs difficult to come by. He arrived at Trent Bridge in the middle of July with 152 in ten innings to his name since the majestic 155 against Surrey. His form with the bat did not improve in Nottingham, but he took another five catches, one of his victims being Colin Wesley, 'brilliantly snapped up by Parks diving low with the left hand.'[30] Poor Wesley 'got a king pair. I dived and just got it in my glove.' Jim made only 16, run out by 'a fine return by McLean from the deep'.[31] Another run-out incident changed the course of the game in the visitors' second innings as they battled to set England a challenging total. Jackie McGlew, the Springbok captain, had put on 91 with Sid O'Linn, when

> as non-striker, he ran into Moss, the bowler, stumbled, and was run out by a direct throw. The England captain, Cowdrey, three times tried to recall McGlew (who never queried the decision), and he asked the umpires to change their minds, but they refused on the grounds that Moss had not wilfully impeded the batsman.[32]

Sid O'Linn was a colourful character. His gutsy 98 was his finest hour for his country, for whom he had also played football in 1947. He made 187 appearances for Charlton in the old First Division and eventually became a director of the club. Like two other Charlton players, Derek Ufton and Stuart O'Leary, he also played cricket for Kent.

England were winning a one-sided series and although Jim was going through a run-drought, his form behind the stumps remained unimpaired. Coming to Old Trafford for the Fourth Test, he had taken forty-seven victims in the season, thirteen of them in the Tests. An especially pleasing haul was at the Central Ground, where, with Hastings Castle as the backdrop and the author rushing down from school so that his dad could let him in free at the gate after tea, he took five catches as Kent were beaten by 8 wickets, Kenny

Suttle making 122 not out and Ian Thomson doing the damage with 5 for 20. Manchester stayed true to its stereotype as the first two days of the Test were lost to rain, and when play did get underway on the Saturday, England found themselves soon after lunch 134 for 5. However, 'fears of a collapse were dispelled by Barrington and Parks, who added 63 in seventy minutes.'[33] Although Barrington pulled a thigh muscle and was limping towards the end of his knock, Jim 'had a quick stand with Kenny and it was a photograph of me slogging Hugh Tayfield for six which was on the front of my book.' In reply to England's barely adequate 260 South Africa made 229, Roy McLean batting beautifully for a century. When Jim was caught and bowled by Trevor Goddard at 101 for 5 England were only 132 ahead but a lame Barrington found a stubborn partner in Allen and a belligerent one in Trueman and the danger was averted. England had taken their run to sixteen matches without defeat, the longest in their history.

Jim's return to the Championship scene came at a propitious time, as the county won the next three games. Although his own indifferent form continued, with the young Pataudi he steered the side to a six-wicket win at Bournemouth and then Middlesex were trounced in the bank holiday match at Hove, a game which 'Ted won virtually on his own.' In front of large Saturday crowd 'Lord Ted' struck 19 fours in an innings of 157. Otherwise, only a pleasant 80 from Don Smith contributed significantly, Jim being bowled by Don Bennett for a duck. Middlesex's reply was stifled at birth as Ian Thomson skittled the top three for 26, and on the last day the visitors were set 329 to win in five hours – a tall order in any circumstances, but made all the harder as the captain 'came up the hill and they were pinging through. He was quick when he wanted and he swung it around.' With Middlesex on 121 for 6 and facing virtually certain defeat, a thunderstorm engulfed the County Ground, but when play was resumed Dexter, who had taken 3 for 1 before the break, had Titmus caught in the deep and then bowled Bennett. When Ronnie Bell took a smart catch at short-leg to dismiss John Warr, Dexter had taken 6 for 12 in 8 overs and Sussex had won by 202 runs. The skipper finished with 7 for 24 – his best figures for the county.

'Dickie' Bird has become one of the game's most respected and much-loved institutions, but he plied his trade for nine seasons as a journeyman, opening bat for Yorkshire and Leicestershire before becoming the game's best-known umpire. At Grace Road that September Jim saw him record what he believes is cricket's quickest-ever king pair:

The game was played in a very heavy atmosphere and the ball swung like a boomerang. We won the toss and struggled to 239, Robin Marlar at number

11 making 39. Dickie opened with Willie Watson and was out first ball, caught by Alan Oakman off Ian Thomson, who finished with 6 for 23. They were bowled out for 42 in 24 overs and Ted asked them to follow on. Only one over of the second innings remained of the first day when Dickie came out looking very nervous. Ian ran in, bowled an unplayable ball, Dickie got a nick and was caught round the corner by Hubert Doggart for another first ball duck. That's the only time I can remember him speechless – but only for a second or two!

The Foxes never recovered and Sussex won by an innings.

Jim had withstood Hall, Griffith and Watson earlier in the year on their home turf but always reckoned Frank Tyson to be the fastest bowler he had ever faced. Twice in ten days he renewed acquaintance with the 'Typhoon' as he travelled to Wellingborough. On a low, flat, turning wicket at the School Ground, the terrifying Tyson bowled nine overs empty-handed as Jim scored 87 in the visitors' first knock. Bell took six and Marlar four in the match and slow left-armer Michael Allen captured 6 for 52 as Sussex were bowled out for 91 in their second innings. Northamptonshire knocked off the 123 they needed and won by eight wickets. Jim's chance of revenge came at Hove a week or so later and he seized it with both hands – or gloves. He was disappointed not to have played the tourists; the game against the South Africans was abandoned without a ball being bowled, the first game at Hove since 1903 to be completely lost. So when Northampton came down to Eaton Road Jim relished his return to form with a sparkling 102 – 'the only one I did get against them.' On the last day Sussex were pushing for a win, but Crump and Tyson added 94 so that there was never any danger of defeat. Tyson's 82 was the highest innings of his career. 'Frank Tyson wasn't the world's worst – he could bat a bit.'[34]

Frustrated that he was unable to take up the cudgels against the South Africans on his home ground, Jim took the field at the Oval for the final Test well aware that selection for the 'A' tour of New Zealand was very much on the MCC agenda. In the end rain was the winner and Jim's disappointing series came to a murky end in south London, but in some respects it was perhaps the best match of the series. Amid sporadic showers Adcock and Pothecary dismissed England for 155, Jim scoring 23. Then, led by Goddard with 99, the South Africans secured a first-innings lead of 264. It might have been less, as 'very early in the day [Saturday] Goddard was dropped off consecutive balls from Statham by Cowdrey and Parks.'[35] Such calamities mattered little as on the Monday 'England turned back the calendar and played cricket of pre-war vintage.'[36] Cowdrey (155) and Pullar (175) put on 290 in four-and-a-half hours and enabled the captain to set Goddard's men

216 to win in three hours. Over the five games, Jim had scored only 154 in 8 innings – a poor summer after the euphoria of Trinidad.

The county season had one last hurrah as 'we beat Leicestershire in two days at Hove, then to Buxton, Blackpool and Margam.' Leicester had the misfortune to meet Tony Buss on a green top at Hove, and following on 165 behind, were all out for 40. Buss finished with 11 for 64 and then went off to the RAF for his national service. Derby and Lancashire were damp draws, then 'we charged off down to play at Margam' – the distinctly drab Steel Company of Wales ground with smoke billowing over the ground from the steel complex – and it rained.

> I didn't think we were going to play on the first day. We'd been in the bar but we started about half past six, and there was a challenge that I could hit the first ball for six. I charged off down the wicket and hit Wooller straight up in the air and was caught and bowled for 0.[37]

The party for the 'A' tour to New Zealand was announced as Jim journeyed home from Margam. It contained some interesting names. Roger Prideaux, later a colleague at Hove, and David Allen, a Caribbean team-mate were there, as were Bob Barber, then primarily a leg-spinner, and David Larter, the long-limbed Northants paceman. J.M. Parks and J.T. Murray were named as wicketkeepers. 'J.T. and I were being given overseas experience of keeping in an international arena as we were challenging each other at that time.' Jim had had a respectable season on the whole – second in the Sussex averages with 1,315 runs at 43.83 – but internationally it had been below par and his pleasure at being selected for another overseas tour was tempered by domestic storm clouds gathering back at Nursery End.

Chapter 8

The Wilderness Years

In December 1960 the MCC party under Dennis Silk left Heathrow for New Zealand, the first major MCC side to fly on an outward journey – but Jim was not on the plane. In November he had travelled out with Irene and the boys on the Nederland liner the *Olden Barnevelt*. Combining a family holiday with Jim's professional commitments 'was an attempt to get back together really. Had we not gone on holiday that winter the marriage would have finished then. We'd been struggling for a bit as I'd been away a lot.'

It was a long voyage, some five weeks,

but very pleasant. Rene went overland from Port Said to Suez, so I had the two boys for about four days. That was hard work. There was somewhere you could take the kids but four days was enough. We got out there about a month before the tour started. In the late forties Dad had been invited to go out and coach: he did one year at Napier and one year down in Christchurch so they contacted me. I played one match for Lancaster Park and got a hundred. I played only one game because their matches started on one Saturday and finished on the next. My wife had a cousin in Lyttleton, so the family stayed with them.

Rene and the boys wintered in South Island while Dad joined the tour party in Auckland. He would have been less than popular, as the first game started on Christmas Eve. He stayed in the north until the first week of January and it was just as well the boys weren't watching, as Jim was not getting runs. He was having fun though, as Bob Barber recalls: 'I remember that the Governor-General entertained us on New Year's Eve. We were racing these Scalextric cars around the banqueting hall, which was quite fun.'

Jim returned to South Island via a two-day game against Marlborough at Blenheim and Rene, Andrew and Bobby were in the crowd at Lancaster Park as MCC took on Canterbury. It is to be hoped that they were having an ice-cream late on the last day as Jim was 'hit by Tony McGibbon. I'd opened up to cut but it nipped back and hit dead centre. That's the only time

I ever got hit in the box. It crept up on me and though I got runs in the next couple of weeks it gradually got worse and I had to see a specialist when I got home.' David Allen of course saw the funny side: 'in the sadistic humour of the dressing-room we thought it was terrifically funny as he had them wrapped in cotton-wool and a jockstrap.' The MCC made heavy weather of chasing the 190 they needed to win, but Russell and Larter were there at the end. Bob Barber remembers:

> We did well to get David Larter on the field. I was rooming with him some-where and come the morning, I said, 'We'd better get up' and he said, 'I can't.' I said, 'What do you mean, you can't?' He said, 'I rolled over and went in the back.' He only used to bowl three-over spells.

Jim showed little sign of discomfort as the tourists encamped in Dunedin for the provincial match against Otago and the first representative game against New Zealand. The province batted soundly to reach 349, including 59 from their skipper Bert Sutcliffe, with Neil Harvey the finest left-handed bat of his generation. When Jim arrived at the wicket at 65 for 4 the possibility of a follow-on loomed, but

> Parks ran into form after a lean spell and his brilliant innings of 92 not out in two and a half hours saved them… In one over from Moir, Parks increased the score by 20 runs made up by 2 sixes and 2 fours.[1]

He was in similarly rich form in the unofficial 'Test'. The first day of four was lost to rain and early on the third morning John Reid declared at 313 for 7. Prideaux opened elegantly with 63, 'but the brightest MCC batting came from Parks, whose 82 took only an hour and fifty-two minutes.'[2] In the end MCC needed 206 in 150 minutes, but despite some brisk hitting from Prideaux and Jim Stewart, they were 39 short at the close with three wickets left.

The second match in Wellington, to which the party had travelled via the exotically euphonious venues of Timaru and Wanganui, was marred by heavy rain on the first day in one of the wettest summers in the islands for many years. Larter and Sayer bowled well on the second day, but MCC batted with-out great distinction: Jim 'got 0 and 2. Dick Motz came on the scene – a good cricketer.' On a green wicket, the visitors were bundled out for 111, Motz tak-ing 5 for 34. When MCC batted last needing 266 in four and a half hours, Bob Barber made a doggedly defiant 39 – 'Jack Alabaster came round the wicket and bowled into the holes made by Dick Motz outside the left-hander's off-stump. I spent my time kicking them away.' Of the others, only Prideaux was able to deal with Alabaster, who finished with 5 for 71 as New Zealand won comfortably by 133 runs. John Murray kept wicket in what was becoming a no-contest. In fact, of the twenty-two fixtures on the tour, Jim kept in fewer than half a dozen. The persistent discomfort from the Christchurch injury meant that 'I kept until I got injured then I couldn't keep at all.'

After the serious representative match and the disappointment of a below-par performance, the party could at least look forward to some light-hearted festival-style cricket before the Governor-General's fixture in Auckland later in February. Jim returned to form in Hamilton where 'Stewart and Prideaux shared a brisk first-wicket stand of 99 after MCC had been put into bat on a damp pitch. Padgett continued the revelry with Parks (85) and hit an attractive 125 not out.'[3] Northern Districts were beaten by eight wickets and the next game against Northland marked 'the official opening of the new ground at Whangarei. I got 107 but it wasn't first-class.'

Perhaps it was this century which secured Jim the gloves for the prestig-ious match against the Governor-General's XI at Eden Park, where, in spite of 'the difficulties of a rain-affected pitch on the first day, Russell, Watson, Parks and Silk all batted in a festival spirit.'[4] Jim top-scored with 57 against an attack which included as a guest thirty-nine-year-old Ray Lindwall. In reply, a hard-hitting 44 from the Governor-General himself, Lord Cobham, and a fluent 74 by Bert Sutcliffe took the hosts to a first-innings lead of 25. Then 32 from Jim, 48 by the skipper and a careful 50 from David Allen enabled Dennis Silk to set New Zealand 253 to win. Despite stubborn resist-ance from Walter Wallace and John Reid, Bob Barber, bowling with control and direction, ripped the heart out of the middle order to finish with 7 for 89. MCC had won by 25 runs. The genial Mancunian told me:

About two months ago, I was going through some old books, and found a New Zealand newspaper report of that game. It was falling to bits but it brought back some memories. Don Wilson and I were asked to toss the ball up to the Governor-General to make sure that he could whack the ball over the top, but David Allen said he hadn't come to New Zealand to bowl donkey drops. Did I get 7 for 89 in the second innings? Goodness me.

Jim remembers that game too, but for a reason not entirely cricket-related:

I never used to eat at lunchtime and the Governor-General laid on champagne in the dressing-room straight after the game. He also threw a party at the end of the match at Government House – more champagne and still no food. I sud-denly started to feel a bit light-headed so I found somewhere in Government

House, lay down and went to sleep. They came in and found me later on. Somehow Jim Stewart got me into a taxi and back to the hotel. We were flying early the next morning down to New Plymouth and going straight on to the field. Dennis Silk and Willie Watson weren't going and I was skippering the side. I remember getting there and thinking 'If I can win the toss, we can bat and I can have a sleep.' I lost the toss so we were straight out in the field. I wasn't in much of a state but fortunately we bowled them out quite cheaply. I got a fifty and David Allen got fifteen wickets – but it wasn't first-class.

After the win over Taranaki, Wanagarui and Rangitikei – and in the state he was in Jim would have had difficulty in pronouncing the names of his opponents – he missed the last game at Christchurch ten days later. 'I had a job standing up, especially at a bar, which was very unfortunate. David Allen was right when he said I had to be wrapped in cotton-wool and a jock-strap. I was in danger of losing one of them but it gradually just got better.' Rain in Christchurch ensured that the game was drawn and that New Zealand won the representative matches. Jim had had an enjoyable tour off the field. 'It was a very social tour – an extremely happy trip', and although he averaged over 37 with the bat the prospects for his international career behind the stumps seemed to have receded in the face of the stiff competition from the stylishly immaculate stumper from Middlesex, who could also bat with polished resolution. As *Wisden* noted, 'Murray, the Middlesex wicketkeeper… came right to the fore.'[5]

Rene and the boys had had a relaxing three months with her relations in Lyttleton and even if Jim was away touring with the MCC they had more opportunity of seeing him than if they had stayed in Haywards Heath. They returned home in mid-March. John Murray remembers:

> Jim saw them off on the boat from Wellington just before we flew to Singapore and Kuala Lumpur, where it was very hot and very humid. Jim got 50 in about a quarter of an hour and he came in absolutely drenched, even through the old-fashioned pads.

The party played a two-day game, and 'somebody was offering a champagne for every six that was hit. I hit I can't remember how many sixes and we had all this champagne in the dressing-room.'[6] The champagne in Malaysia was the last fling of a happy winter, as in 1961 'I wasn't really that fit early on and didn't play particularly well. John Murray had got in on the tour and went into the England side.' Although Jim had suffered a cricketing setback after the winter tour, he had developed another string to his bow. He had become a writer.

'I got to know John Graydon, who was editor of Provincial Newspapers and he ghosted my book *Runs in the Sun* – I didn't write it.' Ghosted or not, it appeared in the spring of 1961 and presaged a three-year association with Graydon, reporting football matches and learning how to write.

That spring held hope and promise. Kennedy had been inaugurated in Washington, Gagarin's space flight had opened new frontiers and closer to home the University of Sussex had been founded. Hard work by the County Welfare Association at Hove had seen the reconstruction of the pavilion and the refurbishment of the changing rooms. New players too suggested an exciting future. Appearing for the first time that season were wicketkeepers Terry Gunn and Robin Waters, Peter Ledden, Mike Buss and an intriguing new bowler, J.A. Snow. When Mike Buss joined his brother Tony in the side they became the twenty-eighth pair of brothers to play for the county.

The season opened with a succession of drawn games and Jim struggled for runs until at the end of May he scored his first county century at Eastbourne in a drawn game against Somerset. Once again the benign Saffrons wicket proved a tonic to a batsman out of form. Jim made 158 not out and remembers 'steering Brian Langford quite often – the ball was turning, but slowly and it was a fast outfield'. Buoyed by his hundred, Jim hot-footed it to Lord's for the MCC match against the touring Australians. They were an exceptionally powerful squad, with few obvious weaknesses. Along with the experience of Benaud, Harvey, Davidson and Simpson, they had elegant and powerful stroke-makers in Booth, Burge and O'Neill, and promising newcomers in Lawry and McKenzie, together with the world's best wicketkeeper, Wally Grout.

Jim did little at Lord's to make his place in the England side secure. Lawry and O'Neill made big hundreds and Jim took no catches, scoring 4 and a duck, leg before to Richie Benaud. Another chance came Jim's way when the tourists took the field at Hove, but it was already too late. The twelve for the First Test had been selected and when the team was announced on Sunday lunchtime, Murray was the chosen man. Jim took a philosophical view: 'I never felt right because of this injury and I was struggling for form.' Jim had a quiet game against the Aussies at Eaton Road, bowled by Benaud for 27, but it was an exciting match and a close finish, with any result possible in the final overs. Sussex totalled 336, thanks to 75 from Kenny Suttle and a stand of 107 for the eight wicket between Graham Cooper (62) and Ian Thomson (56).

The visitors' reply was dominated by Peter Burge with 158. Frank Misson's 6 for 75 in Sussex's second knock of 189 set the Australians 245 to win, and when they reached 184 for 3, they seemed home and dry. Three runs later they were rocking as Ronnie Bell took three quick wickets and Wally Grout was run out. Colin McDonald, with 116 not out, nursed the tail-enders but at the death the tourists were 9 runs short of a nail-biting victory.

Jim was unhappy with his game and, still not fully fit, took a few days off after Nottinghamshire were beaten by 60 runs at Hove, where Suttle kept in the second innings. He kept the gloves against Surrey as Terry Gunn, Jim's regular stand-in, was injured and after Surrey had triumphed by eight wickets, the side won six and drew four of the next twelve championship games. Gradually for Jim the pendulum swung. Towards the end of June, as Elvis Presley's *Surrender* yielded to Del Shannon's classic *Runaway* at the top of the charts, his season turned the corner. An 87 at Bristol and 67 at Guildford (where Surrey were beaten by five wickets) were followed by 74 at Ashby de la Zouch where, despite the cold fish and chips, Sussex won by 215 runs. He then had a 'good July without any big scores' – and thirty-eight victims with the gloves.

The Steetley Company Ground at Shireoaks, a suburb north of Worksop, holds a unique place in Sussex's cricketing story. The fixture against Sussex early in July was the only first-class game ever played on the ground and it was the scene of Alan Oakman's only double century in his long career. 'I got my highest score – 229 – at Worksop. It was a small ground and a very flat wicket.' For the home side, left-handed opener Norman Hill scored 201, *his* only double hundred, as Nottinghamshire made 350 for 4 declared. Sussex declared a run ahead after an unbroken partnership of 145 between Oakman and Jim (57). Left 166 to win, Sussex cruised to a nine-wicket victory.

Three more wins that month, over Lancashire and Kent at Hastings and Hampshire at Hove, took the side in good heart down to Portsmouth. Jim had made another three half-centuries, but for him and the team, the train hit the buffers at the United Services Ground. Late on the second day Sussex were 141 ahead. Jim takes up the story:

> It was nearly half past seven and getting dark. Butch White had been bowling a long time, Ted was facing Malcolm Heath and smashing him all over the place and I was fending Butch off at the other end. I said, 'Let's appeal against the light. This isn't very good.' Ted said, 'No, it's fine.' The next over we lost four wickets, starting with me, so from being 179 for 4 we were suddenly 179 for 8. Portsmouth wasn't a great ground for seeing. The next morning the last two got out, we'd lost six for one run and Dexter didn't get any more of the bowling. He was not best pleased and we lost the match by six wickets.

It had been a bad week for the skipper. He had come to Portsmouth straight from losing the Ashes at Old Trafford and his appearance in the Oval Test meant that he missed the debut of the man destined to become the greatest

English fast bowler of his generation. On a low, slow wicket at Cardiff John
Snow took 2 for 12 as Glamorgan could muster only 95 in reply to Sussex's
270. A century by Alan Oakman helped stand-in captain Don Smith set the
Welshmen 323 to win and despite Jim Pressdee's 115 they went down by 124
runs, Snow taking a further 3 for 67. The rector's son from Bognor had made
his mark, and at Worthing he came across the demarcation, still prevalent in
the early sixties, between amateurs and professionals. He found the dressing-
room where most of the players were changing only to be shown the door.
He was in the pros' room. As a public school boy and a clergyman's son, he
was further along with the amateurs. The match was a famous *tour de force* for
Maurice Hallam, who made 203 and 143, both undefeated. He took many of
his runs off Snow. 'Don advised him not to bounce me. He did though as he
was a bit raw, which was meat and drink to me as I preferred to play off the
back foot.' Eventually Smith took him off, saying 'There's a bit of stick flying around so I'll take it.' Jim could only stand and admire the fluent stroke
play of the man he had first seen at Wyggeston School fourteen years earlier.
'We didn't have a really quick bowler till Snow so we never saw Maurice
play against genuinely fast bowling. He was a fine batsman who never got
a smell of an England place. Had he played for Middlesex or Surrey, more
fashionable counties, it might have been different but there was still that
metropolitan bias.' Hallam's achievement left Sussex chasing 326 to win and
Jack Birkenshaw's 5 for 126 left them 62 runs short. For once it had been a
Worthing wicket made for assured batting, with the hosts on the wrong end
of 1,200 runs in three days.

Jim ended a humdrum season with a seaside jaunt to the East Riding for
T.N. Pearce's XI against the Australians at Scarborough, where at last he got
runs against the tourists. On a 'pretty good wicket with not too much pace'
he made a pleasant 60. But it was all too little too late. Murray had made
the keeping berth his own. It had been a season dogged by injury in which
'Smith, Parks and the left-handed Suttle remained the backbone of the
run-getting.'[7]

That winter, his first at home for three years, Jim worked in Fleet Street
covering soccer matches and preparing *The Book of Cricket*, which Stanley
Paul published in the spring. Jim edited an ideal stocking-filler for a teenage
cricket fan, persuading friends like David Allen, Bob Barber, Brian Close, Ted
Dexter, Geoff Pullar, Mike Smith and Ian Thomson to write short pieces
with titles such as 'Learning the Art of Batsmanship', 'The Art of Spinning'
and 'The Real Value of the All-Rounder'. Comprehensively illustrated, its
128 pages confirmed Jim as, if not a leading writer on the game, a player
who was developing another useful string to his bow.

1. *Right:* James Horace Parks, Sussex and England, 1924–1939.

2. *Below left:* Henry W. 'Harry' Parks, Sussex, 1926–48.

3. *Below left:* Jim Parks Snr, James Langridge and Harry Parks at Hove.

4. Three generations of cricketers – Jim, his father, and Bobby, his son. Jim Snr proudly holds the silver salver presented to him in 1937 to commemorate his unique double of 3,000 runs and 100 wickets.

5. Lindfield *v.* Mark Parks XII on Lindfield Common, August 1945, in aid of the Pavilion Extension Fund. In the front row Jim Snr. has the pads, young Jim sits on the extreme right in his school cap next to his uncle, Mark, and uncle Charlie is in the centre of the second row with the dark blazer.

6. 'No, Parks, that's the Sahara Desert. They don't play cricket there.' Mr Andrew, Jim's housemaster and geography teacher, makes a point to Jim and Ken Dean.

7. Hove County School cricket team, 1947. Jim is seated on the extreme right of the front row – recognise the cap? Geoff Sear, later a football team-mate at Haywards Heath, stands behind Jim and John Stanbrook is twelfth man (in civvies). Mr. Griffiths is the master-in-charge.

8. Hove County School First XI football, 1947–48. Jim is seated second from the left in the front row. Geoff Sear stands behind, second from the right. 'Basher' Bates, Don Bates's father, is the master in charge.

9. Haywards Heath FC at Whitehawk in the late 1940s. Jim and Geoff Sear are in precisely the same positions as they were at school – in plate 8!

10. *Above left:* The boys in blue! Four RAF cricketers. At the top: Fred Trueman (Yorkshire) and Dennis Heath (Warwickshire). At the bottom: Roland Thompson (Warwickshire) and Jim.

11. *Above right:* Jim sweeps his hero, Denis Compton, at Lord's as Bill Edrich and wicketkeeper Leslie Compton watch the ball race to the long-leg boundary.

12. Jim comes of age at Tunbridge Wells, June 1951. His innings of 188 gains him his Sussex county cap.

13. Sussex CCC, 1953, Championship runners-up. Back row, from left to right: Rupert Webb, Jim, Alan Oakman, Don Bates, Ted James, Ken Suttle. Seated: George Cox, Jim Langridge, David Sheppard (captain), John Langridge, Jim Wood.

Chosen For The Third Test

Jim Parks and his wife with the telegram telling him he is to play in the Test match, at their home in Haywards Heath.

JIM PARKS IS 'A BIT AMAZED'

FROM the bedroom window of her home in Wivelsfield-road, Haywards Heath, early today, 76-year-old Mrs. E. M. Parks watched a second generation of her family set out to play cricket for England.

Outside on the bus stop was her 22-year-old grandson, Jim Parks, selected for his country in only his second full season in first-class cricket.

14. *Left:* Jim and Irene with the telegram as he is chosen for his Test debut, July 1954.

15. *Below:* Sussex CCC 5-a-side indoor football team – winners of the *Evening Argus* tournament, February, 1955. From left: Ian Thomson, David Mantell, Don Bates, Ken Suttle, Jim, Gordon Potter and Sam Cowan, trainer.

16. *Right:* Jim in action for Hove Town FC, 1958.

17. *Below:* Jim catches John Warr, the Middlesex captain, off Ian Thomson as he makes his wicketkeeping debut at Lord's.

18. Jim receives the trophies for the fastest century and the most victims by a wicketkeeper from his boyhood hero, Denis Compton, 1959.

19. Jim pulls Ramadhin for four on the way to his first Test hundred at Port of Spain, March 1960.

20. Alan Oakman, Les Lenham, Jim and Ian Thomson off to the nets, Hove, 1960.

21. Jim, with Andrew, and Irene (holding Bobby) about to embark for New Zealand, November 1960.

22. 'My best catch!' Jim dives to snaffle South Africa's Colin Wesley at Trent Bridge, July 1960.

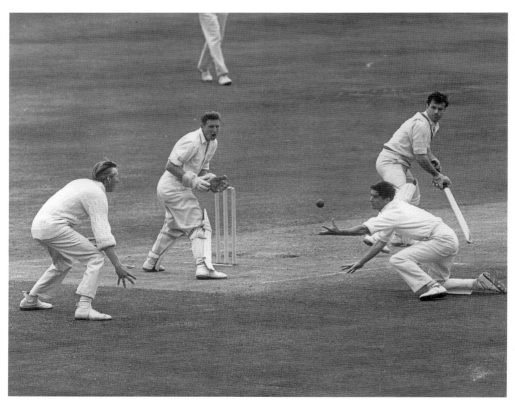

23. *Above:* Sussex *v.* Middlesex,
Lord's, June 1963. Don Bennett
is dropped in the gully by
Richard Langridge, to the
dismay of Alan Oakman at slip
and Jim behind the stumps.

24. *Left:* Gillette Cup *v.*
Yorkshire at Hove, June 1963.
Jim, Man of the Match, is
congratulated by Alec Bedser.

25 *Left:* Barrington and Sharpe salute Jim as he snaps up Deryck Murray off Fred Trueman in the Third Test at Edgbaston, June 1963.

26. *Below:* Sussex win the first-ever Gillette Cup, September 1963. From left to right; Les Lenham, Jim, Alan Oakman, Graham Cooper, Ted Dexter, Richard Langridge, Ken Suttle, Tony Buss, Ian Thomson, Don Bates, John Snow.

27. A smart piece of work as Jim runs out Lawry for 3 in Australia's second innings at Trent Bridge, June 1964.

28. *Above left:* Sussex *v.* the Australians, one-day challenge, Hove, 1964. Jim and Bill Lawry walk out for the toss.

29. *Above right:* Jim acknowledges the applause after reaching his century in the First Test at Durban, December 1964. He went on to make 108 not out, his highest Test score.

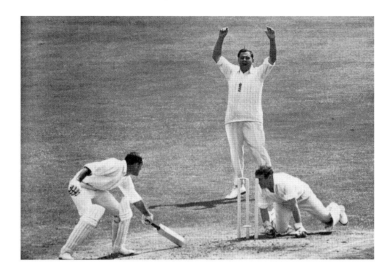

30. Cowdrey celebrates as Jim stumps Colin Bland in South Africa's first innings, Trent Bridge, August 1965.

31. Jim is caught by Wally Grout off Neil Hawke for 15 in the Third Test at Sydney, January 1966.

32. Basil D'Oliviera is run out on his Test debut, Lord's, 1966. Jim's drive bounced off D'Olivera's heel and Wes Hall breaks the wicket as umpire Buller looks on.

33. The First Test at Old Trafford, June 1966. Jim pulls Sobers for 2 in England's first innings. Charlie Griffith is at slip.

34. England's team for Jim's penultimate Test at Trent Bridge, July 1966. From left to right, back row: Geoff Boycott, Eric Russell, John Snow, Basil D'Oliviera, Colin Milburn, Derek Underwood. Front row: Ray Illingworth, Jim, Colin Cowdrey, Tom Graveney, Ken Higgs.

35. Jim wins a trophy with England, Lord's, September 1966. Cowdrey holds the World Cup trophy watched by (from left): Barry Knight, Fred Titmus, Basil D'Oliviera, John Edrich, Peter Parfitt, Jim, Ted Dexter, John Murray, John Snow and Ken Higgs.

36. *Above:* The MCC party in the West Indies, 1967–68. Back row, left to right: J. Jennings (physiotherapist), Alan Knott, Jeff Jones, Pat Pocock, David Brown, John Snow, Basil D'Oliviera, Colin Milburn, Robin Hobbs, Leslie Ames (manager). Front row: Geoff Boycott, Ken Higgs, Tom Graveney, Colin Cowdrey (captain), Fred Titmus, Ken Barrington, Jim, John Edrich.

37. *Left:* Jim and Ted Dexter, Hove, 1968.

38. Old England XI, 1994. Back row from left to right: Roger Tolchard, Geoff Humpage, Bobby Parks, Tom Cartwright, Pat Pocock, Robin Hobbs, Derek Randall. Front row: John Snow, Alan Oakman, Jim, Brian Luckhurst, John Lever.

39. Golf the easy way! Jim and Jenny in Florida, 1995.

Dexter had captained England in India and Pakistan during the winter, scoring over 1,000 runs and making his highest first-class score, 205, at Dacca. He returned in prime form, but his absence had exerted pressure on Jim and his colleagues. The side won twice in May, winning away at Trent Bridge, where Jim made 80 and 83 not out and beating the touring Pakistanis at Hove while they were still acclimatising to an English early summer – but it was the game against Nottinghamshire at the Saffrons which really got the season under way.

Dexter offered the visitors first use of a beautifully flat Eastbourne pitch and 'Norman Hill, their one decent batsman, got a big hundred and the rest were pretty ordinary.'[8] Hill made 193, Andrew Corran declared at 406 for 8, and on the Thursday Oakman (177) and Dexter enjoyed themselves, the skipper plundering 114 in 97 minutes of hard hitting all round the wicket. By tea Dexter was able to declare at 423 for 4. 'We batters liked playing at Eastbourne', said the captain, but the bowlers hated it. 'You could pitch a wicket anywhere in those days and the ball didn't deviate at all. Tommo and I used to feign injury sometimes as it was such a perfect batting track.'[9]

At tea on the second day, Corran appeared in the Sussex dressing-room and said, 'Look, it's a beautiful wicket. If we leave you 110 an hour, will you go for them?' The topic in the dressing-room had been 'How long will Notts bat, and what will they leave us?' As the side took the field after tea, Ian Thomson had a word with his skipper. Knowing Dexter liked a bit of an experiment, he said, 'I think I'll have a change. I'm going to bowl quicker and go round the wicket.' Jim caught Winfield off Bates in his first over, Geoff Millman was farcically run out and soon Nottinghamshire had lost three wickets before the scores were level. Panic set in.

> Batesy would bowl a long hop and they'd hit it up into the air somewhere.
> Next minute they were gone – loads of mistakes, and Norman Hill, the
> opener, who'd got 193 first whack, was at one end, 25 not out and couldn't
> believe what was going on![10]

On an absolutely perfect wicket, Corran's men were all out for 57. 'Yes, we bowled them out but they were a very poor batting side and when suddenly wickets started to clatter it was one of those amazing things that happen in cricket.'[11] Jim and Alan Oakman knocked off the 41 they needed and an incredible game of cricket was over in less than two days. Don Bates thinks it 'was the most remarkable game I ever played in.'

Straight from this triumph Middlesex were beaten by six wickets at headquarters in Alan Moss's benefit and then at Tunbridge Wells Kenny Suttle made the highest score of his long career – 204 not out against Kent. The captain led the way with 6 for 63 and then supported Suttle with 114 of his own as the side led by 206 on first innings. Kent could muster only 185 as Dexter completed his ten-wicket haul plus a hundred in the match. He repeated the feat against Surrey at the Oval in July. Sheppard had returned in a bid to be included in the party for Australia in the winter, but 'both my innings were undistinguished. I was really struggling to get runs anywhere at that moment' and Sussex made only 158. However, when the hosts replied, Dexter took 7 for 38 to restrict them to a lead of only 26. He then smashed 94 in quick time to leave Surrey to score 216 in two sessions. At tea they were 197 for 3 and cruising, so much so that a friend of Mickey Stewart, who had said 'I'll get along later, just after tea, if you'd leave me tickets on the gate,' was told, 'There's not much point, we only want 30 and we've got seven wickets left. It'll be all over.' Stewart was right – after tea when Barrington was run out, Dexter and Bell took three wickets each and Sussex won by 10 runs!

Jim was having a satisfactory if not dazzling season. By the end of July he had made 1,205 runs and had captured sixty victims. More wins over Lancashire and Leicestershire, along with three defeats, most painfully by Kent at Hastings, brought the side to Hove for the Bank Holiday fixture against Middlesex in reasonable heart. Then came a bombshell, the repercussions of which still echoed a decade later.

> They wanted to play the amateur wicketkeeper, Robin Waters. Ted fought the Cricket Committee and I remember him coming to me in the dressing-room and saying, 'I'm sorry, I've lost. They want you to skipper the Second XI to get experience of captaincy.' I retorted, 'Cobblers!' I'd already been skippering the side at different times. That was just their excuse.

So Jim was left out. He did not play at Scarborough nor at Portsmouth, but was recalled *in extremis* against Surrey at Hove after Waters had an absolute nightmare:

> I refused to keep wicket after that and when they asked me to come back and keep, because he had done so badly, I said, 'You can get lost.' I played as a batsman for the rest of the season and I was going to give up keeping.

Surrey won easily and Jim made some runs, but he was disillusioned that 'it was still happening, that late in life – having to make way for amateurs in August. I was getting runs that year and the keeping had gone very well.'

While 'Lord Ted' was taking the Pakistanis for 172 at the Oval, Jim had another chance to gain 'experience of captaincy' at Hove against Hampshire.

Waters was keeping wicket, so 'I bowled all afternoon and took 2 for 37. The problem was that Butch got his second hat-trick in successive years against us. He was a good bowler – used to make it duck in at you.' Robin Waters had the gloves for the rest of the season, enabling Jim to take one last wicket as Gloucestershire won the final game by 7 runs on the penultimate ball.

It had been a disturbing month. 'I was going to pack up keeping and then I thought during the winter, "No, sod it. I'll go in the nets and work hard."' And he did, though Jim still found time to work for United Newspapers and to edit his first *Commonwealth Book of Cricket* for Stanley Paul. Essentially the same format as the *Book of Cricket* a year before, the grander title was justified by the inclusion of articles by Wes Hall, Norman O'Neill and Bobbie Simpson. The first words Jim wrote in the book, in a piece about the West Indian tourists, were curiously prophetic: '1963… a year that could go down in the annals of cricket history as the year when our national game staged a revival.' These hopes for the future of English cricket were to be played out in the renaissance of his own career.

Pivotal in Jim's re-emergence as a Test player was, ironically enough, the birth of one-day cricket. The catalyst for this seismic change was the popularity in 1962 of the Cavaliers, who pioneered swashbuckling cricket played to a finish in one entertaining afternoon. Gillette saw that sports sponsorship was a relatively cheap and unexplored source of advertising and that cricket, with its traditionally wholesome image, was ripe for exploitation. In 1963 the company offered the counties £6,500 as prize money for the first one-day, 65-over competition. Sussex – especially its cavalier captain – embraced this innovation, and 'the new tactics for the Gillette Cup games emerged in Ted's head. Whereas other captains treated it as a form of county cricket cut down to one day, we defended our total from the word go.'[12] Alan Oakman remembers the dressing-room talk:

> Dexter had got us together and he said, 'Look, we're never going to win the Championship, but with our attack, and our batting, we can win this.' He said, 'We will bat first, provided we win the toss. If we don't, you'll find the others will put us in.' So we would bat first, the opening pair would play properly for 20 overs or so, then Parkser, Suttle, Dexter and Graham Cooper would get you runs.

For this new form of the game, Sussex had 'the ideal side – a battery of seamers, Snow, Buss, Bates, Dexter and Tommo – Snowy and Tommo could also hold a bat – Ted, me and Kenny, as well as Oaky bowling off-spin. We were a good fielding side – the only one we had to hide was Tony Buss who

lumbered about at third man and didn't have a very good arm. Richard
Langridge was a good close fielder, as was Graham Cooper.'[13]

Sussex discovered early that good form in the traditional game was carried
over, in terms of confidence and success, into the new format. By the middle
of June the side had won six Championship games and stood on the verge
of a Gillette Cup semi-final. Jim had made 616 runs and had taken nearly
forty victims. Dexter's side had lost only once, spectacularly, by 175 runs to
Northamptonshire at Worthing. Laurie Johnson, the visitors' keeper, held five
catches in each innings to equal the world record and David Larter took 8 for
41 as Dexter's side chased 293 on the final afternoon. Jim had made 82 in an
innings victory over Glamorgan at Hove and Leicester had been vanquished
by eight wickets at Grace Road when the side arrived at the Nevill Ground
as Championship leaders for their first-ever Gillette Cup match.

Batting first on a good wicket, Dexter with power and Suttle with,
well – subtlety – took the score to 127 for 3 at lunch. In the afternoon,
the little left-hander completed his hundred and Jim, driving gracefully off
'Underwood, a promising young bowler, who, on green wickets could dismiss or contain the best batsmen',[14] reached 59 when 'Les Lenham came in
and ran me out.' Sussex hit 97 off the last 11 overs to total 314 for 7. Kent
started quickly but despite Man of the Match Peter Richardson's 127, they
never looked like getting the runs. Dexter's tactics had worked encouragingly, as Underwood recalls:

> They batted first and got a huge total: I disappeared – 0 for 87. When we
> batted everybody went back on the boundary. I hadn't bowled in that form
> of cricket, none of us had, and we didn't know quite how to play it. We were
> venturing into the unknown.

Some felt that Sussex's approach just wasn't cricket: 'We had a letter from
their Chairman afterwards saying our attitude towards the game was diabolical.'[15] Diabolical attitude or not, Sussex kept on winning. Tony Buss's 8
for 65 beat Nottinghamshire at Trent Bridge, where Jim made 41 and 65,
and Hampshire were beaten at Hove. In the bank holiday game at Lord's
Dexter's men won by 1 run, Jim scoring 71 in his best man's benefit match,
but it was the Gillette Cup game against Yorkshire at Hove which set the
season on fire.

This was the best knockout game Jim ever played in. Dexter won the toss
and batted. Sussex made a slow start against steady bowling, but when Jim
arrived at 126 for 3 the innings gained momentum and once he reached his
fifty after seventy minutes, he 'hit Tony Nicholson over extra cover a lot.

The ball was coming on to the bat a bit quickly and therefore it went a little bit finer. I hit two or three sixes square over point off the front foot', one of which landed in the top of the pavilion. Then he hooked Mel Ryan for six, striking a spectator, and Jim had scored 30 off eight balls – 6, 4, 6, 1,6, 2, 4, 1 – before he fell lbw to Nicholson for 90. He had scored his last 40 in fifteen minutes. Geoffrey Boycott was in only his second season at Headingley:

> I had never seen anybody play like that. Tony Nicholson bowled outswing-ers and nip-back balls from the Sea End and Jim hit him inside out twice over extra cover for six into the pavilion. I'd grown up in league cricket in Yorkshire, which was pretty tough and in the sort of climate we have in the north, these were hard-fought matches on green, wet wickets and nobody hit inside out over cover-point. You just didn't do that. It was unbelievable – amazing shots.

The last four wickets added only 26 and the home side were all out for 292 in the 64th over.

Yorkshire started steadily and accelerated. 'That was the first time we saw Boycott and he played all the shots. He'd got 70 when, had we not run him out, I think Yorkshire would have won.'[16] With 30 wanted and two wickets left, Boycott steered Tony Buss to third man where 'off balance, Ian Thomson picked up and in one movement flung a magnificent throw straight into my gloves. I hardly had to move to run him out.' Boycott had nearly won the game but 'we saw Closey running down the stairs and we reckoned that he 'd given him a right bollocking. He'd been looking for runs for himself which of course he did all his life.'[17] In gathering gloom Jim caught Nicholson off Buss and Yorkshire ended 22 short. It had been a famous victory over a Yorkshire side packed with Test players like Trueman, Close, Phil Sharpe, Doug Padgett, Jimmy Binks and John Hampshire. As darkness fell the pitch was invaded by hundreds of the Sussex faithful who applauded wildly as Alec Bedser presented Jim with his Man of the Match award, £50, which he generously and typically shared among his team-mates.

These were heady times at Hove, where the old ground welcomed the touring West Indians a week later. Although Sussex lost by six wickets, Wisden records that

> Sussex fought back splendidly, in their second innings, attacking the bowling from the start… Suttle, who had to retire for a time after being hit on the head, and Parks also batted well, but even so the touring team needed only 113 to win.[18]

Gerald Brodribb, ever the chronicler of the bizarre in this noblest of pas-
times, noted that:

> N.I. Thomson of Sussex gained a… four when he made a hit to square-leg off
> A.L. Valentine. A black dog bounded on to the field, seized the ball and carried
> it over the boundary line. The umpires considered that the hit would have
> reached without the dog's help.[19]

Jim had needed no help, canine or otherwise, to return to his best form.
Murray was injured: 'I had busted my shoulder catching Lawry at Sydney',
and for the first Test at Trent Bridge the normally reliable Keith Andrew
had been drafted. He 'knew by halfway through that first day that I hadn't
made a good impression'. He asked Ted Dexter, '"Shall I stand back?" "No,
stand up", he said… I think he'd got it in his mind, "They say this fellow's a
good wicketkeeper; let's see how good he is".'[20] Dexter might also have been
thinking, 'I know a fellow down at Hove who's likely to get me more runs.'
In the event, with the First Test highlighting the lack of depth in England's
batting, it was inevitable that a keeper with more batting prowess would be
brought in. So Jim was recalled for Lord's. 'We were playing a benefit match
in Seaford on the Sunday. I wasn't listening to the radio and someone came
running round and said "You're in the Test side".'

Chapter 9
Back in Harness

Ted Dexter thinks the Second Test in 1963 was arguably the greatest match ever seen at Lord's: Jim feels it was the finest cricket match he ever played in. 'Fortunes fluctuated all the way through and in the last over you could have had any result.' David Allen, who stood between England and defeat in that dramatic final over, described it as 'a tremendous game.'

The selectors dropped Brian Statham and recalled Derek Shackleton after a gap of eleven years, a controversial choice. 'I'm not saying that Shackleton wasn't a good bowler – he was,' says Brian Close, 'but he'd no pace and that's what you needed at Lord's. If Statham and Freddie had played we would have won that game.' On the first morning Shackleton 'beat the bat so many times it was amazing'[1] and at stumps West Indies were 245 for 6, Sobers, Kanhai and Solomon making runs. The next morning, the total stood at 297 for 7 when Shackleton dismissed Solomon, Griffith and Gibbs in four balls. Allen thought England were unlucky not to bowl them out for less but Cowdrey was more positive: '301 was not a losing total, quite clearly, but the English attack, shorn of a third seam bowler, could be reasonably satisfied with the result.'

The English reply began disastrously and at lunch the home side were 20 for 2. Then 'Lord Ted' played an innings which the author, riveted to a black and white TV in a university common room, will never forget:

> I decided that I was going to take Hall and Griffith on. We'd had a bit of experience of their bowling in West Indies and they were obviously going to be a handful. Some people are better off just fighting them ball by ball, but I liked to get stuck into them

and he did. He hit 70 in eighty minutes against extreme pace – 'sustained violence that took England right back into the game.[2] For Cowdrey, 'it was not a huge score in the Bradman vein; it was not a technical exhibition in the Hutton vein; it was not cavalier in the Compton vein; it was a brand of his own,' and for Jim, what marked it out as special was 'the contemptuous manner

with which he dealt with Hall and Griffith.' He hit 10 fours and wrested the
initiative from the attack. He perished at 102, leg before to Sobers, whereupon
Barrington took command and put on 55 with Jim before being caught in
the covers for 80. Titmus came in and, with Jim on 35, Frank Worrell bowled
him with a straight one. At the close England were 244 for 7. The gates were
closed on the Saturday ten minutes before the start, and they saw Titmus and
Shackleton eke out a last-wicket partnership of 23. England finished on 297
with the tough Middlesex all-rounder 52 not out.

At lunch the West Indies were 15 for 2, both openers having fallen to
smart slip catches by Cowdrey, and soon after the break he took a third to
get rid of Kanhai. Then Jim 'had the great satisfaction of catching the mighty
Sobers off the bowling of Fred Trueman' and Allen 'got Joey Solomon again.
I turned one down the slope and Mickey Stewart caught him round the
corner.' The West Indies were 104 for 5 and seemingly heading for defeat
when Jim believes that one umpiring decision

> changed the course of the game. Sid Buller gave Frank Worrell not out when
> Fred Titmus bowled this little flighter down the hill, Frank dragged his foot
> and I took the bails off. I can remember looking at Sid Buller and pointing
> – he was still out of his ground. Sid gave him not out, he got 30-odd and that
> saved the match for them.

Basil Butcher got together with his skipper and took the score to 214 for 5
at the close. On a sensational Monday morning the pendulum swung again.
Almost at once Worrell was brilliantly caught by Stewart, Trueman rose to
the occasion and the last five wickets fell for 15 in 6 overs in 25 minutes.
Butcher, ninth out, had batted admirably for his 133.

Needing 234 to win, English hopes plummeted when Edrich, Stewart and
Dexter were out for 31, but Barrington and Cowdrey steadied the ship. With
the Kent man on 72, however, Hall made one lift off a length: 'I thrust out
my left forearm to parry the ball and a few moments later I was walking off
the field, disconsolately out of the match.' Doug Insole came to the rescue:

> I drove him down in thick traffic to Bill Tucker's surgery at Park Street to
> have the arm x-rayed and set so that he could come back and bat if necessary.
> I remember parking my car and sticking a sheet of paper on the windscreen
> saying 'Do not tow away – Colin Cowdrey inside'.

Close joined the fray and before bad light ended the day Barrington hit Gibbs
for 2 sixes in one over to leave England 116 for 3, needing another 118.

The Yorkshire legend describes the last day:

> We didn't start till half past two – then we kept having to go off. Frank Worrell rested them each time and they were ready to charge in again. We would have won it if it hadn't been for all the rain delays. Charlie was devastating, Wes was bloody frightening and they bowled all the time. It was a fight for survival and we had to score against the clock.

Hall and Griffith opened up on a lively pitch and 'most of the scoring during these opening exchanges was done by Close, and there was not much of it,'[3] the first hour realising only 18 runs. Then Barrington was caught behind off Griffith for 60, and Jim joined Close, who was playing courageously. 'Parks was freer with his strokes after surviving, off his first ball from Griffith, a concerted appeal for leg-before. He lived for long enough to add 28 with Close and to display two ravishing cover-drives off Griffith.'[4] Jim was beginning to enjoy himself when, at 17, and the score at 158, 'Griffith put one in a bit short, I stepped back for a hook but the ball came through lower than I expected and I was lbw.' At tea England were 171 for 5, with four wickets left and Cowdrey to bat in an emergency. David Allen thought 'things looked a bit iffy. We knew how bad his arm was, but dear old Kipper was going to bat almost one-handed.'

After tea, Titmus helped Close edge the score to 203 before he was caught off Hall. Next ball Trueman heaved at a wide one and Murray took the catch. It was 203 for 7 and Brian Close decided to charge the fast bowlers:

> When the bowler got about five yards from the crease I picked up my bat and walked towards him. We needed about four and a half an over – in Test cricket that's bloody fast – and I was in with tail-enders and I thought, 'I've got to do it. When I walked towards Wes, he picked his head up as it had never happened to him before. Frankie Worrell had to go and put his arm round him and cuddle him. I reckoned that if I got myself in the way of the ball, they couldn't give me out lbw down the wicket that far and I might get a free shot. It worked for a bit because it upset Wes.

Suddenly England had reached 219, with Allen urging Close on. 'I said to Brian, "Keep it going. Keep batting. You've seen it through." ' Then, with about three overs to go he did the same at Charlie. Close says:

> He was a chucker, but he didn't chuck all of them. When he bowled properly you could play him with one hand in your pocket because he was medium

pace, but suddenly the ball would come at you three or four yards quicker and it was either the yorker or the bouncer. I thought if I got one pitched up I could get it through Kanhai at mid-wicket for four runs and we could get the rest in singles… Anyway, I walked down the wicket and Charlie chucked this bloody bouncer in. When you chuck a ball, it cuts. It causes the ball to rotate and it goes against the arm. This bouncer pitched and went up the bloody hill at Lord's – and got the underneath of my bat, went between my upper arm and chest through to the keeper.

Close had played one of the bravest innings David Allen had ever seen. 'You couldn't criticise him – if he'd got the 20 or 30 we needed at that stage it would have been one of the greatest innings ever to win a game. He took his shirt off in the dressing-room and there was hardly a spot on his right-hand side and chest which wasn't black and blue.' No helmets then:

We had bugger-all protection. I didn't even have a vest. The only danger was your head and providing you keep your eyes on the ball you can move your head faster than you can move any other part of your body. I got my hands out of the way every time it lifted. When Wes pitched the ball from the Pavilion End just short of a length, it flew and that's how we lost Cowdrey. Playing quick bowlers, you've got to get behind the line and if it lifts you take the bat out of the way. Oh, the book title! I wanted to call it *I Took the Blows* – you know, from the Frank Sinatra song. I bruise the same way as anybody else – I just don't let it worry me.

Close's heroic 70 had brought England to the brink of a memorable win and David Allen 'scrambled a few singles till we needed 8 off the last over. Shack could bat a little bit, like all the old pros, and at the beginning of the over I said, "Shack, the wicketkeeper's back – whatever happens, the first ball you miss, I'm going to run. There will be no call." The reason for that was, as long as one of us was down at the striking end we knew Cowdrey could come in. We nurdled a couple amid excruciating tension.' Six to win. The fourth ball 'went through to Murray and I ran and I realised too late Shack hadn't set off. I yelled, "For Christ's sake run, Shack, run!" Murray hurled the ball to Frank Worrell and Frank beat Shack to the bowler's end. He daren't throw because there was no one backing up. The West Indies almost started walking off and there was a tremendous hubbub. I just stood there – and in came Kipper.'

It remains one of the iconic images in English sport. Cowdrey walked down the pavilion steps, 'with two balls to go, his left arm encased in plaster, with any of the four results technically possible. England needed six to win, West Indies had one wicket to take, the light was fading fast, the crowd could scarcely cast their eyes upon the scene.'[5]

Allen asked Cowdrey what was happening. 'He replied, "We're one down in the series, we don't want to go two down, but if there's an opportunity, we'll take it." In other words, get as many runs as you can, but don't get out.' Mercifully it was Allen facing the bowling. He pushed the fifth ball back to Hall, who 'in utter silence, tossed it from hand to hand and looked imploringly at the sky. He began to run, gold crucifix flying out behind him. England could win with a six. West Indies could win with a wicket. It was probably the fastest ball of Hall's life. It seared straight for Allen's middle stump. But Allen leant forward like a master and met it with a bold British bat. Cricket's greatest last over was done.'[6]

Jim motored down to Guildford next morning and got a duck, caught by Ken Barrington off Tony Lock, who took 6 for 39 as Sussex were shot out for 139 on 'an old-fashioned county pitch, grassy but not firm, really a club wicket, with each ball taking out little divots.' There were a few Test batsmen on view – Barrington, Edrich and Stewart, as well as Jim and Ted Dexter, and they all struggled. Peter May however, 'head and shoulders above the rest of us... made it very difficult for the bowlers to find any sort of length' and 'had no inhibitions about hitting it over the top',[7] as he stroked 85 in Surrey's 238. Ronnie Bell took five wickets and in a game dominated by left-arm spinners, Lock five more as Jim top-scored with 46. The home side were left only 14 to knock off and won by nine wickets.

England had their only Test success that summer at Edgbaston, where 'Freddie bowled sensationally and got twelve in the match'.[8] In a low-scoring, rain-affected match, Jim had a quiet game but took 3 catches in the tourists' second innings as Trueman, with 7 for 44, took his last six wickets in 24 balls and skittled the West Indies for 91, England triumphing by 217 runs.

Keith Andrew, Jim's colleague from the Caribbean tour, was now Northamptonshire's captain, and on an overcast July day, with rain around, Sussex turned out at the County Ground for the first-ever Gillette Cup semi-final. Dexter won the toss and batted despite the cloudy conditions, but when Jim joined his captain at 49 for 3, his team were precariously placed. The many Sussex supporters who had journeyed from the south coast need not have worried. Exuberant, powerful hitting and enterprising running brought Dexter an imperious century and after Jim had driven Scott for a enormous six he essayed another over extra cover and was caught for a glorious 71. David Larter polished the innings off with a hat-trick and the home side were asked to score 293 to reach the final at Lord's. They never recovered from a farcical start as, in Don Bates's second over, 'they decided that as soon as it came past the bat they were going to run a bye. At the bowler's end Brian Reynolds called for a single and set off. I dropped my gloves and threw the stumps down underarm.' 5 for 1 on a rain-affected wicket – and when Dexter brilliantly caught Milburn at mid-off, only Roger Prideaux with a classy 73 offered any resistance. Sussex would meet Worcestershire in the inaugural final.

Jim made his only century of 1963 – that summer of the Beatles and the Beach Boys, of Martin Luther King, Christine Keeler and the Great Train Robbery – against Kent at Hastings, where the author, now promoted to operating the scoreboard, saw him hit 136 and 49 not out. The game was drawn, and he had to report to Headingley for the Fourth Test, with the series all square.

At Leeds England were simply steam-rollered by the power and panache of the West Indians. Kanhai made 92 and Sobers scored a century which Jim says he will never forget:

> The first ball he received from Derek Shackleton pitched about middle-and-leg and went over middle-and-off. Garry, attempting a forcing shot off the back foot, missed the ball altogether. He turned round to me and burst out laughing. 'Man, that was a good one.' He had a big backlift and brought the bat through so fast – it's the only time I ever felt the wind of the bat. Such a lovely man too – so laid-back. He feels, as I do, that cricket is a game to enjoy.

West Indies totalled 397 and 'England lost their first eight wickets for 93 in the face of the terrific pace of Griffith and only Jim Parks, Fred Titmus and Tony Lock at the end lifted them to 174.' Frank Worrell decided not to enforce the follow-on in the damp conditions and set England 453 to win. To follow his six in the first innings Griffith took three more as Close, with 56 and Jim, who top-scored with 57, led a valiant rearguard action.

> Charlie Griffith hit me on the arm at Headingley – one of the most painful blows I ever had. Closey was at the other end when I went in five minutes before lunch. The first ball was a yorker. The middle stump went flying out of the ground and I thought 'Ohhh!' John Langridge called 'No-ball!' John was at the bowler's end and called him for over-stepping – not for chucking, although it was a chuck. Next ball he bowled me a bouncer which hit me right on the elbow. It took about five minutes to get any feeling back.

Despite these heroics, England were never in the hunt and lost by 221 runs.

Meanwhile the county had lost at Edgbaston and when Jim caught up with them down the road at Chesterfield he came across his old tour captain from Pakistan. Carr's 136 enabled Derbyshire to declare at 339 for 9, then Jim 'went in No.3 for some reason and Les Jackson was bowling short. I was in a hooking mood – I wasn't usually – and I can remember hooking Les and getting a very quick 80 before lunch.' Bob Taylor took 6 catches in the Sussex innings and the match was drawn – as were the next two at Hove, where Jim made solid runs. He had fun as usual at the Saffrons, where

> Kenny Suttle kept wicket and I bowled – against Leicestershire. That was prob-ably the first time I bowled that year – I used to love it. We got bogged down at tea-time and Ted said, 'Take your pads off and have a bowl.' I gave Munden and Inman, two left-handers, the googly and Kenny got both of them. I didn't bother to get the pads back on.

The game highlighted the inestimable value to the county of Suttle's versa-tility. In addition to his victims behind the stumps he made 60 in the second innings and wrapped up a 124-run win with 2 for 17 with his left-arm spin – 'We'd do things like that in those days.'[9] The county won again – at Cheltenham – after which Jim and the skipper drove to the Oval hoping to square the Test series.

It was a vain hope. No batsman had made a century for England that sum-mer and the match at the Oval was no exception. Griffith took 6 for 71 as England made 275, Jim contributing 19, and although Phil Sharpe notched 83 second time around, the West Indies, with Hunte 108 not out, knocked off the 255 to win for the loss of only two wickets. Griffith had taken 32 wickets in the series but Jim and Ted were collecting evidence:

> We both took some 8mm film of Charlie Griffith in slow motion and on a rainy day showed it to the two umpires who came down to do the last match at Hove; one of them was a Test match umpire. He said, 'If we'd seen this we'd have called him.'

For Jim, 'the proof of an illegal action is in the follow-through'. Griffith collapsed sharply to the left in a way 'that the legitimate bowler would find difficult to imitate without doing himself an injury.'[10]

As Jim's season drew to a close, it rained almost all the week before the Gillette Cup final and the festival game at Hastings was abandoned without a ball being bowled. Thus far that summer Sussex had 'achieved their success through attrition rather than attack, which is, of course, contrary to the aims of the competition,'[11] but Dexter had mastered the one-day game.

> He was the first person to do so and it wasn't very attractive to watch. We had seamers that bowled back of a length and made it difficult to score. He was the first to push the field back, to take out second slip and put him in front of the wicket to stop the singles. I remember the initial crowd reaction.[12]

However, at Lord's on that damp and drizzly Saturday

> the atmosphere was full of excitement. It was like Yorkshire and Lancashire with the lid off. There was some of the ribaldry of Eton and Harrow before the war; and at times devotees from Dudley and aficionados from Angmering found themselves reacting to a boundary hit more like West Indians than Englishmen of traditional reserve.[13]

On a day not made for stroke-play, 'only Parks played with the dash and distinction of other rounds. Oakman and Langridge provided a good beginning, with Langridge the more forceful. Their opening stand of 63 had a big influence on the match... The pitch was inevitably slow; the ball would turn, and only Parks' handsome driving gave impetus to the innings.'[14] Certainly it was not easy to play shots 'yet our score of 168 still gave us a chance. People didn't really have a measure of what a par score was.'[15]

When Worcestershire batted,

> Sussex's tactics were unashamedly defensive and insidiously effective. Where Kenyon had, for the opening overs, placed two slips, a gully and a short leg, Dexter had only one close fielder, a slip, for Thomson and Buss. This made for a hard match and a slow rate of scoring.[16]

Although the pitch had dried out somewhat, it still thwarted 'all but the finest drivers and once Kenyon was leg-before to a break-back and Horton had been brilliantly caught and bowled it was up to Headley and Graveney to mount the challenge.'[17] It was then that 'Alan Oakman bowled a great spell', which Jim thinks should have won him the Man of the Match. He bowled 12 overs for 17 runs and in this 'crucial phase in the match... his successful suppression of Headley for two hours and a quarter... settled the issue.'[18] Headley 'kept pushing forward and winking at me. Anyway Tom had come in all huffing and puffing and in the effort to accelerate he hit me down to long-on where it was a choice between Dexter and Les Lenham. I shouted "Captain!" I'd got more confidence in him than Les. He caught it,'[19] and at 103,

> Headley skied Bates to mid-on... After a few lusty hits by Broadbent, Snow took three quick wickets... with 8 overs left and the last pair together, as Worcestershire still needed 36. That they got 21 of them was due largely to Booth... and not until Carter, his partner, was run out a few minutes before seven o'clock were Sussex assured of victory.[20]

It was starting to drizzle, but from the Tavern the massed ranks of the Sussex faithful raised their glasses and 'Sussex by the Sea' rang out in the Stygian gloom. Sussex had won something at last.

Alan Oakman 'had all sorts of feelings. When it gets that close you don't know what to feel. You hadn't played in it before.' Jim thinks Ted had proved his point. 'Perhaps it was not,' as John Arlott wrote, 'strictly speaking first-class cricket. But as entertainment it is with us for the foreseeable future. Let us be grateful for it.'[21]

As a tasty dessert after the main course, the West Indians were beaten at Hove when, sent into bat by Dexter, they lost four wickets for 39 'on a seamers' paradise'.[22] Sobers and Butcher rescued the situation with a century partnership but the total of 177 was not enough. Jim, with 39, Dexter and Suttle confirmed Sussex's status as one-day Champions.

The tactical architect of this famous victory was sufficiently realistic, however, to perceive that his side was still insufficiently strong to mount a Championship challenge. The absence of himself and Jim on Test duty 'was not the whole answer to our failing to hit the jackpot. We still lack something in the spin division... The other lack is a reserve force of any quality. Young cricketers on the ground staff hardly seem to get enough good class competition to bridge the gap into the first side.'[23] This was true, despite the recognition for four decades of 'the need and the difficulty for Sussex to breed from its own nursery'.[24] Sussex had adapted to the brave new world of cricket as a marketing tool, 'thanks largely to a combination of tradition and thoughtful leadership'.[25] The county now needed a vital transfusion of talent to ascend from the one-day plateau to the Championship summit.

That was for the future. Following complaints about the over-blown tour to the Indian subcontinent in 1961/62, the MCC experimented this winter with the first 'short tour', eight weeks in India alone, with only ten matches, five of which were Tests. The party was stronger than the previous one, although Dexter, Trueman and Close, who had featured so prominently in the summer, were absent. Cowdrey was named as captain, although a few weeks later he withdrew with an arm injury and Mike Smith took over. Ken Barrington joined John Edrich, Mickey Stewart, Fred Titmus and Jim as established Test players, Jim Binks of Yorkshire was deputy keeper, John Mortimore and Don Wilson back-up spinners and Jeff Jones, David Larter, John Price and Barry Knight the seam bowlers. Brian Bolus and Phil Sharpe completed the party. Jim sums up the tour succinctly: 'It was the first of the short tours – five Test matches and I think five other matches. All five wickets were so low and flat and slow, it was difficult to play shots.' The hazard of illness or injury exists on all tours, no less on a short than a long one, and an 'additional hazard in India is the risk of stomach trouble'.[26] MCC arranged for tinned food to be brought from England for use in the more remote centres and it 'was in some places very necessary',[27] for the story of the trip reads less like a cricket tour than a medical bulletin.

Jim sat out the first match, against the President's XI at Bangalore:

We were staying at a hotel near the river and we spotted a building further upstream. Someone asked a local, 'What's that?' It was a brewery – in India! So we organised a visit and they very kindly supplied us after that. It wasn't very good beer. They used to put glycerine in it to preserve it, but we used to put bottles of this stuff in the bath, open them, the glycerine would run out and you'd have quite a decent drink...

though how damaging its effect might have been upon already uncertain stomachs can only be surmised.

After a high-scoring draw where Stewart, Bolus and Barrington made runs, South Zone failed against the spin of Titmus, Barrington and Wilson. The latter pair also made centuries and Jim scored 52 as MCC won by an innings and 27 runs two minutes from time.

In the heat and humidity of Madras England had four players taken ill during the First Test, yet had no difficulty playing out a draw. India had made an enterprising start, reaching 277 for 3 after the first day, but curiously played for safety as the Englishmen fell by the wayside, stricken by stomach complaints. Jim didn't 'suffer from tummy trouble very much but in Madras it did get me. I had to sprint off the field several times at short notice – literally, gloves down, panic stations', as on the second day he and vice-captain Mickey Stewart were *hors de combat*. 'When we were 63 for 2 on the third morning,' Stewart recalls, 'only four England players arrived at the ground. The rest were ill in the hotel. They gradually trickled in, Jim arriving just before lunch.' By the middle of the Test, as Michael Melford described, 'England could scarcely raise a quorum and, but for a delaying action by

Bolus and Barrington who spent most of one Sunday denying themselves anything resembling a stroke, England might have run out of batsmen in the middle order.'[28] India's negative approach, exemplified by Nadkarni, who bowled 131 balls without conceding a run, meant that Stewart, the most seriously ill, was not needed till the fourth day. Left 293 to win, MJK made 57, Jim 30, and at the close Sharpe (31) and Mortimore (73) took England to within 52 of victory.

The casualty list lengthened alarmingly at Ahmedabad against West Zone, where Edrich and Bolus both made centuries. The match 'was dissolving into a quiet draw on the last afternoon, when S.P. Gaekwad, brother of the Maharaja of Baroda, slashed at a ball from Price, who had started to bowl quite fast: Barrington put out a hand at second slip and broke a finger.'[29] He was out for the rest of the tour and Smith cabled home for reinforcements. Peter Parfitt was eventually dispatched but failed to arrive in time for the Bombay Test.

Wilson's back was now giving him trouble and on the morning of the game, MCC woke up with ten fully-fit men. Barrington, Edrich and Phil Sharpe were ill in hospital, to be joined shortly by John Mortimore, who was sharing with Jim. 'I woke up about six one morning – I don't think I'd slept very well having listened to John going in and out of the loo all night. He had false teeth as well, and he was pretty slim, so he always looked about eighty.' Henry Blofeld was among the press party, an Old Etonian, Cambridge Blue and a Norfolk opener now on the fringe of an improbable Test debut. This amused the captain. 'Next in line was Blofeld, and that shut him up, to think he might be getting in on the Test scene! I'd have paid to watch Henry fielding for a day and a half.'

In the event England fielded two keepers (Binks and Parks), two batsmen (Smith and Bolus), four quick bowlers (Knight, Price, Larter, Jones) and two spinners (Titmus and Wilson). The team lined up before the game to shake hands with Nehru, including Mickey Stewart, who was then taken ill. 'I lasted until tea and then went to hospital. At one point during the day I dived forward at short-leg trying to catch Manjrekar and threw up on the pitch.' Jim Binks kept wicket, India won the toss and made 300, although remarkably England's depleted attack had them at one time 99 for 6. Jim went in first wicket down only to be run out by his captain, 'although I was past the stumps'. At 116 for 6 the innings was rocking but Fred Titmus made a fighting 84 not out, his highest Test score, and 'we hung on against Chandrasekar with John Price and Jeff Jones, who put on quite a lot of runs for the last wicket.'[30] The deficit was only 67 and when England were asked to score 317 in four hours, they settled for a draw. Binks and Bolus shared an opening stand of 125, and Jim was 40 not out with his captain at the end. Showing fortitude in the face of adversity, Smith's men had saved a bizarre Test and with the cavalry having flown in, moved on to Calcutta in better heart.

At Eden Gardens, in another tedious draw, Jim again played as a batsman, making 30 in a partnership of 81 with Cowdrey for the fourth wicket. Jim was batting when 'suddenly all the crowd were milling about and coming on to the field. Someone had set fire to the sight-screen. We all trooped off and we didn't play again that day.' Cowdrey batted over six hours for 107 and on day three the umpires decided that after a millimetre of rain the ground was unfit. Binks kept wicket, but was not enjoying the experience. 'I kept wicket worse than at any time in my life. I had my chance and did not grasp it.'[31] As India did not begin their second innings till the fourth day, there was no chance of a result. It was a similar story at Delhi, where Cowdrey made 151, Pataudi scored India's first double hundred against England and Hanumant Singh became the third Indian to make a hundred against England on debut – and but for Jim he may not even have been playing. At Nagpur for East & Central Zones 'before he had scored... he nicked the ball which was caught by Jim, who did not appeal.'[32] Had he been dismissed then he might never have been selected for India.

The final Test at Kanpur was notable only for England's highest total in India until the 1984/85 season and for Jim's sole Test wicket.

> Pataudi was skippering India and at the end of the first day we chatted Tiger up. We were about 250 for 3 and we said, 'We'll declare, you declare tomorrow night and we'll try and make a game of it in the last three days.' Tiger thought this was a great idea but the Indian Board got wind of it and said, 'No way – you can't do that,' so we just batted on.

England amassed 559, 'Parks at the end was playing delightfully',[33] making 51 not out, and 'we got them in overnight. We opened with Fred Titmus. Jaisimha decided to charge him, missed it and I caught him.' When India were all out 266 on day four, Smith enforced the follow-on:

> The worst thing he ever did. The umpires weren't going to allow us to bowl them out again. I'd been keeping in the 100-degree heat for three days: at tea-time on the last day MJK said, 'You don't want to keep any more. Come and have a bowl'. I got Sardesai second ball, caught by Edrich and then Morty dropped Saleem Durani at deep square leg in my leg trap.

Titmus and Mortimore had been toiling away for hours, 'having a contest to see who could bowl the most maidens'[34] and complained bitterly that Parfitt and Jim were pilfering cheap wickets when any hope for a result had disappeared in the dust.

Jim had had a tough but reasonably successful tour and although he suffered from lack of match practice he averaged 38.71. He arrived home for the publication of the second *Commonwealth Book of Cricket*, featuring pieces by Charlie Griffith, Lance Gibbs and one by Jim himself entitled 'The Strain of being a Wicketkeeper Batsman'. He also needed to plan the next season with great care. 'It was my benefit year – the first game was at Cuckfield at the end of April. It had rained heavily all week but I woke up to a glorious morning. We had a good game, a large crowd and a lovely day.' There were the Ashes to be regained and along with 'the strain of being a wicketkeeper batsman' in international cricket, stresses emerged during 1964 which were much closer to home.

Chapter 10
Home Thoughts From Abroad

County and village cricketers mingled and played on the lovely ground in Cuckfield where 'wooded country stretches in green and vivid landscape to the foot of the South Downs. In summer the air is sweet, so are the soft country sounds and the songs of the birds.'[1] So Jim writes lyrically of his native heath, and at the start of the 1964 season he had every right to feel pleased with his lot. He had arrived as an international sportsman. He was carving out a promising career as a sports writer. His benefit year held the prospect of just reward for his fifteen years of service to Sussex as a professional player. He had a young wife and family – and yet that year would see emerging signs of a darkening sky.

May began happily enough, with 70 not out and 97 at Northampton and a pleasant bowl at Chesterfield where 'Ted kept wicket in the second innings. We got stuck again and I came up the hill at Queen's Park and got a couple of wickets.' Oakman recalls:

> Parkser wasn't the worst leg-spinner. Dexter said to Jim, 'I'll keep wicket and you have a bowl.' Parkser said, 'I didn't know you could keep wicket.' 'Well, I can,' said the skipper. 'I used to do it at prep school' – which is typical Dexter. So he gets the pads on, Parkser bowls to Charlie Elliott who misses it and it hits middle. It could only happen to Parkser.

Jim then made the acquaintance of the Australians at Lord's for the MCC in what was virtually a Test trial. Jim contrived to play on in the first innings and hit a couple of sixes off Potter in the second as Simpson and co. won by nine wickets.

The format of the Gillette Cup was modified for 1964, with innings reduced to 60 overs and five minor counties included in the draw. Sussex wanted to prove that their success 'was no fluke of hypothesis'[2] and began with a 200-run spanking of Durham at Hove. 'They had a very good fast bowler called Young, who got the first three wickets. We were 20-odd for 3, including Ted. Graham Cooper joined me and in just over an hour we put on 134.' In a partnership of ferocious hitting, exquisite driving and audacious running Jim made 102 not out and was made Man of the Match. 'As it was Andy's eighth birthday I gave him the gold medal. Then when Tommy bowled it was the end of the contest.'

'Here's a good catch question for cricket quizzes – who was my first opening partner in Test cricket?'[3] As Jim drove into Trent Bridge for the First Test, Geoffrey Boycott, making his debut, was pondering the answer too.

> We used to turn up for 3 o'clock nets on the Wednesday and in the practice John *Edrich* stood on the ball by mischance. Next morning his ankle had swollen up: he couldn't walk properly and couldn't bat. We didn't have any reserves apart from David Allen and we didn't want to play two spinners. Anyway, we had to and Fred Titmus opened the batting with me.

In the event, the game was ruined by the rain, which washed out much of the first day's play and the whole of the third. The best-known incident occurred after only sixteen overs when Boycott pushed Hawke to leg.

> I called for a single and Hawke was so quick. He was a great athlete, an Aussie Rules footballer, and he collided with Fred going for the run. Fred's only a little fella – Hawky knocked him arse over tit, picked up the ball and threw it in instinctively to Wally Grout.

Grout sportingly just held the ball for a second or two and said, 'Are you coming, Fred, or aren't you?' He didn't take the bails off, 'one of the funniest things I've seen', David Allen remembers. 'Great keeper, Wally – he was very easy with his talent and his knowledge. John Murray learnt a lot from him' – as did Jim. 'I had a long chat to Wally Grout in '61 – he taught me a lot.' Grout received generous fan-mail for this piece of chivalry, and Boycott thinks:

> Cricket should be played like that. Technically it's up to batsmen to get out of the way of the bowler, but there's no rule about good sportsmanship. It's a matter of judgement for each individual. I'd like to think that there are individuals who would do that today but I know many who wouldn't. I played the game hard and I expected everybody to play hard against me – and many did – but I don't think you should ever take out the sporting element.

Sporting men and a sporting pitch, bad light and dirty weather, but Jim had a bit of fun batting with Phil Sharpe. Coming in at 141 for 5 he 'took 12 in an over off Veivers, on-driving for six and off-driving for four.'[4] But in Veivers' next over he perished by the sword, caught on the square-leg boundary for 15. He fell in similar fashion as England pushed for a declaration on the final morning. When rain closed proceedings that afternoon, Australia were 40 for 2 with O'Neill hurt and Simpson's finger still sore. What might have happened was anyone's guess, but the players never returned.

While the Test was mundane, events at Worthing were almost surreal. There can be few bowlers in the game's history who have taken 10 for 49 and 5 for 26 whose side has lost by 182 runs, but that was Ian Thomson's fate against Warwickshire. Twenty-two wickets fell on the Monday and when Sussex were left 206 to win, Ken Suttle 'thought I'd played quite well to be top scorer with 9. Every ball shot along the floor or lifted off a length', Jack Bannister taking 6 for 16 in Sussex's total of 23. Alan Oakman saw the funny side:

> I filmed the placards outside – 'Sussex bowler's great feat – Christine Keeler freed.' In our second innings half-volleys were lifting and hitting you on the glove. It was a ridiculous pitch. It was soaking wet and skidded through, got knocked about and then dried out. We were all out for 23: we got a bollocking off the Committee for not trying but the Committee then comprised non-cricketers.

Jim rushed south from the early finish at Trent Bridge: 'Ted and I went back and joined them for the last-ever match at Worthing.' The wicket was still untrustworthy, and Jim was 'in the fourth ball of the first over; we were 2 for 2. Andrew Corran's first ball pitched just short of a length, hit me in the chest and a bit of mud hit me in the head.' Bolus and Millman looked solid by contrast in an opening partnership of 89, but when they were dismissed Thomson and Bell wrapped up the Nottinghamshire innings for another 44 runs. Sussex led by a single run and in their second innings 'A dashing not out century by Parks (twelve fours) who, taking full advantage of an early life, hit boldly all round, overshadowed all else.'[5] Jim had spent the night 'in Pagham having a beer with my mate Buster Lloyd. I was between marriages then so I used to go and stay with him.'

Jim had to all intents and purposes left Nursery End, the pressures of professional cricket having taken their toll, as his son Bobby observed. 'It was the fact that he was away for months on end – for years on end, on and off – and it was tough.' Jim regards his 103 not out as 'the greatest hundred I ever got. I just gave it the slog. If it was short I just let it hit me; if it was up

I just whacked it and it all came off. I had an early life when I lapped Bomber Wells to deep square leg who kindly put it down.' Kenny Suttle agrees: 'Jim's was a very good hundred because he thought "This is a bad wicket, I must have a go," so he scored very fast and it won the game.' It was all over soon after lunch on the second day and Thomson ended the week with 23 wickets.

There are few more atmospheric and highly-charged occasions in sport than an Ashes Test at Lord's but that year was a damp squib as 'it rained and it rained, and we didn't start till the third morning. I remember Fred running in to bowl the first ball, and he slipped and it flew down the leg side for four wides.' The great man recovered to bowl Lawry leg-stump in his next over and to take 5 for 48 as Australia reached 176. Then John Edrich made his debut hundred against the old enemy in front of royal visitors, Jim essayed one hook too many off Hawke and was caught at fine leg for 12, and when the heavens opened after lunch on the last day, half the playing time, as at Nottingham, had been lost to the elements.

The test series and domestic problems apart, there was the benefit to be pursued. There were one or two Sunday benefit games during the Test matches, as at Three Bridges during the Lord's game. The MCC had rules about that sort of thing: 'I came down for the match but couldn't play.' A tense second-round Gillette game at Taunton and a draw at Bristol occupied Jim before the Headingley Test. 'We beat Somerset at Taunton – narrowly – we didn't think we'd got enough runs. Ted ran in and bowled quick there and won the game.' In truth, Don Bates (4 for 28) and John Snow (3 for 28) bowled Sussex to an unlikely victory by 16 runs, after the champions had made only 141 on a fast, unreliable wicket.

Australia's only success in an otherwise drab Ashes series came at Leeds when 'Peter Burge batted magnificently – he got 160. We had them on the run at one time at 178 for 7.' England won the toss and batted but had not made the best of what looked an immaculate wicket when Jim strode to the wicket at 163 for 5. With his customary panache, Jim demonstrated his contempt for the new ball, hitting McKenzie for four, and the stand with Parfitt reached 50 in 66 minutes. But Parfitt and then Titmus fell. Enter Trueman to an imperial welcome from his home crowd to adopt an unwonted defensive mode as Jim reached an attractive 50, including 6 fours. Soon, with a lofted cover-drive, straight drive and sweep he took successive fours off Corling, but after sweeping Hawke for another boundary, 'I hit a half-volley to Ian Redpath at mid-wicket – I got 68'. England were 232 for 7 and the tail succumbed to 268. Australia's reply was dominated by Burge's 160 in over five hours, although Titmus took 4 for 69 in 50 overs, and, with a lead of 121, they set about England's second innings on the Saturday afternoon with a

vengeance, Simpson catching Boycott at slip and Parfitt going to hospital
with a broken knucklebone. At the close they were in a parlous position, 36
ahead with four wickets down and Parfitt *hors de combat*. Ten minutes before
lunch on the fourth day, Simpson and Lawry were beginning the modest
task of scoring 109 to win the match, England having folded to 229 all out.
It was a performance lacking determination and good sense. Gifford went
early, bowled by McKenzie: in John Clarke's vivid phrase, 'a nightwatchman
working to rule and departing at cockcrow',[6] and then Jim, at 184, 'with a
delinquent stroke hit a lifting ball from McKenzie into the hands of Booth at
mid-off.'[7] Parfitt appeared bravely, but the rest had no answer to the new ball
and Australia cruised home in a little under two and a half hours.

On duty at Leeds, Jim missed his benefit game at Haywards Heath, an occasion filled with irony. He couldn't be on his home ground to celebrate his
years of service to Sussex, for his success in the game had taken him far from
the place which had nurtured his talent. Success had also distanced him from
his family – but Irene was pregnant again. That summer saw the slow but
inexorable process of estrangement which would be cemented by Jim's selection for the MCC tour of South Africa and the events of the winter. But
now it was mid-July and Northampton at Hastings. On a rain-affected wicket
Cooper and Suttle made fifties in Sussex's 213, against the good left-arm spin
of Malcolm Scott, who took 13 for 94 in the match. It was not a wicket on
which to bowl short: it had no bounce but plenty of movement, and when
Snow pitched one short Milburn hooked it over square leg for four. Dexter, at
short leg, said, 'Why don't you pitch it up, you silly little bugger?' The next ball,
on the same length, rose even higher. The captain took a simple catch off the
shoulder of the bat and Snow inquired, 'Pitch it up like that, you mean?' Dexter
was exasperated, but Jim does not remember the disagreement. 'It's very true
that Snowy didn't take criticism very kindly, but Ted wasn't really volatile. I got
on with him very well, although you could rub him up the wrong way. Snowy
was very much his own man.' The captain's anger abated as Snow finished
with 6 for 39 as Northants were 85 all out. Despite Sussex crumbling for 99
Thomson and Oakman ensured that the home side won by 28 runs.

Jim was going through a lean period with the bat. His runs at Headingley
were the first of any note since the hundred against Nottinghamshire at
Worthing and matters did not improve as the Australians came to Hove
and the Old Trafford Test loomed on the horizon. He got a duck and 14 at
Liverpool, where Suttle made 97 and carried his bat – 'All our fellas were
getting out the other end and I couldn't quite understand it. Ramadhin had
settled in Lancashire, Statham and Higgs, all useful bowlers. I thought we
played a few bad shots', and they lost by 85 runs. Dexter took 124 off the

Australians but for Jim the only bright spot of the tourists' visit to Sussex was 'a ten-pin bowling match against the Aussies at King Alfred. It was a hilarious evening and even here they were just as competitive. It was a lot of fun and we raised a few pennies for my benefit.' Surrey were next at Hove before Jim and Ted had to travel to Manchester and for Jim 55 in the first innings was an oasis in a run desert. David Sydenham took eleven wickets and the visitors won by ten wickets. Arnold Long, who in the late seventies followed Jim and Mike Griffith behind the stumps at Hove, broke the world record with eleven catches in the match, one of which annoyed Suttle:

> It was the only time in the whole of my career I was given out when I knew I wasn't. It whipped in at me, hit me on the thigh, which stung: the keeper caught it and they all shouted. I was given out. Not bad in a long career.

Bill Lawry was a dour, gritty opener who believed that decisions of fact on a cricket field are solely the umpire's responsibility, with which it would be impertinent to interfere. Along with other overseas players, notably the South Africans, Lawry regarded 'walking', which had always been the custom in county cricket, as a quaint English tradition. The issue arose at the end of John Price's first over at Old Trafford, after Simpson had won the toss and batted. 'John Price bowled a beauty. Bill got a thick edge and I caught it and chucked it up. I couldn't believe Charlie Elliott gave him not out.' The gimlet-eyed Victorian stayed put and he and Simpson put on 201 before being run out for 106. 'They batted till Saturday morning and only when Simpson got out did they declare.' Simpson made 311 and Australia made 656 for 8, their fifth biggest total ever and the highest in a Manchester Test. 'Only Parks could get the slightest satisfaction from the tremendous innings, and his achievement, in letting pass only one bye, must have been tempered by the early chance Simpson had offered.'[8]

How would Dexter react in the face of this massive deficit? 'Ted came into the dressing-room and said, "Right – we bat till the close." And we nearly did. Kenny got 250, Ted got 170. I got in on the last morning at about 12.' It must have been an excruciatingly tedious last day, 'for lack of enterprise by the batsmen threw away a golden chance of passing the massive Australian total. Dexter's example counted for nothing. Barrington pushed and deflected when he could have driven powerfully and the opportunity to encourage his partners and thoroughly discourage his rivals was lost. Parks hit only 3 fours in his 60, which occupied three hours and twenty minutes.'[9] Barrington's highest Test score – 256 – and the captain's 174 had saved the game but the Ashes were gone.

From the marathon grind of a grimly-fought Test to the *joie-de-vivre* of a limited-over joust – such was the lot of county cricketers in the sixties. Jim drove overnight to Hove for the Gillette semi-final against Surrey, captained by Mickey Stewart and containing Edrich and Barrington, Test colleagues only the day before. On a slow pitch and with rain interruptions, Sussex struggled to 215, Dexter smiting 84 and Jim 32, but when Surrey replied, 'Ian Thomson got Mickey Stewart first ball, which started the rot – caught Parks bowled Thomson 0.' Snow had Edrich lbw and then Dexter caught Barrington off Bates, and at 36 for 3 the back of the challenge was broken. Sussex were through to their second successive Lord's final.

Before that, when Jim would renew acquaintance with his partner from Port of Spain and skipper in India, as well as Bob Barber and Jim Stewart from the New Zealand tour, Sussex went down heavily at Lord's, losing a one-sided game by 182 runs – but Jim was making runs again. He hit 70 off Middlesex at Hove, 56 at Portsmouth and as usual batted well at the Saffrons, scoring 72 and 43 not out against Worcestershire. Jim found himself skipper at Portsmouth when the match was meandering to a draw, Hampshire needing 207 to win on the last day. Oakman thought:

> Dexter got a bit bored with county cricket now and again. He buggered off after lunch and went to the races. It was a boring game, because they were about 100 for 4 with people like Henry Horton and Peter Sainsbury, who weren't going to win the match. We were all bored and we would quite happily have gone off. He could get away with it – Dexter.

Jim takes Oakman's point. 'He often disappeared racing. Down at Hove he would suddenly go off and watch a race on the television in his little room up stairs and I'd skipper the side till he came back.'

At the Oval, Colin Cowdrey returned after his two-Test exile having scored heavily for Kent and Bob Barber replaced John Edrich. In just over two sessions, a side which on paper batted down to Cartwright at number 10, were all out for 182, Jim making only 10 and Neil Hawke taking 6 for 47. Australia replied with 379, Trueman taking his 300th Test wicket when he persuaded Hawke to give Cowdrey a regulation slip catch, provoking scenes of soccer-style adulation for the greatest English pace man of his generation. In their second knock, England's batsmen applied themselves with the single-minded resolution which their first effort lacked, Boycott making the first of his twenty-two hundreds for England, supported by nightwatchman Titmus (56). Cowdrey (93 not out), who reached his 5,000th Test run, and Barrington (54 not out) remained at the end of the fourth day. There was no fifth, 'so the series ended as it began – rain ruined.'[10]

Fred Trueman was setting one record at the Oval, and at Hove Ian Thomson, Jim's room-mate, took his 100th wicket of the season, equalling Maurice Tate's record of doing this eleven summers in a row. He then went off to the Saffrons, where Jim had driven after the Oval washout. An exhilarating climax saw Suttle take Sussex home to a jaunty victory over Lancashire in the last over. Against Worcestershire, Jim made runs, Don Kenyon made his usual century (158) and Kenny Suttle scored 106 and won a bet: 'I was batting with Les Lenham. We were both on about 45 so I bet him half a crown that I'd get to 50 first. He had a slog and got out for 40-something. I'd won and carried on and made a hundred.' Suttle's friendly wager indicates yet again the relaxed nature of county cricket in the sixties. The Australians showed their more light-hearted side when they took on A.E.R. Gilligan's XI in the Hastings Festival. The author – and Gerald Brodribb – were there: 'T.R. Vievers, of Australia, in a festival game at Hastings in 1964 bowled a tennis ball.'[11] A couple of stumpings and 54 runs were a pleasant warm-up before the serious stuff – the Gillette final against Warwickshire at Lord's.

The day dawned misty and humid with dew glistening on the pitch and 'I was actually going down the steps with MJK when Ted arrived, so he went out in his civvies. MJK won the toss and batted.' With a 10.30 a.m. start the ball swung like a boomerang. When Norman Horner saw the first ball from Ian Thomson swing in 'and nearly end up a wide I knew we were in trouble'[12] – and they were. Jim said to his skipper, 'Come on – normal field – we can bowl them out.' Thomson opened with 3 for 14 in 7 overs: by lunch Warwickshire were 100 for 7 and the match was over. Thomson ended with 4 for 23 and the men from the Midlands could only muster 127. When Sussex batted the haze had lifted, there was no swing for Cartwright and for the watching Alan Oakman 'it was a lovely afternoon. All the crowd wanted to do was to watch Dexter bat.' They had little chance. By the time he and Jim came together at 97 for 2 only 34 were wanted and Sussex retained their trophy at a stroll.

When Dexter lifted the trophy for the second successive year, the MCC party to tour South Africa had been announced and Jim had been given the opportunity to wipe out the disappointment of eight years before. With Cowdrey unavailable and Dexter fighting Jim Callaghan in the forthcoming General Election, Mike Smith was appointed captain. There was criticism that with no Cowdrey, Graveney, Russell, Edrich or Stewart the batting looked vulnerable, though Dexter would join as vice-captain if he failed in his parliamentary ambition. Boycott was on his first tour, Barber was an opening bat of unknown quantity and Mike Brearley had been selected largely on the basis of his university career, during which he had made over 4,000 runs.

Set against that, Parfitt had proved a capable cavalryman in India and the two wicketkeepers, Jim and John Murray, were batsmen of proven international class. Among the bowlers, Tom Cartwright had scored a first-class double hundred, David Allen had shown he could hold a bat and Fred Titmus had been tried and tested in the international arena. Ian Thomson, chosen for his only full tour, had made useful runs for Sussex down the order.

The party would fly out on the day of the General Election – but that was for the future. First Jim wound up his benefit year with games at Amberley, Beeding and Bramber and Rottingdean, interspersed with a one–day challenge against the Australians at Hove. 'I skippered the match because Ted was away campaigning in Cardiff.' [see plate 28]. Jim completed a successful season with an aggressive 84 in 24 overs. His brilliant hitting must have made the umpires swell with pride beneath their white coats. Their names were John Langridge and J.H. Parks.

Proud as he was of his son's cricket, Jim senior was doubtless dismayed at the state of his marriage. For the second time, Irene would pass a pregnant winter alone while Jim played cricket in the sun. Jim had been away from Nursery End virtually continuously since he regained his Test place in June 1963, exerting an increasing strain on his marriage. One of the press corps on the MCC tour was Ron Roberts, the distinguished cricket writer. 'Ron was a great friend of mine – lovely man,' said Jim. 'What we didn't know at the time but other people did was that he had a brain tumour.' Before the tour got underway, Jim met Ann Wembridge, Ron's secretary, at a reception in Salisbury and eighteen months later Jim and Ann were to marry in New Zealand. Although Jim, the true professional, did not allow the situation to affect his cricket, in human terms 'he would be the first to admit that he got it wrong. It's a period he's not very proud of.'[13]

The tour opened in Rhodesia with a game against a Matabeleland XI at Bulawayo, followed by practice on the police ground in Salisbury, where Dexter, whose political career had fallen at the first fence, arrived for nets straight from the airport. Jim had a quiet start: 'We beat Rhodesia by five wickets – I was with Kenny Barrington at the end. The storm clouds were coming up and we got the runs just in time.' Bob Barber hit 108 in his favourite position of opener: 'I was never very comfortable batting down the order. I preferred to open. It was partly that I didn't like waiting but I also preferred the quick bowlers. They brought the field in so if you did happen to hit you had a chance of getting runs'.

Had he been of an historical bent Jim would have enjoyed playing at Benoni, for it was there in 1948 that his idol hit the fastest triple century ever. Against the South African Colts Jim marvelled from the covers as on a good wicket at Willowmore Park 'the young Barry Richards soon got on top of the bowling…[and] played with a confidence that was not far short of contempt.'[14] Set 293 to win, the MCC were holding on for the draw at 241 for 8. Vereeniging holds a special place in British imperial history as the venue for the peace conference which ended the Boer War. Here, at the prosaically named Brick and Tile Company's ground, Jim was beginning to enjoy himself. The two Blues, Smith and Brearley, each made 102 and Jim 50 not out against a Transvaal Country Districts XI, for whom Peter Heine, the veteran fast bowler, hit a rustic hundred including 5 sixes and 11 fours. Jim sat out the innings victory over Transvaal in which Barrington hit 169, and after thirteen nights in Johannesburg headed for Durban.

Against Natal, the Currie Cup Champions, MJK lost the toss in cloudy conditions and although 'there was as much grass on the wicket as that lawn out there', at the end of the third day MCC were still in their first innings. A thunderstorm burst and it became humid; 'we turned up on the last morning and David Allen and Ian Thomson bowled them out.' The Sussex man took eight wickets in the match and MCC won by ten wickets. All the batsmen except Boycott made runs – Jim 'got 80 not out, which got me going on the tour'. Psychologically it was an important result and had a definite bearing on the First Test, now three weeks away. Jim now had ten days off before the Western Province game in Cape Town, time to cultivate his acquaintance with his old pal Ron Roberts before moving to Durban and the Test.

At Kingsmead MCC had beaten Natal on a green top. Mike Smith remembers 'turning up to the first day of the Test and two blokes were on the square taking the grass off. That suited us because Tom Cartwright was injured.' The captain won the toss; Boycott and Barber put on 120 for first wicket and for the Yorkshire opener 'this was magic – I was still living with my mother in Fitzwilliam, a mining village. The only time I'd been out of the county was when I played for Yorkshire and went to a hotel to play against Kent or Sussex or Lancashire – so to go to South Africa…' Barber relished off-spinner Kelly Seymour – 'as soon as he came on Bob smashed him into the stand and never let him settle.'[15] With England 178 for 2 at tea Barrington said 'Wait until we get them on this pitch! The soil is quite loose. If we can bat for two days, it'll get dusty and we'll win by an innings.' David Allen blanched: 'Typical Barrington – "Thank you very much – no pressure – three days to bowl a Test side out twice." Then of course he played a mag- nificent innings, which he would on a slow turning wicket against spinners – as did Jim.' In fact, Barrington and Jim came together at 279 for 5 to put on 206, a record sixth-wicket stand against South Africa. 'We batted til after tea on the second day, because Kenny and I both got hundreds. I was on 99 and

Kelly Seymour was bowling – one of the gentlest off-spinners I ever played against. They brought everyone up to save the single and I lapped him over square-leg for four, then over long-on for four next ball,' whereupon MJK declared at 485 for 5. Jim was slightly lame: 'I did an ankle in Cape Town before the Test and Jack Jennings, our masseur, strapped me up. I was in good form then, and with John Murray hanging around I thought "There's no way I'm not playing".'

At the close, South Africa were 20 for 3 and already there were signs of the wicket breaking up. 'Tommy bowled Eddie Barlow with a magnificent delivery, which pitched middle and hit the top of the off stump.' The captain was at short leg and 'it's always stuck in my mind – that first over Ian bowled in Test cricket. He bowled two or three nipping in and then he knocked his off stump out: he was a very, very high-class bowler.' Price had Goddard caught,

> which brought Graeme Pollock in, and Mike immediately got Fred Titmus on as he always bowled well at him. Fred bowled one or two outside the off-stump which turned. Then he bowled a little arm ball which Graeme was going to leave. He realised too late it wasn't turning and it bowled him middle stump.

On the following day, South Africa followed on, Titmus and Allen each took five wickets and England won by an innings and 104 runs with a day and a half to spare.

The team's success earned them a day off, spent visiting a farm or writing Christmas cards, but Jim 'went water-skiing. I drove the boat!' because Parks, J.M., a fit and healthy international sportsman, superbly talented in any ball game, couldn't swim! 'I tried to swim in the Red Sea. I dived in and spluttered around but I had negative buoyancy, they told me at school.' In fact Jim did not play again until the Johannesburg Test, missing the game at Pretoria 'when we decided my ankle was playing up a bit so John had to play.' The Middlesex man was not best pleased:

> DA, Boycott and I were going with Donald Carr, the manager, to the Kruger Park for three or four days, all laid on by SA Breweries. We stopped for lunch somewhere on the way. There was a message – Jim wasn't fit – he'd done something to his ankle so we turned the car round – and I made 142. After lunch when I'm batting, all of a sudden Jim's in the nets perfectly fit and by the next Test match, he's back in.

England had the upper hand in a draw at the New Wanderers either side of Christmas where South Africa were forced to follow on yet again, saved in the second innings by a powerful 144 not out by Colin Bland and the rain which ended play two hours early. England made a huge 531, Dexter hitting his last Test hundred (172) and Barrington his second in successive innings. Barber almost made a hundred before lunch on the first day. Jim remembers him 'slogging them all over the place, especially Seymour.' Barber laughs heartily:

> Yes, I must be his only wicket. He was one of those fellows you couldn't resist
> – a peaceful non-spinning off-spinner. When I was in the 90's I said to Ted,
> who I was batting with, 'Right, six or out.' He said, 'Don't be so bloody daft.'
> I took a huge swing and got bowled. When Kenny got to 94 he looked up
> at the pavilion as though to say, 'Here you are, Bob' and whack, six over the
> sightscreen – 'That's how to do it!'

– and Barber chuckles again.

With South Africa starting the last day needing 68 to avoid an innings defeat with six wickets left, Smith gave everybody a bowl except himself and Jim. Bland hit straight for 2 sixes and 16 fours and was especially hard on David Allen who took 4 for 87 in 49 overs. 'He was a great attacking player off the front foot and the best fielder I ever saw. He'd sit at night in the pavilion on very hot days with a coke bottle, take the cap off and top it up with gin. When it fizzed he drank it out of the bottle.' It had been a flat wicket and in the end a comfortable stalemate for the hosts.

Forty hours later hostilities would be renewed in Cape Town and after nets at Newlands the tour party and the press celebrated New Year's Eve on the waterfront – and started the Test on New Year's Day! 'The 'Tarnished Test', Charles Fortune called it, and long after the slow and unenterprising cricket is forgotten, it will be remembered for two incidents focussing on the issue of 'walking'.

Goddard won the toss and when Eddie Barlow had made 41 he played forward to Titmus. Jim 'saw him play it straight on to his toe and Parf caught it at slip. It ran up the bat beautifully.' Umpire Warner gave Barlow not out. Barlow was convinced the ball hit his foot – 'My only thought at the time was to get back in my crease to avoid being stumped,'[16] but as Boycott pointed out, 'they'd got into this habit of not walking.' Still more astonishing was 'what happened when I was on 73. I played forward, the ball hit me on the glove and Bob Barber at short leg caught the ball and tossed it back, and no one said a word! I thought I was out that time, but to my amazement there wasn't a single appeal, so I went on batting!'[17] In a massively slow 501 for 7 Barlow and Tony Pithey made big hundreds.

England, one up in the series, decided to bat it out. On an extremely flat pitch with no pace MJK played his finest innings, scoring 121 and Barrington, on 49, played a wide ball from Peter Pollock. Robin Hobbs was behind the wicket filming for Jim as he was waiting to go in. Jim saw 'the ball deflect off the bat, it took a thick edge and Lindsay caught it in front of first slip. The umpire refused the appeal, Kenny waited a good eight seconds and then walked.' Was he making a sporting gesture or was he making the umpire look a fool? Opinions differed, but the Surrey man's desire to do what was right overcame any potential embarrassment to Warner, to whom he later apologised. Bob Barber and Jim thought that most English players walked because they knew it was in their interests for when they did stand their ground, they were believed. Dexter made 61, Jim 59 and when England were all out for 442 with just over a day left, the Test 'died a slow death to be buried eventually as a bad joke.'[18] For the first time in Test cricket twenty bowlers were used, Barrington and Boycott recording their best figures. Jim 'liked to keep to Boycs. He used to bowl little swingers.' David Allen thought 'Boycott wasn't a bad bowler. He used to bowl little in-duckers and he was as tight with his bowling as he was with his spending.'

To Bloemfontein where 'the only thing I remember was driving a speed-boat around the lake while someone was water-skiing.' Jim might also have recalled his 89 in putting on 154 with Boycott and his old friend Barrington captaining MCC to a seven-wicket win over Orange Free State. 'Through the three days in Johannesburg preceding the Fourth Test the tourists lived life to the full. Practice daily and strenuous nets at the Wanderers' came first but thereafter everybody went the rounds.' Jim 'went down a gold mine with Boycs. Somewhere there's a photo of us in hard hats' – perhaps the thrifty, single-minded Yorkshireman felt at home. 'He *was* a very selfish player but in a Test match you could afford to be selfish if you were going in first. He still did a marvellous job for England.'

He did a marvellous job in the Test as England hung on for a draw, playing out time with Cartwright after England had lost 124 for 6 on a pitch taking spin. Jim calls it 'the green-tinted spectacles Test'. On the first morning, 'MJK went out with Dexter, Barrington and Carr: they thought it had a bit more grass but it was a good track. They'd misread it.' Bob Barber quipped, 'MJK must have been wearing green-tinted spectacles. It wasn't very green at all.' Cartwright, chosen to exploit the conditions, was not convinced, as he told David Allen. 'They've selected me because there's something in the wicket but you should be playing.' Boycott thought that MJK chose to field because 'Tom played for Warwickshire and Smith had great confidence in him.'

In any event South Africa made 390 for 6 declared in two days, and in reply Parfitt made 122 and Barrington 93 in England's 384. After Goddard had scored his maiden Test hundred England were left to chase 314 to win. With an hour left, England stood at 106 for 5, with Barber out of action with a shattered little finger – 'Trevor Goddard hooked one and I caught it on the knuckle.' Jim, who, with 0 and 10 'didn't have a very good match', lasted 25 minutes then watched as 'Tom Cartwright saved England with the bat. He had entered the game as a batsman, played very straight and was a great sweeper.' But Boycott's 76 was the sheet anchor: 'we were in danger of losing it all the time. Wickets went down like ninepins as the pitch just got worn, with cracks and an unpredictable bounce.'[19]

During the game Jim wrote home to Lorraine Whitehead, a Sussex cricket fan, 'We are having a most pleasant tour, and the cricket has been extremely successful.'[20] England stood one in the series and as the rest of the party headed off to Kimberley, Jim flew to Cape Town with Titmus. For Jim, the social side of the tour had been 'very hectic. It is naturally difficult to refuse the hospitality, but rather necessary at times.'[21] It was certainly the tour he enjoyed most, as did Bob Barber; 'Life was good – you went into a restaurant and you could eat, and drink all the wine and port you wanted and it cost peanuts.'

Cartwright once more showed his capabilities as a batsman in Cape Town, when 'only determined resistance by Smith and Cartwright on the last day prevented the strong Invitation XI from breaking MCC's unbeaten record.'[22] Adding 105 in three hours, he made 42 not out to go with his unbeaten 53 in the first innings. The game ended on a miserable note when, completing a run, the Warwickshire bowler stumbled and damaged a knee and was out of the final Test in Port Elizabeth, the windy city, to which the party flew and arrived in a howling gale. 'The walk of about a hundred yards across the airport apron into the reception hall was a battle against the elements which, if it achieved little else, confirmed that half the touring team sadly needed haircuts.'[23]

On the morning of 12 February, Jim's daughter Louise Marion was born in Cuckfield Hospital, while 5,000 miles away, MJK lost the toss and on a docile pitch Goddard took no risks. As in Cape Town, South Africa made 500 in nearly two days, Graeme Pollock becoming only the second batsman after George Headley to score three hundreds before he was twenty-one. 'Graeme hit the ball hard with a great big heavy bat and he played very straight.'[24]

Smith's strategy of containment had been forced on him by injuries to Barber, Price, Cartwright and Brown, and Ken Palmer, coaching in Johannesburg, was drafted in. England went into the game with a gentle seam attack of Palmer, Thomson and Boycott, who admired the Sussex stalwart:

> Ian Thomson was very nice to me, the youngest kid on the block. He showed
> great resilience, stamina and mental strength and never moaned about things.
> Even when Jim clearly caught Barlow and he didn't walk Ian just said, 'You
> little beggar.' He was a great guy. Absolutely top drawer.

England responded with 435, employing two nightwatchmen – Titmus and
Thomson. Jim 'batted 9 there – the lowest I ever batted.' Thomson made a
creditable 39, Jim 35 and when England were set 246 to win at 65 an hour,
'a little rain was coming down before Pollock began… The light was poor
and the clouds hung very low'[25] and the curtain came down on a tame draw.
Their comprehensive victory at Durban secured England the series; they
remained undefeated on the tour. Jim felt that the criticism of Smith for his
defensive approach – thirteen draws in fifteen Tests – was unfair. The captain
was not prepared to throw away a hard-won advantage by taking unneces-
sary risks.

Jim had 'spent much of the tour with an ankle strapped – with JT float-
ing around I was determined not to get left out of the side.' While Charles
Fortune accepted that

> there were those who had little doubt that Murray was the better wicket-
> keeper, [I] never heard a suggestion that Parks should be dropped once the
> series was underway. Parks kept efficiently… [He was] a very likeable tourist
> as well; one of the very happy sidelights of the tour was that Parks should now
> do so well whereas in 1956/57 the South African tour had been a miserable
> disappointment for him.[26]

We stumble over ourselves, though, in the intricate tapestry that was now
Jim's sporting and personal life. He arrived home in late February in time
for the publication of *The Commonwealth Book of Cricket*, No.3, this year
with more articles by Jim and fewer guests, although Wally Grout, Sonny
Ramadhin and Garry Sobers contributed, as did Jim senior in a delightful
piece about the family and his early years. On 9 March, the *Daily Telegraph*
ran a headline, 'Benaud accuses Griffith of throwing' – describing an article
by the former Australian captain headed 'Griffith is a chucker'. This both
harked back to Jim's 1963 film and foreshadowed events at Old Trafford on
the West Indies tour to England of 1966.

However, that was for the future. Jim had more pressing matters. 1965
witnessed the first two 'mini-series', against New Zealand and South Africa.

Chapter 11
A Talent Fulfilled

Any resolution of the delicate patchwork which was now Jim's private life was put on hold for a few weeks after his return from South Africa, as pre-season nets and then the early games absorbed his attention. He was back at work – with a vengeance. 'On a bad wicket,' against Leicestershire at Hove in early May, 'I remember slogging Jackie Van Geloven and got the fastest century – 102 in as many minutes.' The rollicking start was not carried on at Bradford, where Jim wrote to Lorraine Whitehead, 'not a very happy Sussex dressing-room here... the score being 16 for 5.'[1] Set 257 to win, Sussex were holding on at 118 for 9 at the end. A pleasing win over Surrey, where Jim made 71, sent the side to Brentwood, where they 'were unlucky not to win... It was so cold there, no one felt like playing.'[2] True enough, for from 95 for 2, chasing 115 to win, Sussex collapsed to 112 for 8, Trevor Bailey taking 6 for 25. At Edgbaston Jim made 70 and wrote, not certain of his Test place, 'Well, we shall know on Sunday whether it is to be Birmingham next Wednesday, or back to Hove. The Test wicket here looks like being a real beauty and there should be plenty of runs going for someone.'[3] There were – for Ken Barrington – but he made his 137 so slowly that he was dropped for the next Test. New Zealand had no answer to England's 435 and although they fought bravely in following on, England won by nine wickets.

'It was around this time,' Bobby thinks, that 'Mum and Dad separated and we moved to Eastbourne where Mum had a guest house. So to see Dad Andy and I had to come over to the cricket, but he made efforts to keep in contact'[4] – not that his father was at Hove much in the next month – which was of course part of the problem. As Jim wrote from Lord's during the Second Test in mid-June, 'I haven't been back to Sussex for over a month now as we have had this long run of away games.'[5] The schedule was hectic, like a rock band on tour – Brentwood, Birmingham, Worcester, Birmingham, Northampton, London, Tunbridge Wells, London, Portsmouth, Eastbourne, Hove. It helped if you were in form, and Jim was. He made 57 and 45 in a three-wicket win at Northampton, aided by Laurie Johnson: 'When Sussex still needed 7 runs [to win]… L.A. Johnson, the wicketkeeper, caught Lenham, threw the ball up and then dropped it, Lenham was judged "not out".[6] At Tunbridge Wells, as Jim wrote, 'Sussex went mad last Monday and scored 421, and yours truly nipped in for a century.'[7]

Jim's batting form deserted him at Lord's, where Sussex provided three players for the Second Test. Tom Cartwright had a stomach muscle injury and John Snow was selected as third fast bowler to support Rumsey and Trueman in the great man's last game. Even with Dexter and Jim in the side, Snow felt a stranger and was not called on till Trueman and Rumsey had seen the shine off the new ball and Dexter had come on as first change. After ninety minutes New Zealand were 28 for 4; Rumsey had taken 4 for 7. Two more fell before lunch, both to Snow, who 'did in fact bowl well in their first innings,' wrote Jim. 'I had the pleasure of catching his first Test victim, John Reid. We bowled them out for 175 and we are going well at 121 for 2 with Ted Dexter having just completed his fifty.'[8] While England compiled 307, Snow was enjoying the dressing-room chat. Parfitt, Allen and Titmus used to love winding up Trueman, who had an encyclopaedic recall of past games, with a favourite line, 'I've got an amazing memory for batsmen's weaknesses.' Jim 'got 2, then Richard Collinge, the big left-armer, did me. Kipper got a ton, Bob Barber bowled well second whack and Boycs and Ted knocked off the runs.' England won easily by seven wickets.

'Next Wednesday', Jim wrote, 'we play Middlesex in the next round of the Gillette Cup, and hope we can go into the next round.' Since it was the day after the Test, 'we stayed up at the Clarendon Court Hotel in the Edgware Road. Most of the time prior to that we used to travel up and down.' Dexter's jest after the 1964 final – 'If we win again next year, perhaps they will give us the cup' – rang a hollow note as Sussex, chasing 281, were annihilated by 90 runs – their first defeat in the cup. It was a black week for the county. On the evening after the Gillette defeat Dexter was pushing his Jaguar off the road under the Chiswick flyover (don't ask) when it ran over him, breaking his fibula and gouging a hole in his leg. With the skipper in the West Middlesex Hospital Jim captained the side in a defeat at Portsmouth and at Eastbourne. When Jim reported for duty at Headingley Pataudi led the side, one of five Sussex captains in an incoherent summer.

Headingley was Edrich's match. On the field throughout, he made 310 not out and scored the most boundaries in a Test innings – 52 fours and 5 sixes. Jim 'sat and watched as Eedy kept playing and missing to Dick Motz and then smashing him over his head for four. MJK just got in, I was next but didn't bat.' Ray Illingworth was recalled on his home ground and:

got four wickets in the first innings bowling seamers. It was a green pitch – I tried 2 or 3 overs of spin but it just kept skidding on. I hadn't bowled seamers for two years but when MJK suggested it I said, 'I'll give it a go.' My first ball pitched just outside leg-stump and took Morgan's off peg. It drizzled and we went off for rain and I didn't get on again.

He hardly needed to. 'We rolled them over twice – Fred Titmus got five in the second innings' – including an astonishing four-wicket maiden.

En route to Hastings to captain the side against Hampshire Jim played in a single-wicket competition at Lord's.

Near the end, Colin Cowdrey against Richie Benaud and the last ball of Richie's six overs, Colin tried to sweep and got a top edge straight in my eye. I drove down that night with one eye and had a job to focus. I thought 'If I win the toss, we bat, and I can go down the order till it clears.' Of course I lost the toss and I don't think I laid glove on ball all morning. Fortunately no-one nicked one and gradually the eye opened up – but for a couple of days the eye was completely closed and I did find keeping rather tricky with one eye.

The eye had recovered enough for Jim to take the field at Lord's as South Africa made 280 and by Saturday lunchtime Jim was writing 'I must be careful what I eat. I have in fact done so little lately that I have been putting on weight and have batted only once in the last three weeks.'[9] Jim had an excellent opportunity to lose some of his excess pounds on the Monday, when:

Bland ran me out. I'd got 32 and was batting with Barrington. I was at the Pavilion End, played it behind square, looked to see Kenny rushing down the wicket. He never called – he was the silent partner. I suddenly realised that Colin Bland was there. He had run from in front of square leg to backward short leg to throw with one stump to aim at. I thought 'I've got to get in line with the stumps', which I did and it went straight through my legs and hit the wicket. I was run out by two or three yards. I vividly remember that.

So does Colin Cowdrey: 'Bland drew back his arm like an Olympic javelin thrower and hurled the ball under Parks' feet as he ran. Parks was still out of his ground when his middle stump went cartwheeling into the air. It was the most breathtaking piece of fielding I have ever seen.'[10] Barrington had suffered a similar fate on Saturday. Jim had been going well, 'scoring with increasing freedom and forcefulness'.[11] Left 191 to win in 235 minutes,

England were never up with the rate. Edrich retired, hit by Pollock, Jim made 7 and they managed a draw.

Jim's August was dominated by two Tests and a century off the tourists at Hove, but not before he led the side in a bizarre game against Middlesex. Lasting 130 overs with three freak declarations, his opposing captain was his former best man and after Titmus took 7 for 15 in the only completed innings, Brearley and Parfitt knocked off the runs for a nine-wicket win. Colleagues again at Trent Bridge, Jim and Fred were in the thick of the action as England went down by 94 runs. The game will be remembered for 'Graeme Pollock's beautiful 125', which according to Swanton was:

> fit to rank with anything in the annals of the game. Pollock came in when after 50 anxious minutes, South Africa's score stood at 16 for 2. Between this point and lunch he batted easily and without inhibition or restraint while two more wickets fell, and his companions struggled in every sort of difficulty.... I can imagine either of two other left-handers playing such an innings as his 125, Frank Woolley and Garry Sobers: no one else. [12]

The Springboks made 269: 'I stumped Colin Bland off Fred' and Cowdrey made 105 in England's 240. Then 'Cartwright broke a thumb, Boycott bowled a lot of overs and on the third evening we were 10 for 2. Titmus was nightwatchman, got out and Snowy went in.' Wanting 318 to win, 'we lost comprehensively. I was 44 not out at the end. When David Larter came in I knew it was all over. It was a bad Test match.' Back at Hove for the game against Glamorgan, 'Snowy had a bad back and I can remember saying to him, 'They're picking the team for Australia. Whatever you do, just go out and play because you're in the frame.'

When the tour party for the Antipodes was announced on 15 August, Snow had missed out: David Larter was preferred. Many people, including the captain, now believe Snow should have gone: 'There was a bit of a tradi-tion of taking a young player, but bugger me, we didn't take John Snow in front of Arty Larter, who had been on the previous tour. We got it wrong and missed his potential because John became a very great bowler.' Jim blames Snow: 'He had a little niggle, but he can't have been more injury-prone than Larter, who played in three matches, went in the leg and did it again get-ting off the massage table. He didn't make a great effort to get fit after that.' Jim, who would renew his acquaintance on tour with John Murray, had a gentle net for the Oval Test with 106 not out against the South Africans at Hove: Snow played, but the die was cast. The Oval Test was 'Statham's last and he bowled beautifully.' The great Lancastrian took seven wickets and after Bland hit 127, 'we had a great chance of winning on the last day and it rained and rained. We were going well at 308 for 4 and it would have been a famous win to tie the series.' With 91 to get in 70 minutes and Cowdrey and Smith well set, England justifiably felt robbed by the weather in a miserable summer.

It had been a poor summer for Sussex too. The captain wished he 'could have stood down at a better time'.[13] At various times during that season Jim, Dexter and Snow had been on Test duty and then Dexter 'disappeared from the scene after the... brush with his Jaguar – "retired, ran himself over"',[14] as John Clarke wryly observed. The side finished next to bottom of the Championship, with team spirit far from high. Pataudi had just been appointed captain for 1966 and Mike Griffith was uncertain whether

> Jim felt that he should have had the job rather than Pataudi, who was a won-
> derful player but had not grown up in the Sussex environment. I sensed a
> slight resentment, which made life difficult. Some of the players noticed that,
> because when Jim resigned the captaincy, I don't think he got their fullest sup-
> port, because if he hadn't seemed to be angling for the job at the time Pataudi
> became captain... do you see what I mean?

Certainly Jim had misgivings, as he expressed to Lorraine:

> Writing on a very wet day during the Hastings Festival... I am at present hav-
> ing a little bit of trouble with the Sussex Committee over what I consider bad
> treatment, all tied up with the selection of Pataudi as captain of Sussex next
> season. I am not complaining about the selection, but it would take rather
> too much paper to explain it all. Anyway, I think I shall still be a Sussex player
> next year.[15]

It is a revealing letter. Jim goes on to explain that 'my home life was strug-
gling considerably and we decided that there was no way of making the peace, so I have a divorce coming up next month. In the meantime I have met someone from Taunton who I am very fond of and I am getting married... at the end of the tour.'

On Friday 15 October the tour party met at Lord's. It had been a busy month for Jim. At a National Sporting Club dinner Jim received the Café Royal Centenary Cricket Trophy and a cheque for 100 guineas for scoring the fastest century of the summer. He was pictured in December's *Cricketer* with Cardiff light-heavyweight Eddie Avoth, later British and Commonwealth Champion – 'the only time I've ever been in a boxing

ring'. He had also 'been training very hard and lost a lot of weight'[16] and had been house-hunting so that he and Ann had somewhere to live the following spring.

The monsoon was breaking as the party landed in Colombo to show the flag. The second game was farcical, with players tucking trousers into socks, others rolling them up to Bermuda-shorts length. 'When we were abroad,' says David Allen, 'there was a feeling of "Let's get this crowd on our side." I'm down at long-leg walking round with an umbrella. We had a bit of fun in the rain – and Cowdrey would have seen the joke.' Jim celebrated his thirty-fourth birthday 'with a few beers on an Air Ceylon Comet to Perth but Boycs, who was twenty-five on the same day, had tummy trouble and was none too well.'

Black clouds of flies and bush-hatted farmers swelled the population of Moora for the MCC's light-hearted slog before the tour began in earnest against Western Australia at the WACA. On one of the best wickets Jim had ever played on, Graham McKenzie bowled the 'first real ball of the tour to Bob Barber, who hit it one bounce into the crowd straight over his head. That set the pattern for the tour.' Barber was 'physically a strong man, and he enjoyed the confrontation and challenge of taking on the quicks.'[17] Driving magnificently, he hit 126 out of 197. 'You really have to try to dominate Australians and you have to show them that you're not going to be walked over – that's true even today.'[18] MCC then lost wickets and momentum, and when Jim joined his captain, they were 272 for 5.

> Smith and Parks… played with delightful freedom, and… rattled up 60 runs by the close. [The next morning] Parks built on his overnight 37 with an ease and grace and at a pace that even Dexter would have been pushed to better. Using the lofted off-drive as his principal weapon, he reached 50… Taking 15 off Jenner's sixth over, his shots including a marvellous drive high over extra cover for six.'[19]

MJK admired all this at close hand. 'Jim fancied leggers. The Australian leg-spinners, led by Benaud, tended to bowl off-stump and outside whereas the Indians bowled much straighter so it suited him.' An hour produced 70 runs and 'Parks romped to 97. Next over he drove Mayne through the covers for three to reach a hundred scored in 126 minutes and including 12 fours and a six.'[20] Jim's innings put MCC 'right back on top where we'd been in terms of domination. It was a very important innings psychologically.'[21]

'The interesting thing about that game in Perth was they didn't have sight-screens at the far end. David Brown hit John Inverarity on the head and I

remember Cowdrey ducking a yorker closing his eyes. It was quite dangerous, especially with people like McKenzie bowling.'[22] Laurie Mayne bowled
fast on this lively track and 'had Kenny caught at slip trying to defend a quick
bouncer though Kenny was such a good hooker.'[23] Jeff Jones also bowled
well, taking 5 for 9 in 6 overs at the end of the state's first innings.

At the death, WA wanted 10 to win off the last over with two wickets left.
Then Larter bowled Jenner 'and the last man, Mayne, came in. Larter ran
up to bowl, and Mayne, so cool in defence in the first innings, flicked out
his bat to give Parks a catch. The minute hand on the clock was showing
six o'clock, and MCC had won by 9 runs with five balls to spare.' Said MJK
to John Clarke: 'You don't mean to say you thought we weren't going to
win, do you?'[24] Rex Alston was much heartened: 'The fact that our two best
forcing batsmen – Barber and Parks – both came off at the first attempt is a
matter for much rejoicing.'[25] Rejoice they did. Right next to the WACA is
the trotting circuit and Jim 'went to the trotting that night – the only time I
ever went.'

Adelaide, with its parks and church spires, is the most English of all
Australian cities and the MCC would have felt at home, greeted by rain and
high winds on their arrival for the game against South Australia. They were
in good spirits. At a civic reception, Sir Don Bradman paid tribute to MCC
for their approach to the game and at the Adelaide Oval 'the pitch… had
the kind of slightly murky case history you would find written down about
delinquents in a probation officer's notebook… It was damp and deceitful.'[26]
Jim saw it as an Australian 'sticky dog – the only one I ever played on, apart
from one at Eastbourne, strangely enough. We bowled them out for 50-odd
and I was keeping to David Allen and taking them up near my shoulder
– they were rising off a length.' Allen concurs: 'I took 4 for 24 – you couldn't
have hit the wicket unless it was a half-volley.'

In reply, Boycott played his first innings since arriving from Singapore,
where he had had a bad back and ended up in hospital. Batting fluently,
he made 94 and Barrington 69 as MCC led by 207. The hosts made a better fist of their second knock, with Brown and Higgs taking four wickets
each. Totalling 364, they left MCC 158 to win, which they did at a stroll,
Barrington making 51, leaving Cowdrey and Jim to finish off the job, earn-
ing 'for everyone an afternoon off that came in handy for dealing with
Christmas cards.'[27] After hitting 75 – 'a gem of an innings'[28] – at Hamilton
against Victoria Country Districts, Jim had a lot more time for Christmas
cards, as Murray deputised against Victoria at the MCG. Actually, he and
Parfitt played golf, with hilarious results:

I played with him once at Royal Melbourne; on one of the holes you had to
play between two lines of trees. He drove, hit one tree and it came back to
him. He drove again, hit the other tree and it came back again – one of the
funniest things I ever saw on the golf course.

While Jim was having fun with Parfitt, Barrington made 158 as MCC lost by
32 runs and flew east for a tough assignment – New South Wales in Sydney.
Barber took the match by the scruff of the neck, treating the bowling with
'a beefy, cheerful, arrogance'.[29] He was run out for 90, going for a hundred
before lunch, and Russell, Cowdrey and Smith kept the momentum going.
At 328 for 5 Titmus joined Jim 'and there were 67 minutes left for play – time
for Parks to put on a show of cultivated big hitting off the old ball and the
new that almost took the breath away.'[30] He hit 14 off Leslie's first over with
the new ball and had reached 56 at the close. Next morning, 'Parks, having
looked to do his best to give a wicket catch off one ball from Renneberg, was
caught behind off the next.'[31] All out for 527, MCC rocked NSW as Larter
and Brown each took a wicket in their first over. Doug Walters struck a defiant hundred as NSW replied with 288. Of more potential import was the
banning of Jeff Jones. Umpire Burgess took him off in mid-over for running
on the pitch, roughing up the ground in the 'danger zone' under Law 46 on
'Fair and Unfair Play'. With Larter out with a bruised heel and Brown having stubbed his toes on the beach, MCC sent for Barry Knight, 'a very fine
cricketer', but the wrong choice, Jim feels. 'Snowy was still available and we
needed the extra pace out there.' In the event, Jim took one of his 'best-ever
catches, diving full-length to hold a snick from Booth' and Titmus took 5 for
45. MCC cruised home by nine wickets and headed north to Brisbane.
    Murray stood in again for the Queensland game where Russell and Edrich
both made hundreds, enabling Jim and Parfitt to have another eventful game
of golf, where Jim 'hit a particularly fine drive only to find the ball lodged
in the coils of a snake!' While Jim enjoyed his golf, Cowdrey's sick-bed, to
which he had taken with a virus infection, was the venue for the selection
meeting prior to the First Test. The main topic was the batting order, the aim
being to accommodate Boycott's usefulness as a relief medium-pace bowler
without the added responsibility of opening the innings.
    As it happens, he had to. Russell split the webbing of his right hand while
fielding, but by then it was day four with the match heading for a draw.
Australia, with Lawry and Walters making weighty hundreds, declared at 435
for 6, but the story might have been very different. Brown opened the bowling and on the seventh ball of his first over 'I caught Lawry off his glove
down the leg-side. I appealed but it was turned down. Lawry was the first

of the non-walkers.' In reply, 'England, unsettled by the pace of Hawke and Allan, lost four wickets for 115, but Parks, who drove Veivers straight and to the off for 3 sixes, played such a fine attacking innings that his side afterwards was not in serious danger.'[32] Jim hit 52 in a partnership of 76 with Barrington in 68 balls and, although forced to follow on, England ground out a draw. Relaxing by the pool at the Travel Lodge overlooking the Brisbane River, Jim reflected that life had scarcely been better. He had a tour average of 88, the golf handicap was diminishing, Christmas was coming and there was a merry round of up-country games before the Second Test in Melbourne. His divorce was finalised that week, leaving Ann free to join him in the New Year for a wedding in New Zealand. Then, playing against the Prime Minister's XI in Canberra, Jim was stricken with the same violently bilious headache which laid Cowdrey low before the Brisbane Test, and had no cricket til after Christmas.

Though suffering from a recurring stomach upset which kept him out of the South Australia game, Jim was well enough to enjoy Christmas Day golf at Kooyonga with Sir Don. On Christmas morning:

the press, as was the custom, gave a champagne-cocktail party... during which Murray auctioned players in a golf competition to be played in the afternoon.... So good was Murray at the job that £98 was invested.[33]

Jim partnered his best man and had

a good start, until we discovered there was a bar on every third tee. With temperatures in the 90s it was thirsty work. Fred and I won the first nine and retired at the 14th bar, sorry, tee. The Don was about the only one that finished.

For John Murray the ghastly experience still rankles:

Never forgiven him, I haven't, Bradman. By three or four o'clock in the afternoon, we were all fairly well-oiled and part-time golfers anyway. Of course he won it easily – he was a 1-handicap golfer, a teetotaller, and it was his own golf course. The lads were pissed and having a bit of fun. Bradman took the money and buggered off. You'd have thought he'd have said, 'Boys, have a Christmas drink', wouldn't you?

Jim was more philosophical. 'Sir Don played golf like he played cricket – to win. Anyway, it was good fun.'

The scorching arena of the MCG in front of a huge crowd was just the sort of place to banish any lingering Christmas crapulence. Just to increase the pressure, Higgs fell victim to the Cowdrey/Parks lurgy, so England's opening attack would be Jones and Knight. Things went from bad to worse when MJK lost the toss, and at 57 'England missed a chance for which the price they might have to pay hardly bore contemplating.'[34] Simpson had leapt out at Titmus, missed and was stranded. 'Unsighted, I aimed to take the ball on the off-side, but instead of it going into my gloves it bounced rather high and hit my forearm.' Simpson, Lawry and Cowper all made runs in Australia's 358, Knight taking four and Jones three wickets. Boycott and Barber opened with a quick 98, Edrich and Cowdrey made centuries in their own style – the one combative, the other graceful – and at the close of the third day England were 516 for 7, with Jim on 66, playing 'strokes that were a joy to watch'.[35] Eventually England had a lead of 200, and when the home side batted again Ken Barrington stood in for Jim, who had a recurrence of his stomach trouble, and caught Simpson off Barry Knight. With about four hours left, Australia were 18 ahead with four wickets down, when Burge, 'on 34, went down the wicket to a wide one from Barber and hit over the top of it, but the bounce beat me and it hit me up near the shoulder.' The chance was gone, and Burge and Walters made hundreds to save the game. Jim took some stick in the press, because had Burge 'been out then, England surely would have won the match',[36] but as he points out, 'no stumping is quite as easy as it looks from the stands.'

The party flew to Sydney with the ascendancy regained, and the moonlight cruise round the harbour provided by Guinness, accompanied by large quantities of black velvet and oysters, did nothing to dampen the spirits. Confidence was high at nets the following morning and when Simpson went down with chickenpox, the Test omens were propitious.

'303 for 1' – at 4.50 p.m. on the first afternoon England supporters had to rub their eyes to believe the scoreboard. An hour later, they didn't want to. A day of glory had turned to ashes, yet nothing could dim the grandeur of Barber's innings. When he was bowled by Hawke, the Warwickshire opener had 'completed a chanceless innings of 185 out of 303 in just under five hours, his 19 fours finding the boundary at all points of the compass'.[37] Boycott 'just stood and watched as Bob Barber, in tremendous form, came down the pitch, hit the spinners over the top and the pace bowlers on the up and took the attack apart.' Barber, 'a very strong character',[38] always felt that 'as an Englishman if you wanted to have a go at the Aussies Sydney was the place. The ball ran for me and sometimes I think you just know.' Their opening stand of 234 was England's third highest against the old enemy, and one which Jim enjoyed watching, though not from the start:

I reckoned to watch the cricket when I was two away from going in. I put my pads on then and relaxed. We were interested in watching Sincock, who bowled chinamen and Bob annihilated him. That really got things going and we all went out to watch then.'

All except for Allen and Titmus, who unaccountably were playing shove ha'penny.

The boys said — and this is typical of the dressing-room — 'You get on with your shove ha'penny — we don't want you changing our luck,' so I saw one ball of Bob's magnificent knock. Graham McKenzie bowled a bouncer and he pretended to lap it, almost taking the mickey out of him.

At length Hawke bowled a weary Barber, whose brilliant belligerence belied a ruthless efficiency, and then hauled Australia back into the match, dismissing Barrington, Cowdrey and Smith. At stumps England were 328 for 5 and honours were even after a memorable day.

John Edrich then piloted the ship towards a total of 448 with a second successive Test century. 'With that total we knew: Titmus and Allen were a very good pair of spinners and Sydney was traditionally a turning wicket.' However, David Brown bowled well in the first innings, taking 5 for 63, one of them 'a wonderful diving left-handed catch'[39] by Jim to dismiss Burge. Jim snaffled five victims and 'kept magnificently', says Allen. 'He had two stumpings, Cowper and Walters, both coming down the wicket trying to attack me.' Jim was pleased with Cowper 'because it turned and lifted and I had to drag it back.'

Australia, all out for 221, had to follow on and, as England walked out on that last morning with only seven wickets to take, the captain said to Allen, 'I'm going to have a couple of short legs in straight away. You're opening up.' Allen replied, 'Skipper, I know it'll turn. But give me an over to settle in and we'll move him in second over.' 'No, I'm having him there now.' Allen immediately bowled Booth through the gate 'then Mike caught three at short leg. This was the wonderful communication we had — there was a lot of trust in each other.' The off-spinners took four wickets each and when Barber caught McKenzie off Titmus England had won by an innings and 93.

Normally the players give way to the bowlers, but when we came off the field that day we clapped the captain off, which shows the respect and the regard we had for him. And Titmus didn't suffer fools gladly.[40]

With England one up and two to play it was a moment to savour.

Jim, David Allen and a couple of colleagues now had a week off in one of the world's most stunning cities before enjoying a week's cricket in Tasmania. It was a chance to get into batting form against some friendly bowling and, at Launceston, Jim made 91 and 58, 'full of beautiful strokes',[41] before flying to Hobart. Murray kept wicket against a Combined XI and Boycott (156), Lawry (126) and Cowper (143) all indulged in some lengthy batting practice before moving on to the Adelaide Oval, where Australia outplayed the heroes of Sydney. Jim wrote home, a week after the defeat, 'we were naturally all very disappointed to lose the fourth Test, ... but we have no excuse at all, we just batted badly.'[42] Nearly forty years on, it still hurts:

> We blew it. We played shots on such a good wicket. It was the way we played on the whole tour. I can remember Boycs getting out flashing at one, which was very unusual for Geoffrey. I was run out by Kenny Barrington in the second innings, running a second with no apparent danger. They did play well there, though Jeff Jones bowled well and I caught three of them.

In fact Simpson (with 225) and Lawry (119) batted Australia out of sight after England's collective death-wish had them all out for 241. A fighting hundred by Barrington in his last Test in Adelaide took the tourists to within 9 runs of Australia's 516, but they won easily in four days and Jim wrote to Lorraine: 'It is going to be a difficult task now to win the last game and bring the Ashes home, but in this game of cricket, you never know.'

The Windsor Hotel, a lovely old building not far from the ground, was the party's base for the last Test in Melbourne, and it was an ebullient group of players who pitched camp there after a display of batting full of *joie de vivre* on the last day against New South Wales. Having been forced to follow on, Russell made a century and Barry Knight hit 94 out of 120 in 71 minutes.

With the series at stake, the last Test was a boring draw.

> We just batted once and I got to 89 riding my luck when I was run out batting with Fred. He pushed one round the corner, I hared off for the single, but Fred, who's a bit hard of hearing, didn't hear my call. I was stranded. Kenny got a 100 with a 6, the first batsman to do that twice. He was the best player I toured with – he knew the pace of overseas wickets.

England made 485 and insured themselves against defeat, the fourth day was washed out and when Bob Cowper batted for over twelve hours for 307 it was clear that 'the fear of losing frustrated the good intentions'[43] of both sides. Even Boycott found it tiresome. 'Bob Cowper got 307 – it was very boring. You can't knock a guy for getting 300 in a Test match but I'd rather watch Graveney play a couple of maiden overs.'

On to New Zealand, 'and we can at last relax a little', wrote Jim. It had been a tiring tour, four months of effusive hospitality and intense cricket and Jim was left feeling that 'we played such good cricket on the whole tour we deserved to win that series – but we didn't.' Barber was typically forthright: 'We should have won it – we were the better side.'

Jim expected the Tests in New Zealand would 'be rather an anticlimax', but the first in Christchurch was unexpectedly tense. England, at 47 for 4, were rescued by the captain and Parfitt, then Allen made a solid 88:

> I was dreaming of a hundred. When I was on about 80 the twelfth man came out twenty minutes before lunch and said, 'MJK wants to know if you've ever got a hundred in Test cricket.' I said, 'Tell him no.' 'Well', he said, you'd better get a move on – we're declaring at lunch.' I got out soon afterwards. My own fault – but it was a marvellous moment – typical of MJK.

Bev Congdon got a hundred and Jim took 5 catches in the hosts' first innings, equalling his own and Binks' England record, and England set them 197 to win. They collapsed like a pack of cards to 22 for 7 as Higgs took four wickets for 5 runs in 9 overs and they were in peril of being dismissed for less than 26, the record lowest total (at Auckland in 1955). Parfitt got 2 for 5 with his off-spinners and Jim 'bowled three overs because we couldn't get the last two out – Russell probably took the gloves.' New Zealand 'were 48 for 8 at the end – there was a bit of grass on the wicket.'[44]

As Boycott, MJK, Cowdrey, Parfitt, Murray and David Allen *et al.* gently played out a rain-affected draw in Dunedin, Jim and Ann were 'married quietly, at Edinburgh House, the registry office there. We went back to the hotel and had a champagne reception.'

An unenterprising draw in Auckland where 806 runs were scored in twenty-four hours' play ended Jim's extremely demanding tour, with the newly-wed 45 not out as the curtain came down. The voyage home aboard the *Rangitane* did Jim 'the world of good as it gave me time to relax. With three years of continuous cricket behind me, life had been hectic: '66 would be my last home series.'

Chapter 12
Taking the Blows

Jim arrived back at the end of April. Along with many of the MCC party, he was tired. The pitches they encountered overseas in the previous three winters – low and slow in India, fast and bouncy in South Africa and Australia – had put extra strain on the physique and threw into stark contrast the inadequacies of the county wickets on which they earned their bread and butter. However, only five days after docking at Tilbury Jim was in Gillette Cup action against Somerset at Taunton. He wondered if he was holding a bat or an umbrella in a four-wicket defeat.

Dexter, still recovering from his accident, had relinquished the captaincy to the Nawab of Pataudi, another university man and then the youngest captain of a Test side. He had captained India in the Caribbean in 1962, but Sussex was a difficult appointment. He was being asked to lead a team of players vastly more experienced in English conditions. The county had finished sixteenth in 1965, Thomson had just retired, the side was weak in spin bowling and would be further weakened by Jim's absence on Test duty. Pataudi felt he would need to adopt a psychological rather than a physical approach; he had a light touch which left members and some team-mates with an impression of too casual an attitude. He believed they played too much cricket; this dulled anticipation and the game became a chore. This belief expressed itself in his dealings with his leading bowler. In short, Snow thought he was being over-bowled and damaging his England chances. The captain saw this as fair comment, but felt the team's success had to come before that of an individual.

It was up to the senior pros to lead by example and though four games were lost in May, Jim made 403 runs and the eight-wicket win at Leicester exemplified Kenny Suttle's commitment to the cause. Suttle was on the field the whole game, made 89 and 139 not out and

> got three wickets in the match. When you do something quite good like that you don't get knackered. It's more knackering to get out for two. We had to get 265, quite a target with the wicket wearing.

Jim was in fluent form as the Old Trafford Test approached, warming up with
119 against Lancashire at Hove, but he admits that it was not a series which
many England players anticipated with relish – or, in retrospect, that many
enjoyed. Sobers was at his peak and the West Indies were no longer the exuberant cavaliers of 1963 but match-hardened champions. When Mike Smith
lost the toss at Manchester on a wicket which would turn, England were
seemingly doomed from the start. 'That disastrous match at Old Trafford',
David Allen calls it:

> My last with Jim and MJK. We lost in three days. Lance Gibbs bowled mag-
> nificently but I had an unhappy match – 2 for 100. After a very good tour, we
> were shattered. But cricket was great fun. I wouldn't *really* know if I was tired
> or not – I enjoyed it all.

It was the debut of a man who enjoyed it too – with an abundance of swash
and not a little buckle. Colin Milburn hit 94 after being run out for a duck
in his first knock. The West Indies dominated from the first and totalled 484,
Sobers hit 161, Hunte 135 and 'we lost by an innings. I made 43 and 31, but it
was Garry's catch at short leg to dismiss Eric Russell', which Jim remembers
– as does Basil D'Oliviera: 'Russell played forward to Lance Gibbs and got
an inside edge. Sobers, already close at short leg, was actually moving in
when the stroke was made. He changed direction and caught the ball at full
length.'

Some ten days later Jim had his revenge in an extraordinary game at Hove.
While Jim described the wicket as the greenest for three years he felt it was a
sporting pitch. After all, Hove always helped the bowlers early on and, while
it suited Don Bates, Tony 'Omni' Buss and John Snow, the visitors could
field Griffith and Sobers himself, who was quick and could swing it. Pataudi,
mindful of giving the capacity Saturday crowd the chance to watch Sobers,
Nurse and Butcher bat, put them in. He may also have been worried about
letting Griffith loose on a side which, without Dexter, was seen as 'a pretty
ordinary bunch'.[1] By mid-afternoon West Indies were 123 all out; Snow,
who took seven for 29 'was at times unplayable as he got the ball to rise off a
length'.[2] Dexter takes the credit for that:

> In 1965 he had an exaggerated leap out to the left and bowled big in-dippers. I
> told him, 'That jump to the side is not doing you any good.' He went to South
> Africa during the winter and taught himself to bowl more side-on, thereby
> developing an outswinger and bowling straighter and faster.

Joey Carew, with 56, scored almost half his side's runs: Jim remembers that 'every time they flashed they nicked it and got out. Garry flashed at a wide one from Don Bates and I took the first of six I got in the match.'

When Sussex replied, neither Griffith nor Cohen matched Snow's menace. 'Charlie Griffith was under the microscope between Test matches for his action so he didn't bowl as quick as he could have done in the first innings. They weren't particularly ferocious when I was batting,' says Peter Graves, who at twenty made an unbeaten 64. 'At that age you're more fearless and oblivious to speed.' Useful runs from the captain and Alan Oakman took Sussex to a respectable 185.

Monday dawned humid and overcast, and in no time the visitors were a sensational 20 for 5. Tony Buss, with his deceptive medium pace, had shot out McMorris, Carew and Nurse. 'We were more adept at coping, better equipped to exploit the conditions,' Graves reflects. After lunch, when Jim snapped up Joey Solomon off a lifter from Snow, the West Indies were 55 for 7, still three runs short of their previous lowest total in England – 58 against Yorkshire in 1928. The injured Hendricks was last out and the cream of the Caribbean had been dismissed for 67, 'Omni' and Snow each taking 4 for 18. With match figures of 11 for 47, Snow had earnt a recall for the Third Test at Trent Bridge.

With his side needing 6 to win, Pataudi took a bath, saying to Jim, 'Leave your pads on just in case.' Suttle and Lenham strode out to knock off the runs. Graves thinks Sobers was determined to make a statement – 'he was saying "Look, you've stuffed us out of sight here, but we *can* bowl." In Griffith's first over there were nine men behind the wicket – and he bowled one of the fiercest overs of all time.' Kenny Suttle was facing: 'Charlie banged this bouncer in. Rather than ducking I stupidly tried a hook, got a top edge and the world spun round. I had been hit on the hardest part of my head, luckily – if it had been my temple I could have been in trouble. I staggered a bit and went to hospital for an X-ray which showed severe bruising.' Suttle, whacked for the second time in three years, says, 'He wasn't as quick as he was in '63. Then he hit me before I had time to play a shot. In '66 he hit me after I'd finished it.' Graves was promoted by his captain:

'You got some runs in the first innings, get your pads on.' In the middle I realised that everybody was behind the wicket but for silly mid-on. The second ball went straight past my ear: 'No ball!' – and I thought, 'Shit, if that had been straight that would have killed me!' and for the first time I felt that element of fear – that this was a real contest. The next ball was a yorker right up in the block-hole, which hit me on the toe. Although it hurt I was very pleased John Langridge gave me out lbw.

Enter Jim.

> I remember Gravesy hobbling off. As I passed Seymour Nurse he said 'For
> goodness' sake, watch out, Jim – Charlie's hopping mad!' Why Garry let him do
> that I will never know. He'd been called for chucking and it was just stupid.

Four balls to play – 'it was probably the fastest Jim had ever faced because
Charlie threw it.' As Jim took guard,

> Lance Gibbs at silly-mid on gave me some superfluous advice – 'Keep your
> head out of the way'. Griffith's first ball clipped my ear. I was greeted by another
> bouncer which I ducked, dug out a yorker and then he hurled down one of the
> fastest deliveries I have ever experienced. I'd hardly moved a muscle when the
> ball screamed over my left shoulder. I was lucky for I don't believe I could have
> got my head away in time if the ball had been another couple of inches to my
> right. Keeper Jackie Hendricks was still going up when the ball hit his finger-
> tips. Griffith glared at me and I glared back. 'What on earth is going on?' said
> the umpire. 'You'll have to call him if he bowls another one like that', I said.

John Langridge went across to Sobers. 'If he bowls another over from the
bottom end we're going to call him.' The crowd was roaring its disapproval.
Sobers took Griffith off: as he said later, 'there was no point in risking someone else getting hurt.'

It was the quickest over that Snow had ever seen and it got Pataudi out of
the bath to watch with young Graves:

> Although I was cheesed off to get out I wanted to watch. A piece of pure thea-
> tre was being acted out there in the middle. We were almost pissing ourselves
> laughing to see Les scratching about, knowing that Parkser wouldn't fancy
> it the other end, but we were also thinking, 'Somebody else might get hurt'.
> Jim, to Les Lenham, 'Come on, get our runs off this over' – and Les played a
> maiden off Solomon's little wobblers, saying, 'I'm staying down this end, mate!'
> Jim's at the other end: 'For Christ's sake, Les, we don't want another over.' Wise
> man, not with Charlie from the bottom end; because he wouldn't have known
> he was coming off, you see. As it happens Joey Carew came on and bowled
> nice little medium pacers and we'd won the match by tea-time.

Sobers held up his hands. 'In a long tour you have to expect to come across
a wicket like this… It was a typical green English wicket and Sussex had just
the right bowlers for it.' His players were solicitous for Suttle – 'when Kenny

got felled,' recalls Graves, 'Wes Hall was already in our dressing-room making sure that he was OK, which was a nice gesture. Wes was a charming man and a great bowler.' However, what irked Suttle more than anything else was that all the West Indians called to see him in hospital – except Griffith:

> I told Charlie when I went to the Caribbean with Christ's Hospital a few years ago that it hurt far more in '66 than it did in '63. He was suspect but he didn't throw every ball. He threw his bouncer and his yorker, but his stock ball was OK.

This made Griffith all the more problematic – Jim found it 'hard to pick up the chuckers' line, because you don't know the angle it's coming from.'

Jim faced the challenge of the chucker anew as he reported to Lord's barely twenty-four hours later for the Second Test, which proved to be 'a draw of more epic quality than many a match of positive result.' Sobers won the toss but when his side were all out for 269, Higgs claiming 6 for 91, England had the advantage. When England replied, Milburn, Barrington and Cowdrey went quickly and the innings was transformed by Tom Graveney's 96 – 'all class and ease on his return after three years out of the England side'[3] – and a cavalier 91 by Jim, as good an innings as any he had played so far in Tests. When he had reached about 20, Hall made him duck smartly to avoid a bouncer and his trousers split at the back. 'I ducked, heard this rip and Lance Gibbs fell about at short leg. I had to drop bat and gloves and rush off to change my trousers. At 203 for 5, when Tom went, Basil came in and I was going like a bomb.' When the partnership had reached 48, with D'Oliviera on 27, Wes bowled Jim a half-volley. 'Jim is a good driver,' says D'Oliviera.

> He has a strange, open stance and his bat comes in from a funny angle, but it swings from high up and he goes right through with the stroke. He hit this ball, straight and as hard as I have ever seen a drive hit.

Sadly, 'it hit Basil on the back of his foot, dropped on the ground and before Basil could recover Wes had got the ball and ran him out. It robbed me of four runs too!' Now, 'Parks, usually a free-swinging batsman, was bowed down under his responsibilities, a gambler who had picked up his chips.'[4] Jim found an unlikely ally in Ken Higgs and their partnership of 59 in 75 minutes gave England a first innings lead of 86. Jim made alliterative headlines in the Sundays – 'Peerless Parks', 'Plucky Jim Parks'.

Monday was a memorable day, especially for Jim, who joined Evans, Waite and Oldfield with 1,000 Test runs and 100 victims when he caught Seymour

Nurse off D'Oliviera. When he pouched Kanhai off Barry Knight, West Indies were in effect 9 for 5 with only Sobers and the bowlers left. The rest was a family affair: the captain was joined by David Holford, his cousin and leg-break bowler, and the pair put on 274 (Sobers 165 and Holford 105) and left England to score 284 in four hours. Milburn, laying about him 'like a sturdy smithy', harboured thoughts of chasing the total but wickets fell at the other end. Barrington went cheaply, then in successive balls from Hall, Cowdrey and Jim, bowled round his legs. At 67 for 4 England had two hours to survive, but Milburn, with his maiden century, and Graveney broke England's fifth-wicket record against the West Indies and a remarkable match was drawn.

Back at base, fine bowling by Tony Buss had won the county two successive games and Jim had time only for a contribution of 72 not out in a defeat at Old Trafford before the Third Test at Trent Bridge. Snow's exploits at Hove had earned him a recall and Derek Underwood's 59 wickets thus far that season gained him his debut ahead of Hobbs and Barber. Illingworth replaced Titmus and when he bowled Barrington with two innocuous off-breaks at nets, it was clear that all was not well with the Surrey man. Overnight it was revealed that he had been seeing his doctor for some weeks for nervous exhaustion. He had been playing cricket almost non-stop for seven years and the strain was beginning to tell.

The events of the first day gave no foretaste of the scale of England's eventual demise. On a perfect batting wicket West Indies were bowled out for 235, Nurse making 93 and Higgs and Snow taking four each. England, left with fifty minutes to bat, ended at 33 for 3, the initiative ceded to Sobers and Hall. Then Graveney, with a velvety 109, and Cowdrey, an uncharacteristically torpid 96, retrieved the position, the captain walking after getting an edge to Hendricks off Griffith. That England led by 90 was due to an exhilarating last-wicket stand of 65 between Underwood and D'Oliviera, who hit a powerful 76.

Then the West Indies turned the screw, Basil Butcher, Kanhai (63) and Sobers (94) flogging increasingly tired bowlers to reach 482 by Monday evening, when Sobers declared. Butcher walked off, unbeaten on 209, and England were left 393 to win on a wearing wicket. They batted badly, falling by their own device rather than fiendish bowling. At lunch they were 142 for 5, Jim caught for 7 mistiming a drive off Hall, and by mid-afternoon Underwood, on debut, stood with Snow between the West Indies and their second Test win of the tour. Griffith bounced Underwood, who didn't see the ball until it rose towards his head. He fended it off with his hand and it caught him on the head. Though he went down dazed, he carried on before, a few balls later, Griffith bowled Snow and England had lost by 139 runs. Underwood laughs about it now: 'Getting hit in the teeth by Charlie Griffith off my glove ensured that I played in the next Test', but Snow felt, along with the crowd – and Sobers – that there was no excuse for bouncers in that situation.

Jim had a poor match – but it was a collective failure. Sobers and Hall, then Gibbs and Griffith had wrought havoc and the attack had no answer to Butcher's bellicosity and Sobers' talismanic effect on the series.

By the time Jim arrived at Headingley for the Fourth Test he was in the slough of despond, having scratched 178 runs in a month. 'I got right out of form and I couldn't get back. I remember going to Hastings and getting 9 runs in four knocks! The wicket was starting to go there and Kent beat us in two days.'

Jim had a little light relief at the Lansdown Club in Bath, playing for Rothmans Cavaliers against Somerset. 'Ted and I played a lot for the Cavaliers – he won the toss and we made a brisk start.' Jim hit 33 in fifteen minutes, when rain forced them off. Ross Salmon, working for BBC2, said, 'Hey, Jim, do you realise that you are in with a good chance of hitting the fastest fifty?' 17 in ten minutes would net Jim the £50 award and on the restart he stroked 3 fours, kept the bowling and got 50 in 22 minutes. Dexter kept wicket and with 9 overs left Somerset needed 100. They did it with a ball to spare, thanks to Mervyn Kitchen's fantastic hitting. For Jim and Ted, Cavalier cricket was a taster for the sponsored 40-over format which would emerge three years later, ideally suited to Sussex, twice Gillette champions, but in which, oddly enough, they struggled.

'By the time I got to Leeds I was right out of form.' Jim was not alone. Apart from D'Oliviera, with 88, and Ken Higgs, with an improbable but spirited 49, England made two feeble responses to the West Indians' 550, in which Nurse (137) and inevitably Sobers, with 174, his highest score in England, put on 265 in four hours' scintillating batting. The supreme all-rounder then took 5 for 41, wrapping up England's first effort with 3 for 0 in 7 balls. It was Lance Gibbs' turn when England followed on, bowling beautifully to take 6 for 39. At 133 he induced Jim to hoist a pull to square leg. His final Test innings in England was over for 16. 'Lance had this lovely high, lazy action and he had very long fingers which he wrapped around the ball.' When Jim departed, England were six down with only Milburn left. 'We lost heavily', says Jim – he could say that again – the margin was an innings and 55 runs and 'if it had been a horse race the stewards would have called for a dope test.'[5] Jim, who loved and lived for his cricket, was suffering the same kind of burnout which afflicted Barrington at Nottingham and he was not sorry to get his cards, along with Cowdrey, Milburn, Titmus and Underwood. Writing during the Test to Lorraine Whitehead, he says:

> I am very pleased with life, but I am looking forward to the end of the season, as I feel just about out on my feet at present and have certainly had enough cricket to last me for a while.[6]

Fortunately for Jim the last laps of the Championship circuit were at beguiling grounds with good wickets – Cheltenham, Eastbourne and Worcester, followed by a festival romp at Scarborough. John Snow and 'Omni' Buss took seventeen wickets between them in the ten-wicket win at Cheltenham, where another significant feature was the civic reception, at which Pataudi responded to the mayor in Hindi. Suttle, irrepressible as ever, took it upon himself to translate, though his knowledge of Hindi was non-existent. 'We had lots of fun, playing then! The Mayor would have thought "This is great stuff – I've got a genuine Indian prince talking to me in his native language!"'

Jim had the Saffrons to thank for some kind of return to form, making 28 and 46, followed by 55 at Hove. Meanwhile England, revitalised under Brian Close, beat the West Indies by an innings at the Oval, John Murray making a hundred. 'Considering we had all those great players then – Boycott, Edrich, Cowdrey, Barrington, Graveney,' says Underwood, 'only one player played in all five Tests – Ken Higgs. It shows we were in a bit of a mess.' Sussex won their last game of the season too, beating Worcester by 31 runs in a low-scoring contest at New Road, Buss and Snow again doing the damage.

All in all, Sussex had had a reasonable season under their Indian prince. They finished tenth and won eight out of thirty first-class matches, beating Yorkshire, the Champions, Worcestershire, the runners-up, and, famously, the West Indians.

Jim caught the sea-air in a carefree coda at Scarborough as he scored a run-a-minute 101 not out in helping an England XI beat the Rest of the World.

> I got my revenge against Bapu Nadkarni, who'd frustrated me in India. He was so accurate there that you daren't take risks against him as umpires don't give batsmen the benefit of lbw calls. He didn't spin it at Scarborough, so I got my front leg well down the wicket and swept four after four to square leg. They then packed the leg side and I hit him over extra cover.

This dashing form took him into the England side as a batsman against the Rest of the World in a Rothmans mini-series at Lord's. Jim made 42 and 33 and with wins over the Rest of the World and West Indies, England took the trophy.

Jim returned home to Hassocks for a bit of a rest before taking up his winter job reporting on football for United Newspapers. He was also busy that winter writing *Time to Hit Out*, which was published in the spring. That summer, 1967, India were to tour and the Nawab of Pataudi would lead them. One morning in November, Spen Cama rang Jim. 'We'd like you to be captain next year.' Cama, chairman of the Cricket Committee and one of the most respected administrators the county ever had, had high expectations. 'We all know Jim is one of the most attacking batsmen in the game, and I particularly want to see him bring that aggressive and purposeful spirit into his captaincy.'

It was an ambition realised. 'I had always wanted to be captain' – perhaps too openly. Certainly, in a letter to Lorraine in August Jim had apologised that his features in the *Eastbourne Gazette* 'have not been so lively. I shall have to rectify this next year, but this season I have had to tread carefully.' With the captaincy clearly going to be an issue in 1967, Jim was reluctant to rock the boat.

He was the obvious choice. He was the best player and was respected as such. Along with Suttle and Oakman he had been on the staff the longest. However, he had broken the mould of Varsity captains and he 'was under more scrutiny than he should have been as regards results. This made it very difficult for him.'[7]

Jim was at the summit, with the Captain's Room and the £1,200-a-year salary. However, he was a realist. Dexter, Pataudi and Thomson had gone and he had instructions to play attacking cricket while rebuilding the side. His innate optimism led him to feel he might have a match-winning combination of bowlers – Snow, Buss and Bates – and he hoped young Euros Lewis from Glamorgan might prove an effective spinner. 'I went down to Cardiff to sign him. In those days you could sign only so many players from out of the county. He enjoyed his beer and enjoyed life. He became a good friend of mine.' Griffith thought he was a useful cricketer, a talented bat-pad catcher and a brave left-handed bat but 'he didn't have a very secure domestic life and got led astray.' Peter Graves had 'never seen anybody spin it more than Euros. He didn't fulfil his potential but he was a real talent.'

Jim sums up his captaincy with disarming candour. 'The first year went so well and in the second year it fell apart. We played excellent cricket in '67 and I was made one of *Wisden*'s five cricketers of the year for the way Sussex played, not me.' The operation was a success but the patient died, sliding from tenth to thirteenth in the table. Jim admitted in his book, published at the start of the season, 'I have a personal problem as to whether I can combine the responsibilities of wicketkeeper with those of batsman and captain' – and prophetically, 'this is something that only time and further experience will resolve.'

The season started with the captain determined that the side should be fit. Jim handed over training to his old schoolmate and ex-Seagull footballer Don Bates, who found it difficult:

> I needed two different programmes – one for the elder statesmen and one for the others: Ken Suttle and Alan Oakman, compared with Peter Graves, who was ten years younger doing a few laps of the County Ground; even then, Mike Buss ran hard but Tony didn't sprint very much.

The rising star in Sussex cricket was a young man from South Africa, Tony Greig. Educated at Queen's College, Queenstown, he had been recommended to the county by Richard Langridge, who was teaching there. On trial during 1966, he was under the wing of Jim senior, then the county coach, with whom he was unable to establish any relationship. Greig perceived Jim senior's self-effacing manner as aloofness and to the self-confident youngster, he typified the establishment ideal. Nevertheless he found Jim senior an extraordinary man, Sussex to the core, with much to impart. Needing to prove himself, this brash newcomer sensed an undercurrent of resentment as the season began. He saw himself as a threat to the older players like Suttle, Oakman, Lenham and Cooper, who were nearing the end of their careers and he detected a palpable tension between them and the younger players coming into the side. One morning after training he joined Jim in the Gondolier Café, where over a hot chocolate Jim told him he intended Greig to bat at number 5. He was in.

The opening skirmish was positive – a two-wicket win at Worcester in the Gillette Cup. Then Lancashire came to Hove, with Statham, Higgs and Lever to face. The match was 'a great disappointment. We batted first. Greigy got this magnificent hundred – the finest innings he ever played.' He hit 156 – but it might have been a duck. Suttle was at the other end:

> Statham was bowling and the first ball rammed into his pads. I had a feeling of 'Oh, my Gawd, that's out,' but he got the decision. If he'd been given out first ball, you don't know what would have happened after that.

Oakman was characteristically blunt: 'Should have been out. Statham bowled him a yorker and hit him right on the bloody foot.' John Snow then took 4 for 6, Lancashire were 21 for 4 overnight 'and then it rained. We could have got off to a flyer.' Greig, buoyed by his triumph, went up to Fenner's the following day and was bowled first ball, to face a sardonic Alan Oakman: 'we told him, 'Funny old game, Greigy.'

Jim had a dismal May, with a highest score of 32 in the win over Glamorgan, where Snow demolished the Welshmen with 6 for 18. Then Peter Graves went down with glandular fever at Leicester and never played again that season. It was a blow: 'I thought he was a future England player. Brilliant fielder, he could bowl as well.'[8] There was progress in the Gillette, however, with Middlesex being beaten at Hove and progress of another kind in June. The second day against Hampshire was the first time county cricket was played on a Sunday at Hove. Jim took 7 catches in an eight-wicket win and Warwickshire were trounced by seven wickets later that week, Mike Buss straight-driving for a handsome hundred. This momentum, however, was ruined by alarming inconsistency: a defeat at the Oval was followed by a close win over Hampshire in the Gillette Cup until the wheels spectacularly fell off at Tunbridge Wells. Norman Graham, 6ft 7in, took 12 for 77 as Sussex crashed to defeat by 208 runs. The wicket 'did a bit that game and Norman got terrific bounce'[9] – as did Snow, except that umpire Lay warned him and his skipper about their excessive use.

Jim's early season famine was supplanted by a mid-summer bloom as ephemeral as that of a desert flower. He scored 577 runs in eight knocks, starting with 150 at Old Trafford, 97 in a thrilling finish against Nottinghamshire at Hove and 107 against Derbyshire, watched by his sons.

'During the summer', Bobby recalls, 'we would be sitting here with grandfather.' He and Andy saw an emphatic win, as Tony Buss bowled Sussex to victory by ten wickets in two days.

> I loved watching John Snow – he really was my childhood hero. I spent hours with the Sussex players as a kiddy – Snow, Les Lenham, Dexter a bit, Kenny Suttle, Oaky, Peter Graves – all Dad's mates. It was a great laugh because my brother would have been here as well.

He might also have been amused by Peter Eyre, the Derby bowler, who was bald. 'He was wearing a wig and decided to bowl in it. As he ran in the wig started slipping. Everybody collapsed so, with his sweater, he handed his wig to the umpire.'[10] Jim then made 78 against the Pakistanis and when

Gloucestershire were crushed by eight wickets, Tony Greig taking 8 for 25, the team was riding high.

Wednesday 19 July was the day of disillusionment when, for Jim, things began to fall apart. John Arlott tells the story of the Gillette semi-final at Canterbury:

> Denness was lost at 3, but Shepherd [77] met the crisis with gay, attacking strokes; Luckhurst [78], acting as anchor-man, nevertheless scored steadily, and Cowdrey [78] batted with a felicity, ease and certainty such as even he has rarely shown before: indeed, no-one on the ground could recall a better innings from him… In the face of a total of 293, Sussex batted with too great anxiety, one eye on the clock and the other on their wickets; they matched the Kent scoring rate for a considerable period, but no batsman played a major innings and, despite some characteristically busy runs from Suttle, shrewd aggression from Parks and some big hits by Greig, they were beaten by 118 runs.

After that defeat, distress signals were hoisted in the camp.

> In late July I can remember going to Hastings and I'd strained my side. I watched Underwood taking fourteen wickets on a cart-track. Gravesy was ill, Snowy had gone in the back, then Oaky was injured and I had to leave him out at Eastbourne.

Sussex failed to win another game and lost four in a row in a dreadful August. Surrey won at Hove and then Jim saw his side lose to Northamptonshire by ten wickets in successive games, at Northampton and then at Eastbourne. Jim made his customary runs at the Saffrons – 49 and 65 not out – but so did Milburn. 'I left them quite a total. I said "If Olly gets runs so be it. If we get him out quickly they'll struggle." Well, he got this magnificent hundred and slogged us all over the place.'

Tony Nicholson was the destroyer when Yorkshire rode into town; with Close at the Test, Trueman led the side. Young Bobby, accustomed to the Sussex players and a little blasé, shook hands with the great man. 'That was big time: he was a famous England player.' The visitors made 210, thanks to 81 from Padgett, and Sussex replied with 142, utterly undone by Nicholson's 9 for 62, including a spell of 7 for 35 in conditions helpful to his skiddy medium pace. Suttle thought 'there was a slight doubt about him because some people reckoned he jerked it', but Jim considered him 'a fine bowler, with a whippy action.' Trueman called him 'the best uncapped seam bowler I played with'. Injured after being picked to go to South Africa in 1964, he paved the way for Ian Thomson to make his only MCC tour. A former Rhodesian policeman, he was tall with excellent control; he died in 1985 sadly young, at forty-seven. Left to chase 350 to win, Sussex strove valiantly but lost by 83 runs. After rain forced a draw against Middlesex in the bank Holiday game, Sussex entertained a Rest of the World XI at Hove and the season meandered to a damp close.

MCC were to tour the Caribbean that winter and the main debate centred on the issue of the captaincy. Close was the incumbent and with five wins in six Tests during the summer he seemed certain to lead the tour, but an accusation of time-wasting at Edgbaston to deny Warwickshire victory and Close's subsequent obduracy sealed his fate. Indeed, Close says:

> It was a cooked-up job. Crawford White of the *Express* rang me a fortnight before it all happened and said, 'For heaven's sake, Brian, watch your step. They want you out and they want their own man in.' I didn't know until we'd won the last Test at the Oval and Doug Insole said, 'I'm sorry, Brian. The selectors chose you to take the team, but MCC have overruled it.' And the bottom fell out of my life.[11]

Colin Cowdrey was the preferred choice.

Jim thought his Test career was over. Apparently not, for he was still in the England reckoning, playing two one-day games against Pakistan and the Rest of the World just as the touring side was chosen. 'It was quite a surprise to me to find I was going back to the West Indies,' but Close described Jim as 'an obvious tour selection. He wasn't perhaps the best wicketkeeper but the fact that he was a bloody good batsman as well meant that the batting strength went down to 7 and 8.' His winter spoken for, Jim turned his thoughts to matters of politics.

Throughout the summer, Fred Rumsey had canvassed through the county dressing-rooms the idea of a cricketers' association. In October, a meeting was held at the *Daily Express* office in Fleet Street to form such a body – virtually a cricketers' trade union, but only forty people turned up. Jim agreed to take the chair for that meeting only. Cliff Lloyd and Jimmy Hill of the Professional Footballers' Association spoke and it was agreed to form the association, with membership confined solely to active, first-class cricketers. In late November

> we had the first meeting of the PCA at Edgbaston. By the time of the meeting in Birmingham I had been appointed captain of Sussex which meant I was *ex officio* on the committee. I said I would love to be chairman but I had to opt out.

Time then to pack for the Caribbean. Alan Knott had kept for England through the summer and as far as Jim knew Cowdrey wanted him 'as back-up for Knotty and for the batting.' By the end of the tour Knott, the best English keeper since Godfrey Evans – some would say the greatest of all – had made the berth his own. For Jim it would be a difficult winter.

Chapter 13
Things Fall Apart

The Magical Mystery Tour was at the top of the charts when, two days after Christmas, Jim left Heathrow for Barbados. While the Caribbean held little mystery for him eight years after his Trinidad triumph, it was magical once again to be touring with MCC when he thought his Test career had ended.

Three days later Jim was driving fluently against Barbados Colts when he fell to a smart catch in the gully off John Shepherd and just after lunch MCC were 55 for 5. Welcome to Bridgetown! Escaping from a poor start with an indifferent draw, things barely improved against a President's XI where, although Boycott and Cowdrey scored centuries, the other batsmen, as yet unacclimatised, took time to settle. There was much to ponder as Jim returned to Trinidad. In Port of Spain Alan Knott staked a claim for a Test place with 'the first of his many sound, well-judged innings in first-class games'.[1] The island, well poised at 290 for 5, collapsed to 321, and at 88 for 5 MCC were in disarray before David Brown (29) and Knott, with 39, ran out of partners and the tourists finished 114 behind. It was not Wes Hall, who had moved from Barbados, who did the damage, but the leg-spin of Willie Rodriguez, who took 6 for 51. Set 319 to win, MCC limped to 188 for 6 when the tropical night closed in to save the Englishmen from further embarrassment. As preparation for Test cricket it was far from ideal and only the two-day match against Trinidad Colts at the Texaco Oil Company's ground in Pointe à Pierre stood between England and the First Test. Jim played on familiar ground at Guaracara Park and made 67, Milburn hitting 139.

It must have been an interesting selection meeting before the Test. Milburn or Edrich? Hobbs or Pocock? Snow or Jones? Knott or Parks? Jim says that he didn't keep wicket until the First Test (although he kept against the President's XI) and asserts that he 'went on that tour as back-up to Knotty and played as a batter in the early games.' That is not the Kent keeper's recollection: 'I was very much the youngster on his first tour, and Jim was an established senior player.'[2]

Whatever the balance of power, Knott was the man in place, but Jim got the nod.

On the eve of the Test, the senior players – Cowdrey, Graveney, Titmus, Ken Barrington and myself, together with Les Ames – decided that we just couldn't put Alan in the Test side. He had done all the keeping (!) but had had an absolute nightmare, punching it all over the place.

Knott was naturally upset, less about the choice than about the fact that he had not been told in advance. After the announcement had been made:

Les Ames took me aside and said, 'We're worried about the batting.' I had a Kent captain and a Kent manager – and with that line-up – Boycott, Edrich, Cowdrey, Graveney, Barrington, D'Oliviera – he was worried?

Cowdrey et al were taking a cautious approach – England could not afford to lose the first Test.

Far from losing, England almost won but 'we couldn't get Wes out. We won the toss and batted and we thought they might be a bit over the hill. Wes had been going a long time and Charlie was no longer chucking it.'[3] At the end of the first day England were 244 for 2 'and we knew they weren't going to be a force in the series.' Graveney stroked a cultured 118, Barrington an efficient 143 and, when he was out at 432 for 4, Jim and D'Oliviera took England past 500. 'We went on to get 568 and I was leg before, beaten by a quicker one from Sobers for 42.' The West Indies, despite Clive Lloyd's 118 and Kanhai's 85, were forced to follow on, Jones taking the last three wickets to leave them 6 short. An hour-and-a-half's rain reduced England's chance of bowling West Indies out again and by mid-afternoon on the last day the home side seemed safe at 164 for 2. Then Hobbs caught and bowled Kanhai and Brown shot out Butcher, Murray and Griffith. Six wickets had gone in an hour for only 16 runs. Hall joined his captain, kept playing and missing and survived. It was a battle of wits between Sobers and the bowlers and when Cowdrey bowled the last over himself, 'even the huge relief that we had at last come good on the tour did not compensate for our deep disappointment.'[4]

Jim had proved his worth with a solid 42 and a catch off Jones. Alan Knott 'thought Jim kept well to Robin Hobbs – he was bowling around the wicket into the rough which not many people did in those days.' Jim had no time to reflect on the fickleness of the rain gods. Up at 5 a.m. for the flight to Jamaica, the party then faced a five-hour coach trip to Montego Bay, not to the seductive pleasures of the holiday playground but a 'barrack block of a hotel' across the road. The real purpose of the trip was a two-day match against Jamaica Colts, where John Snow found a wicket to his liking and

Robin Hobbs took 7 for 97. The rest was a bit of R&R. On the Sunday, the bookmaker William Hill treated the party – and Lester Piggott, who was holidaying in the Caribbean – to a buffet lunch round the pool at his villa in the hills, courtesy of Brian Close, a long-time client of Mr Hill's organisation. Close, covering the tour for the *Sunday Mirror*, was staying with him but 'I still mixed with the lads.'

Out in the West Indies at the time on a supporters' tour was Spen Cama, and 'we heard that Sussex were trying to sign Barry Richards, the overseas player I wanted.'[5]

Richards, then twenty-two and one of the most talented batsmen in the history of cricket, had provisionally accepted a three-year contract with Sussex, 'when we heard from Hove that Hampshire had offered Richards an extra £300 a year.' The Sussex vice-chairman said the county was not prepared to enter into a Dutch auction for his prized signature and Cama and Jim concurred. 'We were too far away to get involved.' The decision still rankles with Mike Griffith:

> If anything sums up the Sussex Committee at the time – their lack of foresight and their reluctance to spend a bit of extra money – it was that incident. I can't begin to think what Sussex might have achieved if he'd been our overseas player – and he was on the verge of signing! I remember asking business people and they were queuing up to pay an extra £100 a year. It was a catastrophic mistake.

In the event Jim recruited Geoff Greenidge, who 'played for West Indies, was a good little batter and could bowl leg-breaks – but he wasn't the personality that Richards was.'

The pitch at Sabina Park for the island game was ill-prepared and a left-arm spinner with the fantastic name of Altemont Beresford Wellington took 6 for 23, bundling out the tourists for 135. In reply Snow, bowling with pace and control, making the ball lift and move away, shattered Jamaica with 5 for 36 and when Edrich and Cowdrey serenely added 201 the skipper was able to leave the island 380 to win. They showed no appetite for the task and England wrapped up a win by 174 runs just into the extra half-hour.

'Then we played the Test where I started a riot.' In 1999 the match at Sabina Park had to be abandoned as the pitch was considered too dangerous. It was little different in 1968. Snow remembers 'an amazing strip with a ridge at one end, zig-zagged by cracks, shining like a mirror'. Close describes the preparation:

The earth dried like concrete and they would water and roll it, water and roll it. The day before the game they'd sprinkle a few grass cuttings on the surface so that it looked a little green and they'd spin the roller on it so it shone like a mirror – you could almost shave in it. As it dried, so you got the cracks.

On this 'near-lethal' wicket, 'which was not suitable for a club match, let alone an international game',[6] it is to England's credit that by tea on the second day they had made 376, largely thanks to Edrich (96), Barrington (63) and a fighting century by the captain. Boycott went early, bowled by Hall, 'a great athlete and a very nice man. He took a huge run and didn't get it right all the time, so he sometimes used to take off with his feet levering him above the screen. He'd come in with his crucifix swinging like a pendulum round his neck, gleaming in the sun.' Then Edrich and Cowdrey put on 201 and when West Indies crumbled to 143 in 49 overs, routed by Snow's 7 for 49, the game looked all over. Ably supported by the menacing left-arm away swing of Jones, and David Brown at his peak, the Sussex pace man was almost unplayable and produced 'one of the most terrifying… spells of fast bowling' Close had ever seen. He was 'fearsome', the bounce unpredictable and life was tricky for Jim: 'I can remember Snowy bowling to Garry, pitching outside the off-stump and it hit one of these cracks and went down to fine leg for 4 wides.'

West Indies followed on 233 behind and when they came to Sabina Park on the Monday Seymour Nurse determined to hit them out of trouble. He smashed a ferocious 73, before at 174 for 4, Sobers arrived and survived three chances, one of which split Graveney's finger at slip, before he had reached double figures. Had any one of them stuck, England might well have won. Soon however West Indies were 204 for 5, needing 29 to avoid an innings defeat with only Sobers and the tail left.

I was standing up to the stumps to Dolly and Basil Butcher kept tickling it down to fine leg. Dolly said, 'I think we can do him. Go back.' So I did, thinking if the ball's anywhere near middle and off I'm going. He nicked it, I dived and it went straight in the left hand, full stretch. You dream about it and Basil Butcher stayed there. He was given out quite rightly but had he not stayed – if he'd walked straight away everything would have been all right.

'It was a very good catch,' says Boycott, 'but when Butcher looked round to see if Jim had caught it cleanly and then at the umpire, it gave the crowd the impression it might have been dodgy. They were losing the game, their heroes were not coming up to scratch and all sorts broke loose.' Front-page headlines in the *Daily Telegraph* read 'RIOT STOPS PLAY IN TEST' and the chaos in Kingston 'was considered in retrospect to have been fomented by elements demonstrating against authority.'[7] As the crowd rained bricks and bottles on to the field, Cowdrey and Sobers walked across and tried to calm then down – whereupon the police arrived and attempted to restore order by firing tear-gas towards the rioters. This was a misjudgement, for the wind was in the wrong direction. Jim had grabbed his ciné-camera and 'as I got out there the tear-gas hit me. It burnt my throat and I had to run back in and get to a sink so I never saw any more of it.' Snow's remedy was to stand under one of the showers. However, Jim Swanton's report was written 'with eyes and nose affected by tear-gas since although the little Sabina Park press-box had been fitted with an air-conditioner – a unique experience for all of us – the door could not be held against spectators escaping from the fumes!'[8] The disturbance would have been laughable had it not been so serious, for the tear-gas reached the parliament building, causing the Jamaican cabinet to suspend its sitting.

Then Cowdrey made a crucial, if understandable, mistake. He agreed to resume play, but England's aggression and momentum had dissipated. Sobers fought his way to a courageous century and with Holford, as at Lord's in 1966, rescued his side and pushed for victory. He declared at 391 for 9, leaving England 159 to win in 155 minutes. When Sobers dismissed Boycott and Cowdrey, leg before off his bat, in the first over, Barrington fell victim to a dubious lbw and Hall bowled Edrich, England stared defeat in the face, 19 for 4 overnight with seventy-five minutes to survive on Wednesday. Graveney and Jim led the rearguard action and added another 19, when Jim was 'hit in the throat by Wes off a top edge. Fortunately it wasn't on the chin, but it meant I couldn't breathe properly.' Thus incapacitated, he fell to another questionable leg before – off Gibbs. The last overs of the game were played out in a febrile atmosphere, which seemed to unsettle the umpires, one of whom 'had moved over to point instead of his usual position at square leg, and when Titmus played a ball in his direction, he stopped it and flung it back to the bowler.'[9] When Sobers bowled Brown, England were 68 for 8 but with a minute left there was no time for Snow to get to the wicket and the match was drawn.

It had been a fraught contest and Jim now looked forward to Antigua. The holiday isle, fringed by white sandy beaches, warm sapphire sea, swaying palms and luxury hotels welcomed the weary tourists – and put them in a run-down establishment with unpalatable food and unpredictable plumbing. This was a disappointment in itself, but an even greater one for Jim was that 'they made me twelfth man and had a little chuckle about it.

I think they did it as a joke.' It was scarcely funny. Jim ran around in the humid heat as Livingstone Sergeant took 127 off MCC. The prisoners in the local gaol next door to the ground prepared the strip – 'and it was the best we'd seen.'

Never mind, there were four days off in Barbados before the island match, time for sightseeing, golf at Sandy Lane, swimming and beach parties. The skipper, Compton, Brian Johnston, John Woodcock and Fred Titmus were mucking about on a boat while Jim was further up the beach:

> It was one of these boats that they use for water-skiing and Fred, not realising they had the propeller in the middle, jumped over the side and the next thing he knew his toes were floating past him.

John Woodcock fished him out but Jim didn't know anything till the evening when someone told him Fred was in hospital. Jim had a Banks's Brewery car which he'd been lent 'so I charged off to the hospital. Fred's sitting up in bed there with his foot all bandaged up, smoking a cigar with a gin and tonic. He said, "I didn't feel a thing."' Nevertheless, the vice-captain had lost four toes and Tony Lock was summoned from a Tasmanian hotel.

Graveney, now vice-captain, led MCC on a near-perfect wicket against Barbados and told Boycott to go and bat all day. 'So I did – he was my kind of captain. I carried on next morning, but I got a lifter and it caught an edge – a pity.' He had scored 243 in nine hours and Snow recalls Boycott complaining when he was out that he'd 'missed valuable batting practice'![10] While Edrich, Barrington, Milburn and D'Oliviera all made runs, 'the failure of Parks with the bat... must have brought Knott close to selection for the Test.'[11] Jim had made only 10 and when he took the field at the Bridgetown Oval on Leap Year's Day, it was to be his last Test.

He had kept well but, for an exceptional player of spin, against Gibbs, Sobers, Holford and Rodriguez, had not made a decent score. Furthermore he was injured. 'Jeff Jones hit me in the back in the nets and I had to have cortisone injections on the morning of the match to get me on the field.' Knott was standing by, but 'Cowdrey... seemed keen for Parks to play and talked him into it.' Once West Indies batted into the third day for a turgid 349 and Edrich with 146 and Boycott (90) ensured that England started the fifth at 412 for 8, a draw was inevitable. England had their chances. At 169 without loss they began the fourth day with 500 as the target and when Jim joined Edrich at 319 for 4 that was still a viable hope. They were dashed when the next ball from Gibbs induced Jim to play across the line, leg before for 0. It was an ignominious end. England ended 100 ahead and when Snow had West Indies 79 for 3, victory loomed on the horizon. But then Butcher, with 60, and Lloyd, with a belligerent 113, made the game safe. To add insult to injury, 'Clive Lloyd gloved one to me off Jeff Jones and was given not out and went on to get a hundred.' Then, to add injury to insult, 'somebody threw it in, I pinched the index finger and broke the top joint. I kept the rest of the game but had to have an x-ray. It was chipped.' Jim did not keep wicket again on the tour. He 'gave way,' says Boycott, 'to the person I believe was the greatest wicketkeeper batsman ever – Alan Knott.'

If the hotel in Antigua had been one-star Fawlty Towers, the one on Malabar beach in St Lucia was five-star paradise. The players had suites with banana and coconut palms outside the door and golden sands were yards away. Only the rain spoiled the party, washing out the last day's cricket, but not before the Windward Isles had reduced MCC to 85 for 7. Jim was caught by Laurent off Charlemagne for 2: these gloriously-named medieval knights shared seven wickets and only aggressive 40s from Higgs, Brown and Hobbs took the score to a respectable 215. Lock's 3 for 62 put him in the frame for the Fourth Test in Trinidad at the end of the week.

For the West Indies, Hall was dropped, and Carew and Rodriguez came in: they expected it to turn. On the eve of the match, Cowdrey rang his predecessor. 'Who would you play, Brian?' Close replied, 'You'd better play both spinners, they're the ones that might get wickets.' In the event, caution prevailed. Lock was in for Pocock.

This extraordinary game has passed into cricket folklore as 'Sobers' blunder' – an unfortunate epithet, as it obscures some fine batting from Nurse (136) and Kanhai (153) as West Indies rattled up 526 for 7 declared. In reply England were 260 for 5, still needing 67 to save the follow on when Knott joined his captain. The Kent pair put on 113, when Butcher removed Cowdrey for 148. England crumbled from 373 for 5 to 404 all out to Butcher's occasional leg-breaks, but the young keeper batted on with unconcerned assurance to remain 69 not out. England were 122 behind and when the West Indies had reached 92 for 2 on the last day, Sobers threw down the gauntlet, and as Close puts it, handed England the match.

I was doing a radio broadcast with Learie Constantine when he declared and I said, 'He's thrown it away. We'll win this without breaking into a sweat. Garry's misunderestimated [sic] the target. They had no bowlers. Charlie Griffith was injured and who the hell was going to bowl us out? They had a leg-spinner that bowled two or three bad balls an over that you could get runs off and Clive Lloyd opened the bowling in the second innings.'

England were set to score 215 in 165 minutes. It was giddy stuff, all the more exhilarating for being so unexpected.

Jim was with Robin Hobbs 'by the swimming pool at the hotel. We were listening to the radio and when Garry declared, we rushed down to the ground.' They saw Edrich and Boycott give England a sound start and then a great innings from Cowdrey, full of expert timing and stroke play. He hit 71 in seventy-six minutes and with 42 needed in thirty-five minutes, Boycott took control, When England won by seven wickets with three minutes to spare, he was 80 not out, having timed his knock to perfection. Sobers had reckoned without the Englishmen's ability to chase a target, a skill developed week by week in the County Championship. He also let his heart rule his head, feeling that another draw would demean the game of cricket, and trusting his gambler's instinct that England were vulnerable to Butcher and Rodriguez. Jim felt that justice had been done because 'we should have been three up by then.'

Jim was now playing out time, though tropical storms alleviated a programme of thirteen days' cricket out of fourteen in the steamy Guyanan heat. The Colts match was curtailed and against Guyana, Pocock and Hobbs spun MCC to a ten-wicket win. In his final knock on an MCC tour, Jim made 16 before Boycott and Edrich cruised to victory in the second innings.

The final Test was a cliff-hanger as Sobers, Kanhai and Gibbs took West Indies to the brink of victory, to be thwarted again by Cowdrey and Knott, with magnificent support from Lock and Pocock. Kanhai (150) and Sobers (152) hit the home side to 414 and England were 259 for 8 before Lock, with his highest first-class score of 89, and his Surrey team-mate put on 109 and reduced the deficit to 43. A peerless 95 not out from Sobers meant that England had to make 308 to win on the last day. At 41 for 5, their three months' hard work was threatened with annihilation, but Cowdrey and Knott ground out 127 together and Knott was there at the end, having made 73 mature and sensible runs.

In only his fourth Test, the Kent man had secured the wicketkeeping berth for a decade. Jim's international career was over and he returned to Hove in the last week of April 'with back trouble, a finger injury and noticeably overweight'.[12] Jim had not been playing very much 'and I wasn't very fit. I had a lot of treatment.'

Jim arrived back to a dressing-room whose morale was at rock-bottom. Richards had slipped through the committee's fingers and by the end of June only one championship win had been achieved. In that time Jim had scored 333 at an average of 18 and he felt things had started to go wrong, but there were three occasions of note, one good, against Yorkshire, one bad at Lord's and one ugly, illustrating how Jim's habitual equanimity was being frayed. Suttle was batting at Bradford when Greig came to the wicket.

> He was 6ft 8in and I went up to speak to him. Freddie Trueman came up behind me, lifted me up nose to nose and held me there. I said to Greigy, 'You want to watch old Fred. He's a bit quick and his away swinger's quite good'. Then he put me down and we carried on with the game. Doesn't happen now – no laughter.

At Lord's the season ended for Peter Graves, breaking his knuckle when Lofty Herman made one lift off the ridge and there was more trouble against Glamorgan at Hove when the visitors thought Suttle had been caught,

> but neither umpire gave him out and Suttle stood his ground. Parks was batting at the other end and angry words were exchanged between him and Glamorgan's skipper, Tony Lewis. The situation grew so fraught with annoyance on both sides that umpire Phillipson warned the players.[13]

Letters flew between the chairmen of the two counties and while the team continued to make progress in the Gillette Cup, beating first Derby with ease and then Northamptonshire by only 7 runs, Jim's emotional and physical resources were being sapped by the struggle to keep the side together. Ironically it was at the Saffrons, traditionally for Jim a happy haven of sun and runs where 'the crisis all blew up after we lost to Lancashire.'

On a rain-affected wicket all four innings were under 90 and although Allan Jones took 11 for 64 on debut, Higgs captured 11 for 69 and Statham and Bond saw the visitors home by two wickets. Jones, only twenty and slightly built, had endearing idiosyncrasies:

> He would come in the Sussex Cricketer with a black coat over his shoulder like the bloke in that Sandeman ad and he used to drink gin and tonics. We told him, 'You'll never bowl bloody quick drinking that stuff'. When he got left out of the first team he said to Grimston, 'Colonel, I'm wasting my time in the second team.' Grimston said, 'Well, go and get another job' – and he did. He went down and played for Somerset, Middlesex and Glamorgan.[14]

After the second defeat in Eastbourne Week, by Worcester, four national papers reported 'a tough-talking team meeting at Hove' and although Jim believes there was no players' meeting in a formal sense 'that Eastbourne Week finished me off'. Writing in the *Eastbourne Gazette,* Jim spoke of his bitter disappointment that he had 'felt it necessary to resign... I wanted very much to be captain of this county.' Going on to discuss the burden of the job, he says:

> the total effect has been to cause me considerable misery for it is simply not possible to forget the troubles of the cricket field once the game is over. I believe my own batting form has suffered badly... At present I just feel completely shattered.

The week at the Saffrons had been the last straw:

> No-one could have visualised the incredible bad luck that befell the county. To be caught on a wet Eastbourne wicket in one innings is unpleasant enough, but to have to bat on a treacherous rain-affected wicket in all four of our innings during the week made the players feel that fate is really not on our side at the moment. Add to this fact that John Snow was on Test duty, Tony Buss injured and early on during the second game Alan Jones damaged a heel and could not bowl again, and you may well understand just a few of the tribulations that had to be faced.

He was at pains to point out that Sussex's poor form was not an issue. 'I am not leaving a sinking ship; my heart is in Sussex cricket, it always has been and always will be' but 'it has been getting me down mentally. It has got to the stage where it is messing up my life and cricket.'

Sussex were bottom of the table: the *Sun*, the *Daily Express* and the *Sketch* reported dissension among members and John Vinicombe, a long-time friend of Jim's, quoted a player as saying, 'It has been building up for some time.' Tensions exist in every team and:

> There were some vociferous personalities – Snowy, Tony Buss, Greigy; it wasn't a happy dressing-room and I gave up. We'd lost Peter Graves and we did suffer a lot from injuries. It wasn't an easy summer, but there we are.

Graves' observations are enlightening: 'he might not have been the flavour and he was putting on weight as well. Jim doesn't make enemies and it's possible that he was too nice a person to be a captain.' His successor concurs:

> I think Jim had a dichotomy – he wanted to play and I don't think he quite grasped the implication of also being captain. Peter Graves was right – they all looked up to him as a player but not always as a leader. Jim was so close to the

players, having been around for eighteen years, and he wouldn't say, 'To hell
with you lot, you're going to do as I say and you either like it or lump it.' I've
learnt over many years that you've got to be a little detached and unpopular
as a leader and, yes, to be a bit of a bully at times and I don't think that was
in Jimmy's make-up. On reflection, I think it was a poor choice to make him
captain but he wanted to be and so it was quite difficult – but the players
didn't support him when he resigned.

Jim was a victim of the growing influence of player-power. At odds with
many team-mates on his approach to the game, he became the target of
sniping by those who thought someone else could do a better job.

Waiting in the wings was Mike Griffith, who when he was made captain
said he never wanted the job:

I was much too young and I was thrust into it. I don't think the Committee
considered what was involved. I was struggling to keep my place in the team.
I hadn't been part of the Sussex scene; I was slightly different in that I was a
reversion to what Sussex had had in the fifties and early sixties, the Marlar,
Dexter mould.

Prone to nonchalant flippancy, Griffith lacked the strength of character to be
a successful leader and strove in vain to weld together a disunited team. Jim
felt that 'Griffith was thrown in the deep end and I backed him as much as I
could' but it was a difficult situation.

Jim's last game at the helm was at Northampton, where he notched a rare
half-century in that depressing summer and travelled south to Hastings relieved
of a burden, to renew acquaintance with Lord Ted. What happened at the
Central Ground against Kent is the stuff of legend. Colin Cowdrey had rung
Dexter some weeks earlier warning him of a possible recall to the England
team, which was suffering a rash of injuries. 'You would need to play a couple
of county matches,' he had told him, 'and hopefully make a few runs.'

So Dexter turned up, dumped his cricket case (which was suffering from
mould and dry rot after three years' retirement) and with his same old brown
bat made 203

... on a nasty turner... Admittedly things looked a little bleak, going in at 6
for 2 and losing two more partners, with only 27 scored. The pitch was turning sharply and Underwood had the ball... An innings of some substance was
needed if I was to justify the confidence of the England captain. I decided that
counter-attack was my best ploy and had some success.[15]

Dexter punished Underwood severely and 'batted magnificently, hitting Undies over the sightscreen. It was a strange one because all through his career Ted was not a great starter against spin bowling.'[16] Underwood said:

> [Hastings] was a pig of a wicket when it was wet – it really did go, hence my 8 for 9 and 9 for 28. Ted hit the ball so hard that he was ahead of his time in terms of power. The bats in those days only weighed 2.2/2.4 maximum compared to what they weigh now, which is almost 3lb. That's why spinners have gone out of the game, I think.

Sussex were closing in for a much-needed win with Kent eight down but ran out of time and proceeded to lose nine of the last eleven games, one them heavily, at Ebbw Vale, where Ossie Wheatley demolished Sussex with 9 for 60 in their second innings.

The Gillette campaign rolled on however, and a comfortable 48-run win over Gloucester took the county to its third final in six years. No longer the skipper, Jim, at thirty-six, was looking at life beyond cricket and as the team journeyed west to the Cheltenham Festival, Jim made a detour.

> About a month previously at Hove Peter Rowe, who was second-in-command of Heineken at the time, was chairing a sponsors' lunch and I happened to be there. I seldom went in, but I must have been out in the morning and sat next to him. He asked me what I was going to do in the winter. 'I'm looking around', I said. He appeared at Hastings a bit later and said, 'We've got a job for you. Can you come up to town some time?' So I went to Trafalgar Square on the way to Cheltenham. I met Tommy Toms, the MD, and it was decided that I would be working for Heineken, part of the Whitbread set-up.

It was a damp festival, with less than eight hours' play.

> I didn't know Whitbread's had a box at Cheltenham. We had a lot of rain and Tommy Toms came round and said, 'Come and have a drink'. So I did. It was bucketing down; we weren't going to play again that day. Suddenly I looked out of the window and saw the players on the field and I'm supposed to be keeping wicket! I missed about two overs.

It mattered little. Gloucester declared and between the showers Sussex disintegrated to 44 for 9 declared before more rain put the game out of its misery.

A gloomy end to a disappointing season was enlivened by the return of a very unfit Robin Marlar, brought back, so rumour had it, to keep an eye on the young captain, but probably 'because Oaky had packed up when I gave up the captaincy'. Nothing was going right for young Griffith, for in the week of the Gillette final Warwickshire had a pleasant warm-up at Hove, gaining a psychological edge with a three-wicket win on the eve of the big day.

Don Bates is indignant – 'The '68 Final we absolutely threw away' – as Sussex did against the same opponents a quarter of a century later. Batting first, Jim made 57 and Greig 41 as Sussex made 214, which Griffith acknowledges 'was never enough. On a good Lord's wicket, you should always get 250.'

Bates recalls: 'I'd got Bob Barber and then Jim Stewart for about 18 off 7 overs and I was in a nice rhythm. I was used to bowling the whole 12 overs straight away so you didn't stiffen up in the outfield and I was dying to keep going.' Griffith, inexperienced in the job, was possibly unaware of this. With Warwickshire 60-odd for 2 after 15 overs there was a conference in the middle. 'We had about three captains that day – it was farcical. Griffith was nominally in charge but Jim took over and then Dexter. The outcome was I was taken off much against my better judgement.' Jim concedes that 'Perhaps it was a little bit like captaincy by committee,' and Griffith agrees: 'It was a shambles really – Don's probably right, too many people putting in their two-penn'orth.'

'Anyway, I was taken off and Snowy and Bussy had a go.' Mike Buss had made 36 and at the heart of the Warwickshire innings took 4 for 42, including the vital wicket of Kanhai. In any other game he might have won the Man of the Match award instead of slipping away with the rest of the team to drown their sorrows. As it was, with six down, Warwickshire needed 60 off 13 overs when Alan Smith joined Amiss, hit boldly and took them home by four wickets. Bates was 'brought back when they were in a desperate situation and Alan Smith came in and slogged. He chipped the first ball I bowled to Dexter at mid-on and it fell just over his head. I was so stiff – if I'd bowled my 12 overs when I was loose and felt confident...' Ken Suttle agrees – 'if we'd had any other captain perhaps it would have been different.' To rub salt into the bitter wound, Sussex lost money on their share of receipts from the whole competition.

It had been Jim's most disastrous summer as a Sussex professional. The loss of the captaincy, the Championship wooden spoon and the disappointment of defeat in his third Lord's final were difficult blows to take – and to cap it all, his father suffered a stroke and was forced to retire as the team's coach.

With the county in dire financial straits at the end of that summer the committee delivered a rallying call:

Let each player, from those of Test match class to the most junior apprentice, know that the county will demand that he give every ounce of his endeavour at all times… and that if he is not prepared to give 100 per cent support to his captain… then he would do better to seek his fortune elsewhere.[17]

While he had always been totally loyal to the cause, Jim nevertheless heeded this sound advice. That winter he went and worked for Heineken.

Chapter 14
Put Out to Grass

In 1969, both for Jim and the county, the only way was up. As if in response to the committee's call to arms, the team rose from bottom to seventh in the Championship table. This was a considerable achievement, given that no Championship game was won until mid-July and Snow was away on Test duty. The 40-overs-a-side John Player League was launched, tailor-made for Sussex, but they finished bottom, winning only three games all season. Jim was mystified: 'I had a chat to Ted but we never worked out why we did so badly; we just couldn't play the JPL.' Although Jim made 1,210 runs, he remembers not having a great season. The five victories after mid-July were far outweighed by the dismal start and the woeful one-day form.

May was depressing – 'my highest score was 31' – but at least the travelling was gentle, the farthest trip being to Worcestershire after Whitsun. Worcester was flooded: it had been raining heavily. 'We decamped up the road to Kidderminster and Brian Brain bowled very well against us.' Norman Gifford took 7 for 40 as Sussex were dismissed for 105 before the rain took pity on them. Jim's form picked up in June, with four half-centuries, but the team won only twice, thumping Gloucestershire by eight wickets in the Gillette Cup at Hove and coasting to a regulation nine-wicket win over Cambridge University, John Spencer making his county debut against his *alma mater*. Though Jim missed the university match, as was his wont, he came to appreciate the blond all-rounder's virtues. 'He bowled little away-swingers. He didn't used to like me standing up, but I did: he could bat too – hit it very hard.'

June comes just too late for the bluebells which carpet the Forest of Dean like an azure sea, but Sussex's thoughts as they crossed the Severn dwelt less on the transience of floral beauty than on two games against Gloucester at Lydney, the gateway to this ancient woodland. The wicket at the Recreational Trust Ground was red 'with a lot of marl on it and would obviously turn. We got hammered.' The Championship game was over in two days, David Allen destroying Sussex's second innings with 8 for 34. All out for 88, Griffith's side went down by an innings and 39 runs. They had fared no better on the Sunday, for Allen, skipper for the day, said to seam bowler David Smith, 'Smithy, every time Parksy gets down there would you bowl?' 'It worked great because Jim couldn't get at him like he could Mortimore or me.' Though Jim made 56, Sussex scratched together a woefully inadequate 126 for 8 against a side containing Milton, Pullar and Procter. However, there were some silver linings and July began well with Gillette Cup progress, Leicester being beaten at Hove by 60 runs. Jim followed 51 in that game with 46 at Trent Bridge and fell 4 runs short of a century back at Hove, bowled by Peter Lee in the defeat by Northamptonshire.

There was something unique about the Central Ground at Hastings – the back gardens of Devonshire Road running down behind the old pavilion, the concrete stand along South Terrace a challenge to hitters like Arthur Gilligan and Collie Smith, the wooden benches and the marquees, overlooked by the Victorian Gothic town hall and the striking ruin of the Conqueror's castle on West Hill. The ground stood at the heart of Hastings, and cricket, for at least two weeks in the year, made that heart beat. And there were the ghosts: the place exuded a faintly Edwardian air of flat caps and waistcoats, scarves tied round the waist and waxed moustaches, and as a boy I learnt with wonder that Grace and Fry, Ranji and Duleep, Hobbs and Sutcliffe, Hutton, Bradman and Compton had all graced the turf. When the sun blazed down on an August afternoon, and Cowdrey drove Gilchrist to the cover boundary five balls in a row, or Jim hit Halfyard over extra-cover with effortless power into the old pavilion there was no better place to be. For me, even a dull morning with a sea fret running held the promise of some interesting cricket on a wicket which was 'doing a bit' – and if it rained, spending sixpence on an orange juice in a tent pungent with damp canvas and trodden grass, perhaps chancing upon Frank Woolley chatting with Percy Chapman – and mumbling for a shy autograph at the feet of great men. The seagulls had the best view, of course, providing musical accompaniment to a raucous commentary on the antics of the flannelled fools below.

Down the years Jim enjoyed his visits to the ground, but in 1969 'we were done by Glamorgan'. On a real spinner's wicket, Euros Lewis took 6 for 101 against his old county, which he had joined in 1961 as a bold left-handed opening batsman, before his sharp off-spin supplemented that of Don Shepherd. Jim had heard of him after a memorable match against Sussex at Cardiff in 1965. Lewis began with a quickfire 80, before returning the remarkable figures of 2.2-1-1-4, polishing off the Sussex second innings in the space of just 14 balls. Sussex ceded a first-innings lead of 96, Shepherd taking 6 for 52 and when set to chase 301 to win, Sussex, despite a brave partnership between Graves and Lewis, were beaten by 72 runs.

The tide turned, not at Hastings but on the Army Ground at Colchester where Jim remembers 'hooking Boycie when he started whacking it in short,' to such effect that he made 77 in Sussex's 291 and then 59 as Griffith tried to set a target. Needing 232 to win, Essex were devastated by a rampant Snow, who finished with 6 for 20 as Griffith's men claimed their first win of the summer by 90 runs. On the Sunday of the game, in a masterpiece of scheduling, the side drove up to Leicester for a John Player match, stayed overnight and came back on Monday morning!

No wonder they lost at Grace Road, but it was an entertaining day, as Maurice Hallam recalls:

Peter Marner was opening the innings with me and was holding the bat in a baseball grip! He hit 99 in 53 minutes, including 8 sixes. He asked me if I thought he was doing the right thing and I said I would just watch from the other end! Snow did not take kindly to this treatment so he took steps. The players had been on and off the field with rain and remarked to each other, 'That ball's just like a bar of soap.' What only Snow and Jim knew was that John had this round red bar of Wright's Coal Tar soap. We went out again and he bowled it to Peter Marner as if it was the bouncer. Peter hooked it and it burst into a million pieces. He was horrified and everyone fell about except umpire Charlie Elliott, who was furious, but eventually even he saw the funny side.

Following the series win over the West Indies, Snow was unaccountably dropped for the First Test against New Zealand and Hampshire felt the backlash. Jim hit 84 and Greig 93 in Sussex's first innings of 209 then Snow took 5 for 29 and 5 for 51 as Sussex won by nine wickets. July had indeed been better and it ended with a Gillette Cup semi-final at Chesterfield. This time Peter Eyre had the last laugh as Sussex slumped to 49 all out, then the lowest total in Gillette Cup history. Jim top-scored with 16 as the medium-pacer from Brough took 6 for 18 to take Derbyshire to their first Lord's final by 87 runs. This humiliating débâcle left the team in no psychological state to face Surrey at the Oval, which Jim regards as the lowest point of the summer. Alan Hill turned up to the game to be greeted by a despondent Sussex member, 'So you've come to watch the worst team in the Championship.' He was referring to the signs of insubordination in the ranks and the drift towards anarchy which Griffith seemed powerless to stop. Jim saw this too – but 'remember,' he says, 'Mike had had the captaincy thrust on him and had difficulty coping with Snowy, Greig and Buss.' Spectators at the Oval saw a Sussex player kick lumps out of the ground in frustration, while on another occasion Griffith had to run after a player to speak to him as he marched to the boundary. He never stopped walking and only when the skipper had finished did he turn round. Ken Suttle was made the scapegoat for a four-wicket defeat and was dropped after 423 consecutive games for the county. Three weeks later he made 127 against Middlesex at Hove, but 'for some in the committee room the days of Suttle were numbered'.[1]

From this nadir in South London a fraught season slowly turned the corner. A half-century against Kent at Hastings was followed by an unbeaten 109 in a partnership of 152 with Peter Graves against Lancashire at Hove, where rain at lunch on the second day robbed Sussex of a likely win. Jim then went west to Taunton, familiar territory because of the Whitbread Wanderers, the brainchild of Tom Graveney and Frank Twiselton, managing director of Whitbread, who that summer got together some former England players to play Sunday games for charity around the West Country villages. It was Jim's sort of cricket and he would go down and have fun with his old mates. This time Sussex met Somerset in the John Player at Torquay, where he opened the batting 'as we had a theory that we'd try and get on with it from the word go. It wasn't a great wicket, we collapsed to 54 for 8 and lost easily.' After the game, Jim suggested to Graves and Euros Lewis that they had a beer in the Sea Trout at Staverton, which he knew from his Whitbread trips. Had he not done so, he might never have met his wife of thirty-one years, for:

I think it was about the first time I ever met Jenny. She was there with her husband Tony, who I know very well. That was just a brief chat… but Jennifer Rogers, a teacher from Cardiff, mother of my step-children, Scott and Sian, was not forgotten.

The steady improvement continued and, *mirabile dictu*, Sussex won a John Player game, and in style. The game against Middlesex at Hove saw the highest aggregate of runs in the JPL that year – 519 in 76 overs. Sussex raced to 288, Buss, Cooper and Greig making runs and John Lush from Hampstead, in his one and only game for the county, scoring 22. Brearley hit 71 but his side finished 57 runs adrift. Lush may have played only once, but it was a memorable game.

There was now a momentum and in a September crescendo the side won a hat-trick of Championship games and the last John Player against Glamorgan. Sussex often played Yorkshire near the end of the season as people used to come down from the north for a week's holiday: they often saw a dramatic match and 1969 was no exception. Right at the start,

Snowy broke a bone in Boycott's hand. He tried to hook Snowy and gloved it. I caught it and threw it up. Geoff didn't walk and Charlie Elliott gave him not out. He played the next ball down to third man and I watched it. I didn't know what was happening but I heard something going on at the other end. Apparently as Geoff put his bat down, Snowy kicked it away and Geoff clipped him on the shin. Snowy then announced, 'I'm going round the wicket' and bowled the best bouncer I ever saw. Geoff couldn't get out of the way and it broke his wrist. I suppose you could say that was justice – I don't know.

Yorkshire managed a decent 188 and Jim compiled 57 as Sussex secured a 7-run lead. 'I remember Copey bowling off-spinners. I swept him and hit Brian Close in the head at short leg. He just shook his head and had a right go at Copey for bowling down the leg side!' Jim had a good match. Chasing 174, Sussex got home by 6 wickets, Graves and Jim, with 91 not out, seeing them to victory.

A happy week at the Saffrons, where Derbyshire were despatched by 5 runs and Gloucestershire by seven wickets in a game in which twenty-two wickets fell on the first day, rounded off a strange season. The appalling performance in the one-day league was inexplicable and whereas the ascent to seventh in the Championship was praiseworthy, it masked an underlying malaise, which did not escape the attention of *Wisden*:

> Often it seemed that a lack of co-ordinated effort had a stifling effect. Rumblings behind the scenes led to Jones leaving the club midway through the summer because he disagreed with the selection policy… News also came that Col. Williams, the secretary, was to retire once his contract expired in early 1970, and this, though it had nothing to do with the playing side, could not have helped towards a settled outlook.[2]

In the winter Jim was reasonably settled, still living in Hassocks with Ann and working for Heineken, but the media detected signs of mismanagement and muddle behind the scenes at Hove, centring on a fundamental issue – how should Sussex County Cricket Club, with its proud traditions, be set on a secure financial basis in a world of increasing commercialism and sponsorship? This question was especially acute in 1970 as the cancellation of the South African tour meant the loss of several thousands of pounds from the TCCB at a time when the club was already losing money and members.

Against this background of discontent the team had a decent season and after the disaster of 1969, Jim started off well. By the end of May he had scored 473, making 5 half-centuries. Nottinghamshire and Glamorgan were beaten at Hove and while the team continued its doleful form in the John

Player, Essex were defeated by four wickets at Chelmsford to set Sussex on the road to its fourth Gillette final. Jim made another fifty against Hampshire in a seven-wicket win at the County Ground and, at the end of June, Sussex were second in the table, only 5 points behind Surrey. Peter Smith, writing in *Playfair Cricket Monthly*, attributes this to the solid starts given by Geoff Greenidge and Mike Buss, while:

> Jim Parks has regained his touch helped, no doubt, by the hot weather and hard wickets which has encouraged rival sides to turn to spin more frequently. I doubt if there is a better player of spin bowling than Parks as he ably demonstrated during his 166 not out… against Warwickshire at Hove.[3]

It was one of Jim's best innings. 'I remember hitting Browny and Bill Blenkiron off the back foot and the runs just flowed. It was one of those dream innings when everything goes right.' Rohan Kanhai hit an undefeated 162 in Warwickshire's 277, then Jim's innings gave Sussex a lead of 75 and when Tony Buss took 6 for 54 Sussex needed only 47 to win.

Jim looked back on June with mixed feelings, however. In the John Player League against Derbyshire at Buxton 'I was one of Alan Ward's 4 in 4 balls at the start. It's a beautiful little ground but it rains so much up there.' The side did beat Northamptonshire in the JPL at Kettering but it was there that Peter Willey hit Jim 'with an in-swinging yorker. It was one of those low slow wickets where you had to get forward all the time and it dipped in and hit my toe.' When Graves and Mike Buss pulled leg muscles, Sussex could manage only 85 for 8 in their second innings and Jim missed the next two games, as did Tony Greig, who won his England cap, joining John Snow against the Rest of the World at Trent Bridge. Few counties could sustain the loss of players of this calibre at the height of the season and only the Gillette Cup gave Sussex any success over the next two months. In the quarter-final at Canterbury Sussex made only 199, which Jim felt 'wasn't enough, when you think they had Kipper, Denness, Luckhurst, Asif, John Shepherd and Knotty,' but Greig's 5 for 42 bowled Kent out for 152 in 'the only time I ever went to Canterbury with Sussex'.[4] The semi-final at the Oval was a close-run thing. Snow took four wickets in Surrey's seemingly inadequate 196, but wickets fell regularly until Pataudi, making a welcome return, and Graves saw Sussex home by two wickets. Jim made intermittent runs: 'I got 79 on a beautiful wicket at Worcester – one of my lucky grounds' and against Essex at Eastbourne 'my fiftieth first-class century and my last for Sussex'. Against Keith Boyce and John Lever Jim stroked a classy 150. Otherwise his form reflected that of the team, with regular John Player defeats and heavy

Championship losses – to Kent by ten wickets at Hove, by an innings and 125 runs at Blackpool, where Tony Buss took his 100th wicket of the summer, and to Glamorgan by nine wickets at Swansea.

The off-stage murmurings had rumbled on through the summer as no South African tour meant no money. At the end of the season a Special General Meeting was called, at which the auditors were asked to investigate the club's finances. Griffith was appointed assistant to the new secretary Arthur Dumbrell and instituted a weekly news conference to explain what was going on. He might first have dealt with an inconsistent end to a season not without merit. Somerset were crushed at Hove. After Roy Virgin had scored 109 in Somerset's 222, Buss and Greenidge equalled Oakman and Smith's post-war Sussex record with an opening stand of 241 to give Sussex a lead of 105. 33 for 3 overnight, on the final morning Somerset lost their last seven wickets for 21 in 37 minutes, Snow finishing with 5 for 18. Sussex won the John Player game too, Jim hitting 96 not out, his highest JPL score. And so to Lord's, where Jim took the field in his fourth Gillette Cup final, probably the most disappointing. Two years earlier against Warwickshire they should have won but in 1970 Sussex barely turned up. Jim made 34 and Suttle, Griffith and Snow were run out in a very uncompetitive 184. Then 'Kenny dropped Clive Lloyd at cover. I know they had a good side.' Wood, Lloyd and Engineer made runs and Harry Pilling, with 70 not out, secured a comfortable six-wicket victory.

The pain of this second defeat in a Gillette final was eased for Jim by a further encounter with Jenny, at a Whitbread Wanderers match in the West Country. All was not well on the home front as his marriage to Ann had been increasingly unstable throughout the summer. Griffith says:

> It's very difficult to keep that totally hidden. We lived so close together for such a long time in the summer and it was playing havoc a bit with his sleep pattern. I think getting runs is one thing but he was juggling four or five balls in the air at one time.

Soon after the season ended he and Jenny 'sort of got together'. He was still working in the licensed trade, though by now Whitbread's were brewing Heineken in Britain and became Jim's main employer for the next sixteen years. Jim was looking beyond cricket: at thirty-nine, his career was running on borrowed time.

For many reasons 1971 was not a good year. Before the season began the senior players spent an hour or more with Arthur Dumbrell, the secretary, who listened and made notes. He was asked if he would raise the points made with the full committee. Amazingly, he said no – he thought they had made no valid points! John Snow tried to talk to Doug Wilshin, the chairman, and Eddie Harrison, who chaired the Cricket Committee, even suggesting that they might do better under a new captain, but to no avail. Griffith was offered a further two years: as events later in the year would show, the Committee was growing more aloof and indifferent to success.

On the field Roger Prideaux arrived from Northamptonshire, but the middle order lacked experience. With 267 runs by the end of May, Jim had made a mediocre start. Trouble loomed in the very first game, against Warwickshire at Hove. John Snow had come back from Illingworth's triumphant Ashes tour in bad physical shape. Used as a stock bowler on the hard tracks Down Under, he had an injury to his right hand, a strained back, his right shoulder had gone and he couldn't throw. 'John complained,' Jim recalls, 'that Griffith expected him as the main strike bowler to bowl a lot' and was annoyed at being put down at fine leg. John Jameson kept running the ball down to Snow and his measured trot around the boundary to retrieve it upset members and the captain, who reported him to the Committee for 'not trying'. Jim supported Griffith,

> as you needed Snowy to perform for you. You did look after him though and when I was skipper I used to bowl him in short spells. You couldn't motivate Snowy; he motivated himself. He was the most intelligent fast bowler I ever kept to because he knew exactly how he would bowl to each batsman.

Hauled before the Committee, Snow was 'convicted' of not trying and dropped. Furthermore, he was made to write and apologise, but the committee's claim that his attitude 'might jeopardise morale was a laugh if you knew how the dressing room was feeling at that time.'[5]

Jim sums up the prevailing mood: 'We were having a very bad time as a team. I remember being thumped by Essex at Hove.' Trailing by 116 on first innings, despite Greig's 99, Sussex were set 326 to win but Lever and Hobbs, with four wickets each, clinched a win by 199 runs. Further Championship defeats by Warwickshire (twice), Somerset, Surrey and Middlesex were offset by two rare John Player wins but when Lancashire came to Hove in early June, the gloom lifted a little. In response to Lancashire's sizable 344 for 6 declared, Buss, Greenidge, Prideaux, Jim and Greig all hit half-centuries and when Harry Pilling's 100 set Sussex 237 to win, they got them with five wickets to spare. It was the last championship win for six weeks and even the Gillette Cup went sour, in the first round against Gloucester at Hove. Sussex went out in style though, losing extravagantly by 123 runs, Procter hitting a

hundred in the visitors' 252. Jim made 81 against Surrey at Hove, a game in
which Miss Stapleton noted that Snow 'took a much shorter run than usual
and only a few balls were really fast'. Alan Ross put it exquisitely: 'Others
can look distracted or detached, Dexter for one, but Snow in some curious
manner that seems almost a Zen or Yoga technique, managed to become
non-apparent.'[6] For Jim, life seemed pretty black. The team was playing
poorly, he was out of form and at Grace Road the back flared up again and
he missed the next two or three games. To cap it all, 'the marriage was going
a bit haywire and by July we were finished. It wasn't really that Ann decided
she was decamping; the marriage to Ann had been a volatile affair. I'd met
Jen by then. We just broke up and that was it.'

Jim saw a JPL win at Harlow and Kenny Suttle score a hundred in each
innings against Cambridge at Horsham, runs which would come back to
haunt him. Then Jim hit 4 fifties in a row in the second half of July as the side
won at Westcliff and walloped Middlesex by 130 runs in the John Player at
Hove. Sandwiched in between was a crushing innings defeat by Illingworth's
Leicester at Hove. Steele, Tolchard and the captain all made runs in 416 for 8
and not for the first time the tough, shrewd Yorkshireman was exasperated.
That season there had been much talk about penalties for slow over rates and
Illingworth told Doug Insole at the MCC, 'Give us a chance to put our own
house in order'. At Hove he announced to the Sussex Committee:

> It won't be popular but I intend to bat on in the morning, for two reasons.
> One is that I think I can bowl you out and the other is that your over rate is a
> disgrace – and you had an off-spinner called Joshi who bowled 30 overs in the
> day off about three yards.

He didn't declare and 'I got stick from the crowd. There was one bloke at the
far side in that little old stand giving me stick most of the match. When we
won Brian Davison walked over, picked him up and said, "Now then, what
have you got to say?"'

The rest of the summer was dominated by the shameful way in which the
end of Suttle's distinguished career with the county was mishandled. A senior
professional with twenty-four years' service was treated in a manner border-
ing on the feudal. After his hundreds at Horsham, he got another at Trent
Bridge. He arrived at Hove for the Derby game to be met by the chairman
of the Cricket Committee, Eddie Harrison, who told Suttle, 'You're rather
embarrassing us, you know, by the runs you're getting.' 'Oh, why's that ?',
inquired Suttle. Harrison went on, 'Well, you're not playing today because
we're not keeping you next year.' This was a blow to the left-hander. He

had wanted to finish in 1972 – he had a joint testimonial with Jim. 'No,' said Harrsion. 'We've got so many up-and-coming players' – which 'wasn't true,' recalls Suttle, 'because very few of them made it. So Jim and I had our testimonial but I never played for Sussex again. I've never known anybody not play in their testimonial year.' Jim made 60 in the draw against Derbyshire but for him it was almost a side-issue.

> I chose the team at the time with Harrison and Mike Griffith and I was a bit late getting to the ground. Mike gave me the team – no Kenny. I said, 'I assume you've made your decision', and of course they had. Essex were keen to have Kenny and I had a blazing row with Eddie Harrison. My argument was 'How do I run a testimonial with one player in Essex and one in Sussex?' So he was given another year's contract but never selected. It was the start of my bust-up with Harrison. It demonstrated Sussex's inability to manage professional sportsmen: they would simply dispense with services with no thanks for what you have done.

Echoes resounded of the 1950 AGM, the Committee being accused of lacking leadership, enterprise, communication, ambition and general competence. The hierarchy of the club had not kept pace with the growing professionalism and commercial impetus within the game.

However, Jim's bitterness at Suttle's treatment did not induce a general malaise as the season wound down. Eastbourne Week produced a hat-trick of wins, the first an exciting 2-run defeat of Kent. Featuring 113 from Greig in Sussex's 294, when the visitors were 211 for 6 chasing 219 England's new all-rounder wrapped up the innings, finishing with 6 for 42. He did it again as Somerset, set 255, were dismissed 46 runs short, Greig taking 5 for 26. Unusually, apart from 50 against Somerset, Jim had a meagre week with the bat, but he took seven catches in the match. As a bit of icing on the cake Surrey were beaten in the John Player game!

The last few games exemplified this pendulum of a season. A tremendous finish against Middlesex at Hove kept the bank holiday crowd on the edge of their deck-chairs. Parfitt entertained them with a century and Sussex were 123 behind on first innings. Snow, with 5 for 34, rescued the side on the Monday, skittling the visitors for 101 to leave Griffith's men 225 to win. They were 208 for 7, then 223 for 8 and 224 for 9 in the last over, when the captain and Mike Buss got home with a ball to spare. It had been a terrific advertisement for the game.

Peter Graves recalls driving the ball

straight back at John Price, who touched it on to the stumps. In a split second, I left my ground and after an appeal, Dickie Bird gave me out. But I knew at the moment the bails came off, I was still in my crease. I didn't say anything but as I walked off Dickie said to Mike Brearley, the Middlesex captain, 'I am sorry but I am going to call him back, I made a mistake.' Brearley said, 'You're correct.'

Jim remembers Brearley's gesture – 'typical of the man, one of the old style of gentleman-captains, and probably the last man to captain England because of his captaincy rather than his ability.'

If Middlesex was the Lord Mayor's Show, the Northants game was what came after, as Sussex were undone by Mushtaq, brother of Hanif, Sadiq and Wazir Muhammad. Geoff Cook's 122 was instrumental in setting Sussex 296 to win, but they collapsed from 181 for 5 as Mushtaq rounded up the tail and Sussex lost by 101 runs.

It had been a chaotic season. Jim scrambled 1,023 runs but Sussex had finished eleventh in the Championship and there was much rebuilding to do for 1972. It was a young side: Pataudi, Dexter, Oakman and Thomson were yesterday's men, Lenham was now coach and Suttle was no more. Jim too was at the veteran stage and the next summer would be his last for his native county. He was rebuilding his personal life too:

I was working for Whitbread's, based in Romsey, travelling as a rep and in January Jenny and I got a place in Ringmer, renting a cottage on a farm on the Laughton road. The Bluebell at Shortgate was our local, and was one of my calls. A Yorkshireman called Bill Sykes had it and we always went in on a Sunday for a couple of drinks.

In 1972, in an attempt to cash in on the commercial success of the Gillette Cup and the one-day league, MCC launched an early-season 55-over regionally based tournament, sponsored by Benson and Hedges. It included the Minor Counties and the universities and was an attempt to spread the appeal of the limited-over format beyond the first-class game. Surprisingly, in view of their John Player pedigree, Sussex reached the quarter-final, where the glue came well and truly unstuck. After a reasonable start, in which Surrey and Middlesex were beaten at Hove and Essex at Chelmsford, Sussex travelled to Bradford with high hopes. Dexter and Thomson were back and Graves was batting at number 7, but they succumbed on a green wicket to Hutton, Wilson and Nicholson. All out for 85, only Prideaux, Greenidge and the captain reached double figures and although Greig took 3 for 15 when the Tykes replied, Sussex were beaten by five wickets.

Sadly for the cricketing public with the Australians on tour, there was a lot of rain that summer. Four of Sussex's games in May were seriously affected or abandoned and the side's from was as depressing as the weather. Apart from the B&H Cup, there was only one win, over Surrey in the John Player League. Sussex were breaking records, though, albeit unenviable ones. At Dudley Worcester beat them by 170 runs, the biggest defeat ever suffered in the John Player League. Turner and Headley had romped their way to 258 for 4, and Jim top-scored with 26 in a paltry 88 all out. Two days earlier, Sussex had played at Gloucester 'and it was bitter. I wore a long-sleeved sweater on mid-summer's day.' With Snow, Buss and Spencer unavailable, Andy Henderson, ex-Hove County Grammar School, opened with John Denman. He played for Montefiore in Hove and occasionally for Sussex II. He had a decent spell, trapping Arthur Milton lbw for 45, but when Procter took 5 for 20 Sussex faced a first-innings deficit of 143. Set 313 to win, they crumbled to 83 all out, Jim top-scoring with 21.

These two back-to-back débâcles were hard to stomach but there were bright intervals amid the showers. Jim's divorce went through in July, enabling him and Jenny to develop and cement a settled domestic life – and suddenly Sussex won a game! On a treacherous track at Hastings Sussex assembled 244, Jim making 25 after finding himself at the wicket with 3 for 2 on the board and Prideaux out 5 runs later. Kent fell to Greig (6 for 20) and Snow (3 for 14) and, 54 all out, followed on 190 behind. Greig, with 5 for 26, and Snow again wreaked havoc, and they were all out again 199 – a comfortable ten-wicket win. It remained the only Championship win when the Australians arrived at Hove in late July.

Lacking only Lilllee and Massie from the side which started the Fourth Test two days later, the tourists' XI looked powerful – Stackpole and Edwards opening, followed by the Chappell brothers, Walters, Sheahan and Marsh. Sussex did well therefore to restrict them to 294 and responded with vigour. Graves and Greenidge posted a century partnership and when the Barbadian was caught at the wicket one short of his hundred, Griffith declared 2 runs ahead. Graves remembers it well:

They were good days, sunny days and Geoff nearly made 100 in each innings. Jim brought Geoff to Sussex and believed in him, but he wasn't a headliner, not a typical West Indian explosive player – he was more methodical.

Jim agrees with Graves that he 'was an under-achiever, which is not to demean his achievements with Sussex.' Keith Stackpole raced from 35 to 135 before lunch on the last day to set Sussex 261 to win in three hours. In an exhilarating pursuit, Greenidge and Graves opened with another century stand, and with the last hour called exactly 100 were needed. Despite a middle-order slump, Greenidge made sure of his ton and against a tiring attack the skipper hit the winning runs with an over to spare. Sussex became the first county to beat the Aussies and though Jim had a poor game it was a memorable win.

Jim's swan song summer drew slowly to a rain-soaked close as the one-day centenary game at Hove against the Australians was abandoned and games at the Oval, Bradford and Brackley were washed out. So, via a nine-wicket defeat at Canterbury, Jim came to the Saffrons for his last tilt on one of his favourite wickets. It didn't quite work out like that. On one of the most extraordinary final days in cricket, 448 runs were scored, sixteen wickets fell and the large holiday crowd saw one of the legendary overs in cricket history. Surrey had made 300 before declaring and Prideaux hit 106 as Griffith declared 76 runs short. Surrey then rattled up 130 for 5 and left the home side 205 to win in 135 minutes. Graves went early, whereupon Greenidge and Prideaux batted superbly, and at the end of the seventeenth of the last 20 overs Sussex were cruising at 187 for 1. Pocock then bowled Greenidge and precipitated one of the most incredible collapses of all time. Buss and Jim were the off-spinner's next victims and at the start of the last over, 5 runs were needed with Prideaux on 97. Dismissing Prideaux, Griffith and Morley gave Pocock his hat-trick and when Tony Buss was bowled by the fifth, Sussex were 201 for 8. Joshi was run out off the last ball, leaving Sussex 3 runs short of the victory which seemed in their grip fifteen minutes before.

The skipper rationalises the irrational:

> We were chasing runs and it looked to be in the bag. We lost some wickets and then we felt that we couldn't win it by pushing ones and twos. Eastbourne in those days was quite a large ground, Pocock had got a well-placed defensive field and we just played like schoolboys. If somebody like Brearley had been captain he would have explained to the batsmen how to play. One of his strengths was that he could captain the batting side as well as the fielding side.

Even now, Graves still can't believe it:

> In the dressing room people were rushing about saying, 'What's going on?' 'Parkser's out', 'Morler's out' and then Uday Joshi was run out. He was a genial Indian with an engaging smile – Spencer and I were very fond of him. Bowled well against Somerset there the year before, didn't he? Strange signing for an overseas player but every county's had those.

Jim smiles: 'Lovely lad, Joshi. Bowled little off-spinners. Replaced Euros, really. Yes, we were running short of time and going for the runs. Pocock bowled beautifully' – and set several world records. 'He bowled 7 consecutive balls at seven different batsmen. He had taken five wickets in 6 balls and seven wickets in eleven, his last over reading WWW 1 W 1 '[7] and finished with 7 for 67.

As August rolled on into September, the team won four more JPL games and one more Championship match, beating Leicestershire by seven wickets at Hove. Jim suffered his first – and only – pair, when 'Trevor Jesty did me second innings against Hampshire at Hove' and Richard Gilliat's men secured a 156-run victory. After Middlesex had also come to the County Ground and conquered, despite Jim's 56 and 41 not out, the team had a day or two off so Jim took Tony Greig down to Devon to 'play for the International Cavaliers. We joined Garry Sobers and Clive Lloyd and we had a few days cricket down there. Then we came back to Bournemouth for my last game.' It was unfortunate that Jim's career, largely marked by bonhomie and fun, should end on a sour note, the dispute centring on Griffith's refusal to declare Sussex's second innings, in which Gilliat used nine bowlers. Jim hit 70 not out in his final first-class knock for the county, but Hampshire, left 214 to win, were left 110 for 4 at the close.

Jim had scored 1,014 runs and *Wisden*'s summary of Sussex in 1972 encapsulates Jim's schism with Sussex. 'His place as wicketkeeper may be challenged by Mansell, twenty years his junior, but such a prospect seems unlikely to daunt him.'[8] Typical of the Byzantine machinations which passed for personnel management at Hove in those days, Jim's departure

> ... was couched more in cricketing terms but, as with Kenny, it was the way it was done. I had a great friend on the Committee, Walter Denman, who told me they were going to offer me match money to play as a batsman if I was fit. That season I had gone right through and stayed fit. I felt the offer was an insult so I told them exactly what they could do with it. I suggested that since we were going to lose Snowy and Tony Greig to Test matches it would make sense to bring Alan Mansell into the side and I would stay at slip. My dad rated Alan and I thought he was a good little keeper. I very nearly walked out of the ground there and then, but I thought 'Sod it, why? Just let's see it through and see what they do.' So I stayed on. Generally, things didn't get to me very much but I was upset that fifty years of family association with the club was going to come to an end.

The season over, Jim 'withdrew his registration as a Sussex player so they couldn't hold me' and flew to Rhodesia with an International Wanderers XI, skippered by his old services mate, Brian Close. With Mervyn Kitchen and Tony Greig also on board, and Procter leading Rhodesia, 'it was a lot of fun. The cricket was taxing – we got thumped – but I did catch Duncan Fletcher off McKenzie, though I doubt he remembers it today!' Jim was smarting at Sussex's treatment of him and Close could not understand 'why Sussex let Jim go because he was still a bloody good player.' Jim told Close he was interested in Taunton but he still wanted to make Sussex see sense.

> I um'd and ah'd until about February when I went to see the Sussex Committee. I'd been working in the beer trade so I'd had a few beers that day and was going well. I said, 'All I want is a contract for one year to start as one of two keepers, nothing else.' It was rejected by Harrison: I think the others just mumbled. Unfortunately Spen Cama wasn't there. If he had been I think I'd have stayed and he would have got me through. I walked out saying, 'I'm sorry, but I think you've just lost two for the price of one' – that was Bobby as well of course. I went home and immediately rang Roy Kerslake, the chairman of Somerset, went down the next day and signed – that was it. Sussex could do nothing about it as my registration had gone, though they tried to oppose it.

'So Closey was entirely influential in my going to Taunton.' The wily old Yorkshireman had orchestrated it well:

> I told the Committee to get him down because he strengthened us considerably. He was spreading a bit by then – he was a social guy too. That's how we were brought up and that's how we learnt. After the game we'd go in the bar, have a drink together and we'd talk the game over.

Thus it was that Jim enjoyed the twilight of his career in Somerset, sipping the last of the summer wine.

Chapter 15
The Last of the Summer Wine

Jim first played for his new county at the end of April 1973, against Gloucester at Bristol. It was an inauspicious start. In this local derby in the Benson & Hedges Cup he scored two and Somerset were thrashed by 103 runs.

Having left Sussex partly because they denied him his wish to be 'senior wicketkeeper' and mentor to Alan Mansell, ironically Jim played for Somerset solely as a batsman, except in one-day matches. Derek Taylor was the man in post and was capable of opening the batting. After that initial reverse, 'we had a good year, and I enjoyed it.' His team-mates were a healthy blend of youth and experience. Close, Cartwright and Jim were the veterans, Dennis Breakwell, Peter Denning, Allan Jones (the gin and tonic man), Hallam Moseley and Brian Rose the youngsters and Burgess, Kitchen and Taylor the engine-room. There were also rumours of some useful teenagers by the names of Botham, Marks and Roebuck waiting in the wings and a promising twenty-one-year-old Antiguan called Richards. Close understands why Jim enjoyed his time at Taunton,

> because we knew the game and competed in everything. We were strong all-round and in Tom Cartwright we had a wonderful bowler. Under English conditions he was the best – he would almost bowl fast leg-breaks. The difference between good and great bowlers is the ability to concentrate for long periods of time and Tom could, so we only needed bowlers for a few overs at the other end.

Released from the yoke of captaincy in a side struggling for form, Jim made his best start for years and by the end of June had scored 885 in all matches. Close went off like a train, making centuries in consecutive Championship games, notably 153 in an innings win at Lord's. Jim hit a stream of respectable half-centuries, against the New Zealanders at Taunton and a rapid 69 in a B&H game at the Westlands Sports Ground in Yeovil. He was made Man of the Match – 'I've got a gold medal somewhere which Godfrey Evans gave me'. Somerset then had an agreeable Championship win over their neighbours at Taunton, Jim making 68, avenged in the JPL fixture at Bristol. Gloucestershire won on the faster scoring rate when David Graveney, now chairman of the England selectors, hit the fourth ball of the final over for 6. Tit for tat nearly, as Jim, who made 35, remembers hitting David Graveney for 3 sixes in one over.

It was nearly six weeks before Jim next played at Taunton. Bournemouth was accessible from Chandlers Ford, where he and Jenny were now living, for the B&H game against Hampshire, but then it was Lord's, Sheffield, Bradford, a week at Bath, Chelmsford, Canterbury, Maidstone and Leicester before finally meeting up again with Hampshire for the Championship game at the County Ground. Though the travelling was tiring for what wags on the circuit were dubbing 'Dad's Army', Jim amassed 558 runs on the road, kept in all six of the limited-over games and scored his last hundred, a crucial 155 against Kent at Maidstone, the only time he played there. Results were uneven but there were some excellent games. Jim made runs in a five-wicket win over Surrey at Bath, and at Maidstone Denness (178) and Cowdrey (123) gave Kent a first-innings lead of 294. When Somerset slipped to 79 for 3 Kent held the whip-hand, but then 'I had a big partnership with Budgie as we fought to save it.' As *Wisden* records: 'Parks shattered them with a fine display of attacking shots. He hit 24 fours... adding 163 with Burgess.' Similarly, at Grace Road, in an unconvincing first innings 'Parks provided the backbone, staying two-and-a-half hours for a patient 55' before the English summer washed out any hope of a result. A similar fate befell a potentially attractive John Player game against Nottinghamshire, including Sobers, at Glastonbury and the chance of revenge against Leicester at Torquay. The Foxes, who, with Higgs, McKenzie and Illingworth almost rivalled Close's outfit for the soubriquet of 'Dad's Army', had knocked Somerset out of the Gillette Cup at Taunton. Chasing 213, Leicester recovered from 167 for 8, thanks to a fighting 112 from Chris Balderstone, and won by two wickets. It was the second one-day disaster in three days as Somerset had crumpled to 61 all out against Hampshire at Bath in the John Player League. Cartwright alone reached double figures and, for once, Jim was the only player not out to an attacking stroke.

Then it rained. After a convincing win at Neath, half the matches in August were ravaged by the weather. 'We played three county games and two John Players at Weston super Mare', Jim recalls. 'It was a good festival and we used to get tremendous crowds but '73 was wet.' The Clarence Park pitch, much like the Saffrons, was normally placid but could become spiteful after rain. Between the showers, Glamorgan and Derbyshire were undone by the guile and accuracy of Moseley and Cartwright, who took 22 wickets in two resounding wins. Glamorgan managed only 83 and 92, Cartwright wrecking them with 9 for 40 in a ten-wicket win, and Derbyshire fared little better. After Jim made 91, adding 175 with his captain, Cartwright took 7 for 37 as Derby were all out for 156. Left 312 to win, they fought hard but were again destroyed by the Warwickshire wizard, who ended with 6 for 52.

Jim faced his native county twice in the final fortnight and must have had mixed feelings as his new team-mates cruised to a seven-wicket win in the Championship at Taunton. He headed for the John Player game at Hove via a huge defeat at Bristol. On a low wicket which turned, Mortimore took 10 for 55 and Graveney 9 for 86 as Gloucestershire crushed their neighbours by an innings and 164 runs. Jim's return in opposition colours to the ground he had graced for over two decades was marked by the debut of a cricketing legend – I. T. Botham was lbw to Buss for a couple. It was an undistinguished home-coming for Jim, caught by Greig off Spencer for 4, and Sussex avenged the Taunton defeat, winning by six wickets.

Close remembers Botham's arrival:

We were struggling for players and we hadn't a lot of money when the chairman recollected that we had a lad on the Lord's ground staff – young Ian Botham. I said, 'Get him down here – see what he's made of.' The two Lord's coaches – Harry Sharp [batting] and Len Muncer [bowling] – said that Ian wouldn't make a first-class cricketer!

Nevertheless, he impressed Jim: 'He was a hefty lad – and mischievous. From the word go you sensed this enormous competitive instinct.'

Jim had had a rewarding summer, as *Wisden* noted:

The experience and skill of Parks proved quite invaluable at number four in the order. He passed 1,000 runs in pleasing style, and also produced some good wicketkeeping performances in the shorter games.[1]

His happy year was crowned on 8 December in Winchester.

Jenny and I got married – the best thing that ever happened to me. At last I could settle down – we'd moved to Fairoak just outside Chandlers Ford as I was working in Romsey for Whitbread during the winter. I intended to work full-time in '74 but my boss kept the job open for me so I played an extra year.

Jim's 'extra year', his last full season in first-class cricket, overlapped with the start of two superlative careers. 'For Both and Viv it was their first full season', and already, by the end of April, the young Antiguan was showing his worth. At Swansea in a B&H game Richards hit 50 out of 89, and when Somerset won with 14 overs left he was 81 not out, having hit a six and 13 fours. No such effervescent form for Jim, who could 'hardly get a run in May – it was when I first started getting shoulder trouble.' His 188 runs were a reminder of the dark days six or seven years earlier and were reflected in the team's indifferent form. By early June Somerset had won three John Player and three B&H games only, and not until Kent came to Taunton in mid-June did they record a Championship victory.

It was Richards who captured the imagination. In the B&H Cup against Gloucester at Taunton, after Somerset had lost early wickets, he took the fight to Mike Procter. Jim recalls:

> He stroked the first ball through the covers. Second ball we knew the bouncer was coming – it disappeared over the boundary and was still going up when it went over the organ works outside the ground. Procter's mouth dropped open. We won by 81 – and he got his debut hundred against them when we played at Bristol over Whitsun.

Gallingly, one of the JPL defeats was by Sussex, by four wickets at Taunton, where only Denning and Jim, who added 59, put up any real resistance. Somerset either won or lost limited-overs games in spectacular fashion: they appeared incapable of grinding out results. In his early days Close was a critic of the one-day game, but in the John Player League at Bristol his 128 in less than two hours contained 3 sixes and 10 fours and thrilled the Whit Sunday crowd. When Jim went to Taunton he had

> ... to talk Closey out of attacking in one-day cricket. He wanted to put people at silly-mid off! Fortunately Tom Cartwright in particular knew how he wanted to bowl and to what sort of field so we talked him out of it. We were all brought up playing the proper game, but I'd been influenced by Dexter, who'd worked out the limited-overs game. I don't think Closey ever wanted to try.

Even the Championship win over Kent had a one-day feel about it when Luckhurst set Somerset 270 in three-and-a-half hours. At 131 for 5, with Richards, Denning and Jim out, Close's men were in difficulty but Burgess hit 2 sixes and 12 fours in 67 and Somerset got home by four wickets. The most breathtaking win of the summer is now part of cricket folklore as

Somerset won an epic match by one wicket with an over to spare. In the B&H quarter-final at Taunton, Hampshire had made a modest 182 on a seamers' wicket. Then Somerset, against Jesty and Sainsbury, faltered to 113 for 5, lost three wickets at that score and Botham was left with Hallam Moseley. Surviving a blow in the mouth from Andy Roberts, the eighteen-year-old batted magnificently and 'the amazing thing was that Hallam stayed with him – he wasn't the greatest.'[2] They added 63 in 13 overs before Moseley was lbw for 24. 176 for 9. 'Then Bob Clapp came in, a local schoolmaster, very tall man and a useful bowler.' In giving Botham the strike, 'Clapp had to dive a long way to complete a third run to make it 180, then after Botham had played and missed three times in Herman's last over, he cover drove him perfectly for the winning boundary.'[3] It was *Boy's Own* stuff, and that courageous 45 not out put Ian Botham on the national cricketing map.

While a bitter April morning at Derby is no fun, professional cricketers do get paid for playing the game they love in some delightful places. Jim recalls many with affection – Eastbourne, Tunbridge Wells, Worcester, Cape Town, Durban and Sydney, but for sheer elegance and civility they could hardly rival Bath. Jim now had ten days at the Recreation Ground, hard by the Avon, where Yorkshire were beaten twice, 'we beat Glamorgan easily and I kept wicket against Pakistan.'

It was an entertaining John Player game with Yorkshire as Close hit 131 against his native county and Jim made 46. Chasing 225, Chris Old laid about him for 82 and Jim took centre stage in a hilarious finale, described by Dickie Bird:

Bairstow and Nicholson came together as the last pair, with their side needing just 5 runs for victory. Ian Botham was bowling... [Bairstow] said to Nick, 'I have to get the strike, so whatever happens to the first ball Beefy bowls at you, I'll set off... You run as hard as you can, and hopefully we'll be okay. Just as long as we both know what we're doing.' 'Right,' said Nick. 'Got it. Whatever happens, I run.'

The first ball whistled... through to wicketkeeper Jim Parks, standing back. Off went Bairstow like a greyhound, only to realise with alarm, halfway down the track, that Nick was making no attempt to move. Bluey slammed on the brakes, turned, and made a mad scramble to get back. Nick, meanwhile, had suddenly decided to run after all, charged out of his crease, and had progressed only a few yards... when Parks broke his wicket to give Somerset victory. As the two batsmen made their way disconsolately through the celebrating Somerset supporters, Bairstow demanded of his partner, 'What the hell did you think you were doing?' 'Sorry, Blue,' replied Nick. 'I forgot what we'd agreed.'[4]

From Bath to Leicester, Northampton and Derby, where Jim took the gloves for the last time, the stabbing pain in his right shoulder worsened and he struggled for fitness from then on. The team had not played well at Leicester in the B&H semi-final, losing by 140 runs. Close criticised the state of the pitch but the home side made 270 on it and Illingworth bowled well, taking 5 for 20. Jim, discomfited by his shoulder, was not making runs, but his contributions were vital. Middlesex were beaten by 73 runs at Taunton where Botham made his maiden fifty and he and Jim rescued a middle-order collapse. In the second innings Somerset were 29 for 4 when Richards and Jim put on a quick 45 leaving Middlesex 168 to win. They subsided to 94 all out against Jones and Moseley.

At Westcliff the first day was washed out, Essex made 200 and declared, then Close retired hurt after trying to walk through a plate-glass door. 'It was one of these massive hotel doors,' says Jim, 'and Closey thought it was open. Did the window more harm than he did himself actually and we all laughed about it afterwards.'

Moseley skittled Essex for 93 and Somerset hung on at 57 for 7 for a draw. Jim missed both games at Swansea 'but I went down there and watched from the press box. The shoulder eventually went completely after I retired through wear and tear.'

This patched-up veteran was back for the Gillette Cup quarter-final at Taunton where, after Surrey had made 254, Peter Denning hit 112 and 'Parks proved the ideal foil. Out of form and out of the side previously, he was only picked at the last moment and batted excellently, giving just the solidity and soundness required. He helped Denning put on 85 in 15 overs.'[5] Jim's 42 not out helped Somerset to the highest winning score for a side batting second in the Gillette Cup. Shades of Hove eleven years before as 'I remember being carried off'. Shoulder or no, Jim's last full summer ended in something of a flourish as he scored over 400 runs and made his highest score of the season, against Leicester at Weston. He certainly enjoyed himself, hitting Pocock, his Caribbean colleague of '68, into the playground of Archbishop Tennison's School adjacent to the Oval, making 66 in a partnership with Close at Weston super Mare and 'slogging J.K. at Taunton when someone caught me on the boundary but ran over the line with it'. The 134 he put on with his skipper against Leicester remains a record fifth-wicket partnership for Somerset at Clarence Park. Then against Warwickshire two days later with the side 38 for 4 in the second innings, the pair 'diligently restored order, Parks finally batting two-and-a-half hours for 61.'[6] Then Jim went to Bournemouth:

I got 46 when we were struggling. We'd had a bit of rain so were playing til
half past seven. It was getting dark and in the last over of the match Closey and
I kept getting singles off Andy Roberts. I ended up facing him fifth ball; he let
his bouncer go and it hit me on the arm. In such bad light I didn't pick it up
at all and I had to go to hospital. Panic stations, but it hadn't been broken. I
would have struggled to bat next day but it was rained off.

Jim had made the most of his farewell summer while for Somerset:

> the most heartening point was… that at last some of the younger generation
> of players succeeded, so that Somerset did not rely on Close, Cartwright and
> Parks, almost exclusively… Parks, although making some highly useful runs,
> did not actually obtain a fifty until August.'[7]

In 1975 Jim 'stood by when Viv or Closey were playing Test cricket – or
injured. There was a small staff and I even got a few runs.' He had the pleasure of catching Pocock off Botham at Bath in June, stroking a 'pleasantly
fluent 65' and although the side lost at Leicester and Edgbaston, made a couple of forties. Jim kept his registration for 1976 and when 'Closey was called
back against the West Indies I played at Bath against Worcester'. Jim's last
ledger records that he was 'bowled D'Oliviera 1' and 'caught Turner bowled
D'Oliviera 10', but it was Imran Khan's pace on a green wicket that convinced him it was time to retire. 'Imran whistled past my ear rather quickly
and that was enough. I was nearly forty-five, the eyes had started going and I
wasn't picking it up – you need to have perfect sight.'

At the Recreation Ground in Bath on 18 June 1976, Jim's 'wine of life is
drawn, and the mere lees is left this vault to brag of.' He had left the field
for the last time as a professional cricketer. Over the next fifteen years Jim,
Close, Allen, Graveney and others continued to play together in the Old
England side, raising countless thousands for charity. 'We all loved the game
and it was great to keep playing and meeting together. It was loads of fun.'
After all, wasn't that the point?

Chapter 16
Reflections

It is Hove in high summer, one of those blissful cloudless days, and at tea, in a deck-chair, thoughts crowd in my reverie of great men, occasions and opinions. 'It is the great virtue of cricket,' wrote Arlott, 'that it is a true reflection of the men who play it. Thus, the Weald, where cricket grew up, has always produced cricketers in the original mould. Thence cometh the man to whom a cricket bat or ball in the hand is as natural as any implement of any other Wealden worker.'[1]

Born of a family of Wealden workers, Jim was 'a young man of undoubted talents, even brilliance, who [needed only] to set his mind on wiping out one or two defects in his technique to have a good chance of bridging the gap to Test cricket' – so wrote Len Hutton in 1956. As Keith Andrew told me, 'here was a young man with the potential to be another Compton: he played all the strokes.'

John Murray, perhaps his keenest rival, concurs: 'When Jim did make runs he was so quick on his feet he made 'em bloody quickly for you – that was equally as important as it bought you some time to bowl.'

John Woodcock joins me. 'John was the better wicketkeeper – very stylish – but Jim never let England down.' More than that, 'If you are the best keeper in the world', says MJK, 'and you don't know which end of the bat to pick up you won't be the most valuable man in the Test team, but if you bat like Jim or Gilchrist, overall, you will make a bigger contribution. You would have worried about Knott batting higher than seven, but you would have been happy to see Jim going in a bit higher.'

'You need your keeper to make runs,' says Boycott, a shrewd and demanding critic, 'and he didn't drop many. I really liked him as a man and admired him as a batter'. So did Christopher Martin-Jenkins, for whom 'Jim was a much under-rated keeper and quick, perky, smart, aggressive, fluent, entertaining and a beautiful driver.' Jim learnt much from Godfrey Evans, who believes that:

> If he had taken up wicketkeeping earlier and he had had the opportunity to keep regularly to top-class spin bowling he could have been a truly outstanding keeper. His greatest qualities were his footwork against spin bowling – he was always able

to get to the pitch of the ball and smother spin – and his delicate cuts and glides which were responsible for over fifty per cent of his runs off fast bowling.

In addition, 'nobody in the English game', says Peter Graves, 'had seen a player put their left foot outside leg stump and hit it for six over extra cover.' His approach was old-fashioned, though, as David Allen reminds me. 'He had this lovely grip at the top of the bat and it was flowing. He was never stodgy – tremendous footwork, so well-balanced – the sign of the great players.' Footwork and balance in the field too – 'He was also, apart from Colin Bland, not far off from being the best cover-point in the world – he was certainly the best cover-point in the Championship. England class – no doubt about that whatsoever.'

Let his final captain have the last word before Jim joins us. 'Jim was probably the best batsman of the lot of them. He wouldn't have played for England if he hadn't been a good wicketkeeper. I like Jim very much – he was a good lad. I shall always be fond of those memories we had.'

Ah, memories… and opinions: cricket abounds in both. The ghosts in my reverie fade and as the sun sets over the pavilion, Jim and I talk about the game now, half a century and more since he walked through the gates.

What changes in those fifty years had he noticed most? 'Cricket is big business now. In the old days it was run as a hobby by committees. Nowadays it's run by money, by sponsors.'

Is that not partly regrettable, partly inevitable as cricket is a high-profile game? 'True, but commercialism brought me back into the game as marketing manager when we were on the verge of moving to Wales. I'd had eighteen years in the commercial world so I came back to market Sussex.'

Part of the commercial thrust is the drive for central contracts, in a sense. 'Yes, it is, but you're depriving a county of their top player, so sooner or later the counties are going to say, "We don't want him. He's no use to us." What use was Flintoff to Lancashire this year?'

Like most things in cricket there are arguments both ways. Gradually the Test team is getting more successful. 'Yes, it is – whether we're getting more successful or whether the standard of the rest of the world is coming down to our level I'm not quite sure yet. I think our attack has improved tremendously, especially with Harmison, who's a very fine bowler.'

A more successful Test side in theory should produce more revenue for disbursement to the counties. 'Yes, but will it improve the standards of county cricket? That I worry about. It's interesting how may counties are developing or have got what they call "academies"… Yes, well we've got one here of course and we were one of the first – and it's now proving successful for us. But we've still got too many overseas players in the game.'

But Sussex have benefited as much as anybody. 'Yes, we've had two, especially Mushtaq who won us the Championship. And we have some like Mark Davis... Yes, of course he's not an overseas player. I believe that counties should be limited to one genuine overseas player and if he can't play, bad luck. All it's doing is depriving one of our youngsters of experience, who could become a Test player.'

Have we got to a virtual transfer system in the game? 'Not yet, but I can see it coming and we should do something on those lines, for the simple reason that if you bring a youngster on and you've spent all that money to develop him, so to speak, then you ought to get something back if he goes elsewhere – for more money.'

You would have enjoyed twenty 20, I guess. 'I think I would. I enjoyed one-day cricket when it came in. It suited me.'

It was your sort of game. I imagine, if twenty 20 had been about in the sixties with people like Kenny Suttle... well, he didn't crash it about. 'Well, he could... but he was more the Graham Thorpe, he was a nudger.'

But he wouldn't have been dramatic. 'No, Kenny was a cutter, but Ted would have been magnificent. He'd have hit everything and you would have had a job to set a field to Ted. You see the fields, they are set wide now, but Ted hit so straight. If you hit straight, you can't have anyone fielding in front of the sight-screen.'

It's like a thirty-second ad for the proper game, twenty20? 'I was very sceptical last year when it came on the scene and went to the first one down at the Rose Bowl and it caught my imagination straight away. It really did. It's not a slog because you've got to play good shots. You've got to beat the field so you've got to place it well.'

And of course the fielding has to be top-class and the bowlers have to be disciplined and bowl straight... The coloured clothing, you don't mind that? 'No, I've accepted it I think now. If you've got floodlights, you've got to have something different. You've got to have a white ball and I suppose the background can't be white can it?'

Would you have enjoyed playing under floodlights? 'I don't know, quite honestly. I suppose so. It does seem strange when I look out at them playing with lights on.'

It can't ever be as high quality as perfect sunlight. 'No. I haven't spoken to any of the players about it... You see these high catches taken so they must find the ball all right. In fact, you don't see many dropped catches these days. Fielding has improved dramatically.'

I was reading in The Times *this morning that England have employed Peter Young, a baseball coach. He's been training the one-day squad in fielding skills at Loughborough. He was asking them, 'Why do you walk in and back when you're fielding? In baseball we adopt a pose like receiving a tennis serve.'* 'Fielding at cover, I didn't walk in fifteen yards. I would go a couple of paces, which I think is the right way to do it. He should have seen Learie Constantine pick up and throw in one action, he was the best ever. I've never seen a fielder like him.'

Christopher Martin-Jenkins was writing recently that the one-day league has run its course. 'I don't think the 45-over league has got much to offer these days. I'd still like to see the C&G Trophy go back to 60 overs, just to be something different from the 50-over game. I think you can play a better game of cricket over 60 overs than 50. You can build an innings and you can still fit it into a day. We proved in the twenty 20 that you can bowl 20 overs in an hour-and-a-quarter so why can't we impose that on the rest of one-day cricket? No reason why not. Make them move quicker. There's so much time wasted in all cricket now. They get a wicket and someone comes on with drinks after one over. Nobody wants drinks after one over. But it takes time for him to get out there. You can always hark back, but we did get through 20 overs an hour. All right, we bowled a lot of spinners in those days which helped.'

There's a lot more at stake today, of course. 'I agree – there's so much aggro. One of the things I think you've got to do is to give the umpires more power and if somebody gets really stroppy on the field, you send them off. It's got to happen. They wouldn't do it again. Imagine your prime bowler letting fly at a batsman and the umpire saying, "Off you go and you don't come back this innings." He wouldn't do it again.'

I've often been surprised why an international game with the potential for verbal stuff let alone physical argy-bargy hasn't got a red card/yellow card system… It's crept into rugby, rightly, but because cricket has always had this tradition of a game played by gentlemen… Old cricketers tend to bemoan the lack of characters in the game these days. 'Everything's stereotyped these days. There were individual characters in the old days and people talked and wrote about them. You saw them possibly only once or twice a year when you played them. Miller and Compton – like two peas in a pod. Flamboyant, larger than life. Great friends. I remember playing against Miller in '53. He bowled one a bit short and I whacked it through mid-wicket. He just ambled up and next one, bang, it flew past my nose. He just laughed and went back and bowled again. No animosity or anything. He had let me know what he could do if he wanted.'

Each county had its characters, didn't it? Like Gloucester with its great off-spinners. Did you play against Tom Goddard? 'Yes, I played against Scarface at the end of his career – he used to growl a lot and had these enormous hands. Cook, Morty, Bomber, D.A. too. Yorkshire too, they had so many. If you were having a long hard day in a Test match Fred kept you going out there. He fielded at short-leg and he was continually going on but he was always very funny.'

I suppose till the end of your career there was still humour about in the game. 'Oh yes, a tremendous amount. In the old days, after a Test match against Australia, you'd go into the other dressing-room and have a drink with them, which was lovely. I don't think it generally happens now – they treat them as the enemy – and the same in county cricket. I think it's very sad. Look at the Old England side. They were all my friends from other counties. It was a lot of fun in the old days – there's no doubt about it.'

The golden afternoon has mellowed into a tranquil twilight. Our talk falls silent and as we gaze across the green, A.A. Thomson's graceful words are especially apt:

> The traditions of Sussex cricket are rural and romantic. If you could imagine an idealised picture of the summer game with the sun full overhead, the turf a gleaming emerald, and a court of noble trees on the boundary's edge, it would sit graciously in some broad fold of the Sussex Downs. The names of the villages where cricket lived in early days – Ifield, Oakendene Green, Mayfield, Ringmer – are as sweet to the ear as the sound of bat on ball. In Sussex, too, far more than in any other county, cricket has often looked like a cosy family affair. Quite apart from the innumerable Lillywhite boys, Sussex men may be brothers, like the Broadbridges, the Relfs, the Parkses, the Oakses or the Langridges; or they may be father and son, like Fred and Maurice Tate; Jim Parks and young Jim; and George Cox and George Cox Junior.[2]

We stroll now in the evening shadows, young Jim and I, across the turf on which he swooped and pounced, dived and caught, drove, cut and entertained, the ground he graced for over twenty years. With us walk Jim's father, kindly, solid, sensible, and Harry, the man and the player young Jim so closely resembled and we know that

> The temper of the Weald, whether it has been bringing forth iron, coal, cattle, wool, crops, runs or wickets, has been that of the craftsman who does his job patiently and well every day. On some days the sun shines, the next, equally good work brings no reward. It is not what the score sheet calls 'failure' that counts with your craftsman-cricketer, but a craft mastered and woven into the understanding. So long as such men play for Sussex, no cricketer will ever fail to recognise the county at the game which has its roots there.[3]

Harry, the Langridges, the Coxes and the Tates – these were such men – and Jim's dad, of course, who once told him: 'Cricket's a game, son, and a game to be enjoyed.' Amen to that.

Epilogue

In the saucer of the chalk downs, with the grey hills for its rim,
Where the gorse flames golden glory, while to north the Weald lies dim,
Where the sou'west wind brings in its wings the salt tang of the sea,
They play the game where the game was nursed, in Sussex bold and free,
And with one accord to King Willow their lord they raise their manful
hymn!

from *King Willow's Realm*, by J.N. Pentelow

Appendix 1
Jim Parks –
Career record

Matches 739

<u>Batting</u>
Innings 1227
Not Out 172
Runs 36,673
Average 34.76
Centuries 51
Highest score 205* *v.* Somerset, Hove 1955

<u>Bowling</u>
Runs 2,235
Wickets 51
Average 43.82
Best performance 16.5-6-23-3 *v.* Cambridge University, Horsham 1956

<u>Wicketkeeping</u>
Caught 1,088
Stumped 93
Total 1,181

Behind:
F.H. Huish (Kent) 1,310
D. Hunter (Yorks) 1,265
A.P.E. Knott (Kent) 1,260
J.T. Murray (Middx) 1,527
H. Strudwick (Surrey) 1,496
B. Taylor (Essex) 1,294
R.W. Taylor (Derbys) 1649

Jim Parks –
Career record by club

For Sussex

Matches   563

Batting

Innings	948
Not out	138
Runs	29,138
Average	35.97
Centuries	42
Half-centuries	175

Bowling and fielding

Overs	518
Maidens	109
Runs	1,700
Wickets	42
Average	40.47
Caught	872
Stumped	65

For Somerset

Matches   45

Batting

Innings	72
Not out	8
Runs	1,941
Average	30.32
Centuries	1
Half-centuries	9

Fielding

Caught	11

Appendix 3
Jim Parks –
Test record

Tests   46

Batting

Innings   68
Not out   7
Runs   1,962
Highest score   108* *v.* South Africa, Durban, December 1964
Average   32.16
Centuries   2

Bowling & fielding

Overs   6
Maidens   0
Runs   51
Wickets   1
Average   51
Caught   103
Stumped   11
Best performance   1-43 *v.* India at Kanpur, February 1964

Most Dismissals in a Test match: England

Taylor	*v.* India, Bombay, 1979/80	ct 10	st 0	total 10
Ames	*v.* W. Indies, the Oval, 1933	ct 6	st 2	total 8
Parks	v. *New Zealand, Christchurch, 1965/66*	*ct 8*	*st 0*	*total 8*

Most Dismissals in a Test innings: England

Parks	v. *New Zealand, Christchurch, 1965/66*	*ct 8*	*st 0*	*total 8*
Taylor	*v.* India, Bombay, 1979/80	ct 7	st 0	total 7
Murray	*v.* India, Lord's, 1967	ct 6	st 0	total 6
Russell	*v.* Australia, Melbourne, 1990/91	ct 6	st 0	total 6
Binks	*v.* India, Calcutta, 1963/64	ct 5	st 0	total 5
Parks	v. *Australia, Sydney, 1965/66*	*ct 3*	*st 2*	*total 5*
Parks	v. *New Zealand, Christchurch, 1965/66*	*ct 5*	*st 0*	*total 5*
Knott	*v.* India, Old Trafford, 1974	ct 4	st 1	total 5
Taylor	*v.* New Zealand, Nottingham, 1978	ct 5	st 0	total 5

Taylor	v. Australia, Brisbane, 1978/79	ct 5	st 0	total 5
Richards	v. Australia, Melbourne, 1986/87	ct 5	st 0	total 5
Russell	v. West Indies, Bridgetown, 1989/90	ct 5	st 0	total 5

Most byes conceded in an innings

F.E. Woolley	v. Australia, the Oval, 1934	37
J.T. Murray	v. India, Bombay, 1961/62	33
Parks	v. *West Indies, Kingston, 1967/68*	*33*

Australia
Played 10

inns	n.o.	hs	100s	50s	runs	ave	catches	stumpings	wkts
13	0	89	0	5	483	37.15	17	4	0

India
Played 5

inns	n.o.	hs	100s	50s	runs	ave	catches	stumpings	wkts
7	2	51	0	1	211	42.2	6	2	1

New Zealand
Played 5

inns	n.o.	hs	100s	50s	runs	ave	catches	stumpings	wkts
6	2	45★	0	0	153	38.25	21	1	0

Pakistan
Played 1

inns	n.o.	hs	100s	50s	runs	ave	catches	stumpings	wkts
1	0	15	0	0	15	15	0	0	0

South Africa
Played 13

inns	n.o.	hs	100s	50s	runs	ave	catches	stumpings	wkts
19	2	108★	1	1	537	31.58	28	2	0

West Indies
Played 12

inns	n.o.	hs	100s	50s	runs	ave	catches	stumpings	wkts
22	1	101★	1	2	583	27.76	29	2	0

Appendix 4

Jim Parks –
Centuries

1	1950, May	*v.* Kent at Gillingham	159*
2	1951, June	*v.* Kent at Tunbridge Wells	188
3	1952, May	*v.* Surrey at The Oval	138
4	1952, June	for Combined Services *v.* Worcester	103*
5	1952, July	*v.* Surrey at Hastings	117
6	1953, August	*v.* Derbyshire at Hove	124
7	1954, May	*v.* Warwickshire at Edgbaston	120
8.	1954, July	*v.* Nottinghamshire at Hastings	135
9	1955, June	*v.* South Africans at Hove	118
10	1955, June	*v.* Cambridge University at Horsham	175*
11	1955, August	*v.* Nottinghamshire at Hove	117
12	1955, August	*v.* Derbyshire at Hove	101*
13	1955, August	*v.* Somerset at Hove	205*
14	1956, May	*v.* Warwickshire at Edgbaston	114
15	1956, May	*v.* Worcestershire at Hove	106*
16	1956, June	*v.* Cambridge University at Hove	129
17	1956, August	*v.* Gloucestershire at Cheltenham	102
18	1957, May	*v.* Cambridge University at Fenner's	124
19	1957, June	for MCC *v.* Lancashire at Old Trafford	132*
20	1957, August	*v.* Worcestershire at Worcester	101
21	1957, August	*v.* Worcestershire at Worcester	100*
22	1958, May	*v.* Leicestershire at Hove	104
23	1958, June	*v.* Kent at Tunbridge Wells	127
24	1959, May	for M.C.C. *v.* Surrey at Lord's	103
25	1959, May	*v.* Glamorgan at Hove	157*
26	1959, May	*v.* Gloucestershire at Hove	121
27	1959, July	*v.* Derbyshire at Ilkeston	130
28	1959, August	*v.* Lancashire at Old Trafford	108*
29	1959, August	*v.* Derbyshire at Worthing	113*
30	1960, March	for MCC *v.* Berbice at Blairmont	183
31	1960, March	for England *v.* West Indies at Port of Spain	101*
32	1960, May	*v.* Somerset at Taunton	140
33	1960, May	*v.* Glamorgan at Hove	131
34	1960, May	*v.* Surrey at Hove	155
35	1960, August	*v.* Northamptonshire at Hove	102
36	1961, May	*v.* Somerset at Eastbourne	158*

37	1963, July	v. Kent at Hastings	136
38	1964, June	v. Nottinghamshire at Worthing	103★
39	1964, December	for England v. South Africa at Durban	108★
40	1965, May	v. Leicestershire at Hove	102
41	1965, June	v. Kent at Tunbridge Wells	101
42	1965, August	v. South Africans at Hove	106★
43	1965, October	for MCC v. Western Australia at Perth	107★
44	1966, May	v. Lancashire at Hove	119
45	1966, September	for T.N. Pearce's XI v. Rest of the World at Scarborough	101★
46	1967, June	v. Lancashire at Old Trafford	150
47	1967, July	v. Derbyshire at Hove	107
48	1969, August	v. Lancashire at Hove	109★
49	1970, June	v. Warwickshire at Hove	166★
50	1970, July	v. Essex at Eastbourne	150
51	1973, June	v. for Somerset v Kent at Maidstone	155

(not first-class)

| 1961, February | v. Northland at Whangarei | 107★ |
| 1971, June | JPL v. Nottinghamshire at Worksop | 148 |

Jim Parks – One-day matches, career record

Overall record

Innings	127
Not out	15
Runs	2,901
Average	25.9
Highest score	148
Catches	79
Stumpings	4

Gillette Cup

for Sussex

inns	n.o.	hs	100s	50s	runs	ave	catches	stumpings	wkts
26	3	102*	1	6	826	35.91	31	0	0

for Somerset

inns	n.o.	hs	100s	50s	runs	ave	catches	stumpings	wkts
3	2	42*	0	0	69	69	2	1	0

Total

inns	n.o.	runs	ave	catches	stumpings
29	6	895	37.29	33	1

John Player League

for Sussex

inns	n.o.	hs	100s	50s	runs	ave	catches	stumpings	wkts
52	4	96*	0	5	1031	21.47	38	2	0

for Somerset

inns	n.o.	hs	100s	50s	runs	ave	catches	stumpings	wkts
23	4	46*	0	0	427	22.47	2	0	0

Total

inns	n.o.	runs	ave	catches	stumpings
77	8	1458	21.13	40	2

Benson & Hedges Cup

for Sussex

inns	n.o.	hs	100s	50s	runs	ave	catches	stumpings	wkts
5	0	37	0	0	102	20.4	3	0	0

for Somerset

inns	n.o.	hs	100s	50s	runs	ave	catches	stumpings	wkts
10	2	69	0	1	198	24.75	0	1	0

Total

inns	n.o.	runs	ave	catches	stumpings
15	2	300	23.07	3	1

Other

for Sussex

1963: *v.* West Indies at Hove – 39
1964: *v.* Australians at Hove – 84

Inns	n.o.	100s	50s	runs	ave.	catches
2	0	0	1	123	61.5	1

for England

Inns	n.o.	runs	ave.	catches
4	0	125	31.25	2

Endnotes

Prologue

1 *Clarke's Directory and Yearbook*, p.31.
2 *Ibid.*
3 *Sussex – Environment, Landscape and Society*, p.228.
4 Revd M.A. Lower, *The Compendious History of Sussex*, quoted in Brandon, p.259.

Chapter 1

1 p.31.
2 Ford and Gabe, p.113.
3 *Mid-Sussex Times*, 29 June 1897.
4 Alan Hill, *The Family Fortune – A Saga of Sussex Cricket*, p.99.
5 Marlar, p.10.
6 Hill, *op. cit.*, p.99.
7 Ford and Gabe, *op. cit.*, p.112.
8 Marlar, p.9.
9 Joe Vine, Sussex and England all-rounder, 1896 to 1922.
10 Stapleton, p.85.
11 Jim Parks, *Runs in the Sun*, p.12.
12 *Ibid.*
13 *Ibid.*, p.13.
14 St Wilfrid's school log book, week ending 30 September 1938.
15 DN.
16 *Ibid.*
17 *Ibid.*
18 *Ibid.*, p.54.
19 St Wilfrid's school log book, week ending 15 September 1939.
20 *Ibid.*, week ending 13 October 1939.
21 DN.

Chapter 2

1 St Wilfrid's school log book, week ending 28 June 1940.
2 Bryan Dolbear, letter to author.
3 PW.
4 Hove County School Magazine, July 1945, p.11.
5 *Ibid.*
6 Hove County School Magazine, March 1946, p.16.
7 *Runs in the Sun*, p.17.
8 School-friend, team-mate for school cricket and football teams, and later Haywards Heath FC.
9 Hove County School magazine, March 1946, p. 20 – 'Parks and Dunning were members of Brighton Schools football team'.
10 PW.
11 Bryan Dolbear, letter to author.
12 John Stanbrook, telephone call.
13 PW.
14 Hove County School magazine, November 1946, p.10.
15 *Ibid.*, July 1947, p.8.
16 Sussex Cricket Association, 1948, p.65.
17 Robin Marlar, *Sussex CCC Handbook*, 1998, p.9.
18 Stanbrook, telephone call.
19 Marlar, *op.cit.*
20 *Ibid.*, p.87.
21 *Ibid.*
22 SCA Handbook, 1956, p.50.
23 SCC Handbook, 1948, p.19.
24 *Ibid.*
25 SCA Handbook, 1949, p.18.
26 *Ibid.*

27 *Ibid.*
28 *Ibid.*
29 *Runs in the Sun*, p. 22.
30 President, Sussex CCC.
31 *Evening Argus*, 5 April 1949.

Chapter 3

1   *Runs in the Sun*, p.22.
2   *Ibid.*
3   *Evening Argus*, 13 June 1949.
4   *Runs in the Sun*, p.25.
5   RW.
6   *Runs in the Sun*, p.27.
7   Hill, *op. cit.*, p.125.
8   Marlar, *op. cit.*, p.10.
9   *Daily Telegraph*, 1 June 1950.
10 Fred Cleary, e-mail.
11 Marshall, p.211.
12 *Kent Messenger*, 29 June 1951.
13 *Ibid.*
14 Baily, Thorn, Wynne Thomas, p.613.
15 *Wisden*, 1952, p.526.
16 Marlar, *op.cit.*, p.11.
17 *Ibid.*
18 Bailey, p.158.
19 *Wisden*, 1953, p.338.
20 *Wisden*, 1953, pp.626–7.
21 *Hastings & St Leonards Observer*, 26 July 1952.
22 *Ibid.*
23 *Wisden*, 1953, p.671.

Chapter 4

1   *Runs in the Sun*, p.85.
2   DB.
3   TJ.
4   DS.
5   RW.
6   Bailey, p.49.
7   *Ibid.*
8   JMP.
9   JMP.
10 *Wisden*, 2004, p.52.
11 AO.
12 DS.
13 Westcott, p.119.
14 DS.

15 *Runs in the Sun*, p.85.
16 *Mid-Sussex Times*, 7 October 1953.
17 *Ibid.*, 25 November 1953.
18 *Ibid.*, 27 January 1954.
19 *Ibid.*
20 *Ibid.*, 20 January 1954.
21 *Ibid.*, 17 March 1954.
22 Carew, p.36.
23 Brodribb, p.102.
24 DS.
25 *Daily Telegraph*, 22 July 1954.
26 *The Times*, 22 July 1954.
27 *Daily Telegraph*, 23 July 1954.
28 *Ibid.*
29 Alan Hill, *op. cit.*, p.104.
30 Wilf Wooller (no relation), groundsman at the Saffrons for over half a century.
31 Westcott, p.241.
32 Bailey, p.165.

Chapter 5

1   *Mid-Sussex Times*, 13 October 1954.
2   *Ibid.*
3   JMP.
4   RW.
5   *Runs in the Sun*, p.38.
6   KS.
7   Westcott, p.123.
8   Lock, p.99. Within the quote PT=Physical Training and PTI=Physical Training Instructor.
9   *Ibid.*, p.100.
10 *Ibid.*
11 *Ibid.*, p.118.
12 DBC.
13 *Ibid.*
14 Lock, *op. cit.*, p.121.
15 JMP.
16 *Runs in the Sun*, p.40.
17 Alan Lee, p.40.
18 *Wisden Anthology*, 1940–63, p.629.
19 JMP.
20 Landsberg and Morris, p.79.
21 *Ibid.*, p.85.
22 Frederick Sporrorth, 1853-1926, legendary Australian fast-medium bowler, nicknamed 'The Demon'.

Took 207 wickets on the 1884 tour of England. Emigrated here and played his last first-class match in Scarborough for MCC *v.* Yorkshire in 1897.

23 Coal was in short supply during the Second World War, so it was decided by the then Minister of Labour, Ernest Bevin, that there would be a ballot to determine whether the conscript should go into the armed services or work in the mines. These conscript miners were given the nickname 'Bevin Boys'. Release from conscription had to be authorised by Parliament.

24 Westcott, p.124.

25 *Wisden,* 1957, p.556.

Chapter 6

1 John Marshall, p.228.
2 Brodribb, p.126.
3 *Wisden Anthology,* 1940–1963, p.669.
4 *Wisden,* 1958, p.566.
5 Christopher Martin-Jenkins, *The Wisden Book of County Cricket,* p.68.
6 Marlar, *op. cit.,* p.10.
7 DM.
8 Marshall, p.231.
9 JMP.
10 RW.
11 DM.
12 Jim Parks, *Time to Hit Out,* p.37.
13 KS.
14 Westcott, p.126.
15 Marshall, p.230.
16 *Wisden Anthology,* 1940–1963, p.630.
17 DB.
18 *Wisden Anthology,* 1940–1963, p.631.
19 Poem by Alan Ross, 'Cricket at Brighton', quoted in *Runs in the Memory,* p.164.
20 RW.
21 *Wisden,* 1960, p.574.

Chapter 7

1 Swanton, *West Indies Revisited,* p.99.
2 MJKS.
3 Swanton, *op. cit.,* p.104.

4 Ross, p.99.
5 RI.
6 MJKS.
7 Ross, *op. cit.,* p.118.
8 For the life of him Jim cannot remember whose box he used!
9 *Wisden,* 1961, p.829.
10 Swanton, *op. cit.,* p.240.
11 *Ibid.,* p.243.
12 *Ibid.,* p.248.
13 *Ibid.,* p.249.
14 *Ibid.*
15 DA.
16 Cowdrey, *MCC,* p.100.
17 Westcott, *Class of '59,* p.182.
18 Ross, *op. cit.,* p.271.
19 ERD.
20 MJKS.
21 Cowdrey, *op. cit.,* pp.100–1.
22 DA.
23 Swanton, *op. cit.,* p.267.
24 *Wisden,* 1961, p.808.
25 Ross, *op. cit.,* p.278.
26 *Wisden,* 1961, p.571.
27 *Ibid.*
28 Swanton, *Back Page Cricket,* p.122.
29 *Ibid.*
30 *Wisden,* 1961, p.290.
31 *Ibid.*
32 Brodribb, p.221.
33 *Wisden,* 1961, p.295.
34 JMP.
35 *Wisden,* 1961, p.302.
36 *Ibid.,* p.303.
37 Memory Shift Syndrome – Jim was caught by Lewis off Wooller for 9, but it embellishes yet another cricketing story.

Chapter 8

1 *Wisden,* 1962, p.869.
2 *Ibid.,* p.870.
3 *Ibid.,* p.874.
4 *Ibid.,* p.875.
5 *Ibid.,* p.864.
6 JMP.
7 *Wisden,* 1962, p. 501.
8 ERD.

9 DB.

10 KS.

11 ERD.

12 JMP.

13 *Ibid.*

14 Doel, p.10.

15 JMP.

16 *Ibid.*

17 AO.

18 *Wisden*, 1964, p.289.

19 Brodribb, *Next Man In*, p.204.

20 Chalke, *Guess My Story*, p.104.

Chapter 9

1 DA.

2 Clarke, *Cricket with a Swing*, p.77.

3 *Ibid.*

4 *Ibid.*

5 *Ibid.*, p.145.

6 Ian Wooldridge, *Daily Mail*, 26 June 1963.

7 Dexter, quoted in Alan Hill, *Peter May*, p.164.

8 DBC.

9 KS.

10 *Time to Hit Out*, p.26.

11 *Double Century*, p.148.

12 DB.

13 *Double Century*, p.148.

14 *Ibid.*

15 KS.

16 *Double Century*, p.148.

17 *Ibid.*

18 *Ibid.*

19 AO.

20 *Double Century*, p.150.

21 *The Observer*, 8 September 1963.

22 Alan Hill, *op. cit.*, p.113.

23 Lee, p.219.

24 *Ibid.*, p.218.

25 *Ibid.*

26 *Wisden*, 1965, p.600.

27 *Ibid.*

28 *Sunday Telegraph*, 19 January 1964.

29 Melford, *The Cricketer's Bedside Book*, p.212.

30 MJKS.

31 Quoted in an article in the *Hull and East Riding Mail*, 6 June 2004.

32 Flyle Hussain, letter to author.

33 *Wisden*, 1965, p.816.

34 Westcott, *Class of '59*, p.99.

Chapter 10

1 *Time to Hit Out*, p.123.

2 Lee, p.220.

3 GB.

4 Clarke, *The Australians in England 1964*, p.62.

5 *Wisden Anthology*, 1963–82, p.441.

6 Clarke, *op. cit.*, p.105.

7 *Ibid.*, p.106.

8 Clarke, *op. cit.*, p.129.

9 *Wisden Anthology*, 1963–82, p.9.

10 Clarke, *op. cit.*, p.159.

11 Brodribb, *op. cit.*, p.41.

12 Westcott, *op. cit.*, p. 198.

13 RP.

14 Fortune, p.21.

15 MJKS.

16 *Time to Hit Out*, p.31.

17 *Ibid.*

18 Fortune, *op. cit.*, p.104.

19 GB.

20 Letter to LW, 26 January 1965.

21 *Ibid.*

22 *Wisden,* 1966, p.814.

23 Fortune, *op. cit.*, p.146.

24 DA.

25 Fortune, *op. cit.*, p.161.

26 *Ibid.*, p.165.

Chapter 11

1 Letter to LW, 10 May 1965.

2 *Ibid.*

3 *Ibid.*

4 RP.

5 Letter to LW 18 June 1965.

6 Brodribb, *op. cit.*, p.182.

7 Letter to LW, *op. cit.*

8 *Ibid.*

9 Letter to LW, 24 July 1965.

10 Cowdrey, *op. cit.*, p.157.

11 Louis Duffus, quoted in *The Spirit of Cricket*, p.490.

12 Swanton, *Back Page Cricket*, p.136.
13 Dexter, p.80.
14 Clarke, *With England in Australia*, p.10.
15 Letter to LW, 8 September 1965.
16 *Ibid.*
17 MJKS.
18 RWB.
19 Clarke, *op. cit.*, pp.26–7.
20 *Ibid.*
21 RWB.
22 MJKS.
23 JMP.
24 Clarke, *op. cit.*, p.33.
25 Article in *The Cricketer*, December 1965.
26 Clarke, *op. cit.*, p.43.
27 *Ibid.*
28 *Ibid.*, p.50.
29 *Ibid.*, p.63.
30 *Ibid.*, p.64.
31 *Ibid.*
32 *Wisden*, 1967, p.831.
33 *Ibid.*, p.105.
34 *Ibid.*, p.110.
35 *Ibid.*, p.118.
36 *Ibid.*, p.122.
37 Swanton, *Back Page Cricket*, p.138.
38 DA.
39 Clarke, *op. cit.*, p.134.
40 DA.
41 Clarke, *op. cit.*, p.140.
42 Letter to LW, 7 February 1966.
43 *Wisden*, 1967, p.841.
44 DA.

Chapter 12

1 Clarke and Scovell, p.59.
2 *Ibid.*, p.60.
3 Arlott, p.148.
4 Clarke and Scovell, p.74.
5 *Ibid.*, p.121.
6 Letter to LW, 8 August 1966.
7 MG.
8 JMP.
9 KS.
10 JMP.
11 DBC.

Chapter 13

1 *Wisden*, 1969, p.823.
2 AK.
3 JMP.
4 Cowdrey, *op. cit.*, p.177.
5 JMP.
6 Close, p. 80.
7 *Daily Telegraph*, 13 February 1968.
8 *Ibid.*
9 Brodribb, *op. cit.*, p.152.
10 Snow, p.51.
11 Close, p.102.
12 *Evening Argus*, 17 July 1968.
13 Stapleton, *op. cit.*, p.105.
14 AO.
15 Dexter, p.101.
16 JMP.
17 Lee, p.225.

Chapter 14

1 Lee, p.227.
2 *Wisden*, 1970, p.559.
3 *Playfair Cricket Monthly*, August 1970, p.7.
4 Memory shift syndrome! – see also May 1969, August 1972.
5 Snow, p.116.
6 Ross, quoted in Stapleton, *op. cit.*, p.109.
7 Wallace, *Fifty of the Finest Matches*, p.93.
8 *Wisden*, 1973, p.546.

Chapter 15

1 *Wisden*, 1974, p.525.
2 JMP.
3 *Wisden*, 1975, p.658.
4 Bird, *White Cap and Bails*, pp.326–7.
5 *Wisden*, 1975, p.772.
6 *Ibid.*, p.546.
7 *Ibid.*, p.533.

Chapter 16

1 Arlott, p.83.
2 A.A. Thomson, *The Cricketer International*, 10 June 1961.
3 Arlott, p.84.

Bibliography

Leslie Ames, *Close of Play* (Stanley Paul 1953)

John Arlott, *The Essential Arlott on Cricket* (Willow Books 1984)

John Arlott, *Arlott on Cricket – his writings on the game* (Willow Books 1984)

Philip Bailey, Philip Thorn, Peter Wynne-Thomas, *Who's Who of Cricketers* (Hamlyn 1984, revised edn 1993)

Trevor Bailey, *Championship Cricket* (Frederick Muller Ltd 1961)

Colin Bateman, *If The Cap Fits* (Tony Williams Publications 1993)

'Dickie' Bird, *Dickie* (Partridge Press, 1996)

'Dickie' Bird, *White Cap and Bails* (Hodder and Stoughton, 1999)

Peter Brandon, *The Sussex Landscape* (Hodder and Stoughton 1974)

Gerald Brodribb, *Next Man In* (Pelham Books 1985)

Gerald Brodribb, *Cricket at Hastings* (Spellmount Ltd 1989)

John Burke, *Sussex* (B.T. Batsford 1974)

Dudley Carew, *To The Wicket* (Chapman and Hall 1946)

Stephen Chalke, *Runs in the Memory* (Fairfield Books 1997)

Stephen Chalke, *Guess My Story* (Fairfield Books 2003)

Clarke's Directory and Yearbook, pub. Haywards Heath, 1879

John Clarke, *Cricket With a Swing – the West Indies Tour, 1963* (Stanley Paul 1963)

John Clarke, *The Australians in England, 1964* (Stanley Paul 1964)

John Clarke, *With England in Australia* (Stanley Paul 1966)

John Clarke and Brian Scovell, *Everything That's Cricket* (Stanley Paul 1966)

Brian Close, *The MCC Tour of West Indies, 1968* (Stanley Paul 1968)

Colin Cowdrey, *The Incomparable Game* (Hodder and Stoughton 1970)

Colin Cowdrey, *MCC* (Hodder and Stoughton 1976)

Ted Dexter, *Ted Dexter Declares* (Stanley Paul 1966)

Geoffrey Doel, *Sussex and the Gillette Cup, 1963–4* (unpublished)

Basil D'Oliviera, *D'Oliviera – an autobiography* (Collins 1968)

Godfrey Evans, *Wicketkeepers of the World* (New English Library 1984)

Wyn Ford and A.C. Gabe, *The Metropolis of Mid-Sussex* (Charles Clarke 1981)

Wyn Ford and Lilian Rogers, *The Story of Haywards Heath* (S.B. Publications 1980)

Charles Fortune, *MCC in South Africa, 1964–5* (Robert Hale 1965)

Leslie Frewin (ed.), *The Poetry of Cricket* (Macdonald & Co., 1964)

Bill Frindall, *Wisden Book of Test Cricket, Volume One, 1877–1977* (MacDonald/Queen Anne Press 1979)

Tony Greig, *My Story* (Stanley Paul 1980)

The Guardian Book of Cricket (Pavilion Books 1986)

Alan Hill, *The Family Fortune – A Saga of Sussex Cricket* (Scan Books 1978)

Alan Hill, *Peter May, a biography* (Andre Deutsch 1996)

Hove County School Magazines, 1945–49

Len Hutton, *Just My Story* (Hutchinson 1956)

Brian Johnston, edited by Barry Johnston, *Another Slice of Johnners* (Virgin Books 2001)

Kelly's Directory, 1938

Alan Knott, *It's Knott Cricket* (Macmillan, 1985)

Pat Landsberg and Arthur Morris, *Operation Ashes* (Robert Hale 1956)

Alan Lee, *Lord Ted* (Gollancz and Witherby 1995)

Christopher Lee, *From the Sea End* (Partridge Press 1989)

Tony Lock, *For Surrey and England* (Hodder and Stoughton 1957)

John Marshall, *Sussex Cricket* (Heinemann 1959)

Christopher Martin-Jenkins, *The Complete Who's Who of Test Cricketers* (Orbis 1980)

Christopher Martin-Jenkins, *The Wisden Book of County Cricket* (Queen Anne Press 1981)

Christopher Martin-Jenkins (ed.), *The Spirit of Cricket* (Faber and Faber 1990)

Jim Parks, *Runs in the Sun* (Stanley Paul 1961)

Jim Parks, *Time to Hit Out* (Stanley Paul 1967)

Nawab of Pataudi, *Tiger's Tale* (Stanley Paul 1969)

Mark Peel, *England Expects – a biography of Ken Barrington* (Kingswood Press 1992)

Jack Pollard, *The Glovemen* (Robert Hale 1994)

Ron Roberts (ed.), *The Cricketer's Bedside Book* (B.T. Batsford 1966)

Alan Ross (ed.), *The Cricketer's Companion* (Eyre and Spottiswoode, 1960)

Alan Ross, *Through the Caribbean* (Pavilion Books 1960)

John Snow, *Cricket Rebel* (Hamlyn 1976)

Garry Sobers, *My Autobiography* (Headline Books 2003)

Keith Spence, *The Companion Guide to Kent and Sussex* (Collins 1973)

Laetitia Stapleton, *A Sussex Cricket Odyssey* (Ian Harrap at the Pelham 1979)

Sussex County Cricket Club/Sussex Cricket Association Handbooks 1948–1973, 1998

E.W. Swanton, *A Sort of a Cricket Person* (Collins 1972)

E.W. Swanton, *West Indies Revisited: the MCC Tour, 1959-60* (Heinemann 1960)

E.W. Swanton, *Back Page Cricket* (MacDonald/Queen Anne Press 1987)

E.W. Swanton, *Follow On* (Collins, 1977)

A.A. Thomson, *The Cricketer International*, 1961

The Times, Double Century (Collins 1985, published in the Pavilion Library 1990)

University of Sussex, *Sussex – Environment, Landscape and Society* (Alan Sutton Publishing 1983)

John Wallace, *Images of Sport – Sussex County Cricket Club* (Tempus Publishing 2001)

John Wallace, *100 Greats – Sussex County Cricket Club* (Tempus Publishing 2002)

John Wallace, *Sussex County Cricket Club – 50 Finest Matches* (Tempus Publishing 2003)

Chris Westcott, *Cricket at the Saffrons* (Omni Press 2000)

Chris Westcott, *Class of '59* (Mainstream Publishing 2000)

Wisden Almanac, 1950–1976

Wisden Anthology, 1940–1963

Wisden Anthology, 1963–1982

Peter Wynne-Thomas, *England on Tour* (Hamlyn 1982)

I also consulted the *Daily Telegraph*, the *Evening Argus*, the *Hastings & St Leonards Observer*, the *Kent Messenger*, the *Mid-Sussex Times* and the *Playfair Cricket Monthly*.

Where interviews appear as footnotes, their sources are indicated as below for brevity:

DA: David Allen; KA: Keith Andrew; TEB: Trevor Bailey; RWB: Bob Barber; DB: Don Bates; GB: Geoffrey Boycott; FC: Frank Clarke; DBC: Brian Close; ERD: Ted Dexter; HD: Hubert Doggart; PG: Peter Graves; MG: Mike Griffith; RI: Ray Illingworth; TJ: Ted James; AK: Alan Knott; DM: David Mantell; TM: Tony Millard; JTM: John Murray; AO: Alan Oakman; JMP: Jim Parks; RP: Bobby Parks; GP: Gordon Potter; DS: Lord David Sheppard; MJKS: Mike Smith; MS: Mickey Stewart; KS: Ken Suttle; RSR: Raman Subba Row; NIT: Ian Thomson; DU: Derek Underwood; PW: Peter Wales; RW: Rupert Webb. Dennis Nicholls' personal memoir of St Wilfrid's School, an unpublished monograph, has been quoted *passim* and appears in footnotes as 'DN'. Letters from Jim Parks to Lorraine Whitehead (Voss) appear in footnotes as 'Letter to LW' and dated.

Index

Other titles published by Tempus

Glorious Summer The Sussex CCC Championship 2003
JOHN WALLACE

Sussex have many famous names to conjure with – Ranji and Fry, Ted Dexter and Jim Parks – yet until 2003 they were one of only four county clubs never to have been champions. That was brilliantly rectified in the summer of that year when a refashioned and well-led side lifted the trophy at Hove. This book gives a match-by-match account of their path to the title and serves as a worthy celebration of this historic season.

0 7524 3224 9

Victory England's Greatest Modern Test Wins
ALAN BONE

With a foreword and commentary by the inimitable Christopher Martin-Jenkins and a wealth of illustration, this book highlights the most memorable occasions on which England has triumphed, be it a consummate thrashing of the opposition or an epic against-all-odds comeback from the brink of defeat. Featuring match reports and scorecards from thirty fine victories, this is a source of great nostalgia and delight for all England cricket fans.

0 7524 3415 2

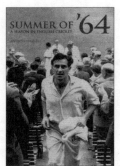

Summer of '64 A Season in English Cricket
ANDREW HIGNELL

The halcyon summer of 1964 saw Graveney, Boycott and Wilson all make over 2,000 runs, while Shackleton, Harman, Cartwright, Titmus and Illingworth were the most lethal exponents of the art of bowling. After one of the hardest-fought contests in living memory Australia very narrowly took the Ashes, while Worcestershire finally saw off intense competition to take the County Championship. This is an affectionate and nostalgic look back at one of the finest seasons on record.

0 7524 3404 7

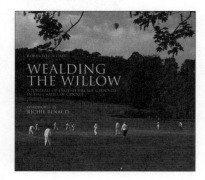

Wealding the Willow A Portrait of English Village Grounds in the Cradle of Cricket
ROBIN WHITCOMB

The Weald area of South East England has been known as 'the cradle of cricket', being the place where the game first started, and in many communities there the cricket ground is still at the very centre of village life. With a foreword by Richie Benaud, this is a beautifully illustrated record of the great game and the places where it all began.

0 7524 3457 8

If you are interested in purchasing other books published by Tempus, or in case you have difficulty finding any Tempus books in your local bookshop, you can also place orders directly through our website

www.tempus-publishing.com